# Bitches
## on a
# Budget

ROSALYN HOFFMAN

# *Bitches* on a Budget

SAGE ADVICE FOR SURVIVING
TOUGH TIMES IN STYLE

 NEW AMERICAN LIBRARY

NEW AMERICAN LIBRARY
Published by New American Library, a division of
Penguin Group (USA) Inc., 375 Hudson Street,
New York, New York 10014, USA
Penguin Group (Canada), 90 Eglinton Avenue East, Suite 700, Toronto,
Ontario M4P 2Y3, Canada (a division of Pearson Penguin Canada Inc.)
Penguin Books Ltd., 80 Strand, London WC2R 0RL, England
Penguin Ireland, 25 St. Stephen's Green, Dublin 2,
Ireland (a division of Penguin Books Ltd.)
Penguin Group (Australia), 250 Camberwell Road, Camberwell, Victoria 3124,
Australia (a division of Pearson Australia Group Pty. Ltd.)
Penguin Books India Pvt. Ltd., 11 Community Centre, Panchsheel Park,
New Delhi - 110 017, India
Penguin Group (NZ), 67 Apollo Drive, Rosedale, North Shore 0632,
New Zealand (a division of Pearson New Zealand Ltd.)
Penguin Books (South Africa) (Pty.) Ltd., 24 Sturdee Avenue,
Rosebank, Johannesburg 2196, South Africa

Penguin Books Ltd., Registered Offices:
80 Strand, London WC2R 0RL, England

First published by New American Library,
a division of Penguin Group (USA) Inc.

First Printing, January 2010
10 9 8 7 6 5 4 3 2 1

REGISTERED TRADEMARK—MARCA REGISTRADA

Library of Congress Cataloging-in-Publication Data
Hoffman, Rosalyn.
  Bitches on a buget: sage advice for surviving tough times in style/Rosalyn Hoffman.
    p. cm.
  ISBN 978-0-451-22917-5
  1. Consumer education. 2. Home economics. 3. Shopping. 4. Beauty, Personal. I. Title.
  TX335.H517 2010
  640.73—dc22          2009020576

Set in Whitman
Designed by Pauline Neuwirth

Printed in the United States of America

PUBLISHER'S NOTE
While the author has made every effort to provide accurate telephone numbers and Internet addresses
at the time of publication, neither the publisher nor the author assumes any responsibility for errors, or
for changes that occur after publication. Further, publisher does not have any control over and does not
assume any responsibility for author or third-party Web sites or their content.
    The recipes contained in this book are to be followed exactly as written. The publisher is not respon-
sible for your specific health or allergy needs that may require medical supervision. The publisher is not
responsible for any adverse reactions to the recipes contained in this book.

    The scanning, uploading, and distribution of this book via the Internet or via any other means with-
out the permission of the publisher is illegal and punishable by law. Please purchase only authorized
electronic editions, and do not participate in or encourage electronic piracy of copyrighted materials.
Your support of the author's rights is appreciated.

*Acknowledgments*
......................

ONCE MY GIRLS no longer allowed me to turn daily experiences into life lessons, I was forced to take pen to paper to share my wisdom and worldview with anyone who would listen. These words are for you, my sweet, brainy, and beautiful daughters, Allie and Julia. To my husband, Warren—forever bewildered by all the bitches in his life—thank you for your support and your patience as I disappeared for weeks on end. To my mom, Ruth, may she rest in peace, for her tender heart and bestowing the gift of recognizing the important things in life; although we grew up without money we never felt poor. Thank you to my brother Robert for encouraging me from the very start— you were the bitch's first cheerleader and an easily amused (and amusing) reader; and to my dad and sister bitches—Bev, Gail, and Deb—for your gift of humor.

Sarah Braunstein, my teacher, reader, adviser, and friend, I will forever be in your debt for your wise help and counsel that allowed me to complete this book. Thank you to Tracy Bernstein, my editor, for your light touch and clear guidance. To my agent, Alanna Ramirez at Trident Media Group, for believing in this project and for your carefully thought-out advice. I am so appreciative of the help from my all-things-book-related-adviser and friend Jan Constantine.

*v*

For encouraging me to pursue my passions and for her kind-hearted friendship, I am deeply grateful to Barbara Pizer, as well as to my dear friends Linda Glassman, Marty Wallace, Carol Efron-Flier and Nadine Bernard Westcott, for your patient listening to all my drama and kvetching. To my old friend and gifted plastic surgeon Dr. Leonard Miller, for your time and knowledge. To Hacin and Associates—David Hacin, Kate Kelley, and Jenn Clapp—for thoughtfully sharing your design perspective. Thank you to everyone on my e-mail list who wrote back with your budget tips or answered my existential queries about why you traveled and why you lusted after those crippling Manolos. And, of course, to Polie, my faithful little man—daily he sat perched in my lap critically watching the computer screen to make certain I stayed on budget.

*Bitches on a Budget* is dedicated to Karen Conner, who began this book with me.

# Contents

# Bitches
## on a
# Budget

## Introduction
....................

## WELCOME, BITCH!
....................

**FOR YEARS YOU'VE** been hearing the message that you're entitled to a future that's nothing less than fabulous, a steady parade of five-hundred-thread-count sheets, French Burgundies, and Jimmy Choo shoes (with matching bags, of course). You witnessed the tech boom, the biotech boom, and the luxury-market boom, and you contributed with label-loving glee. You watched smugly as your stocks split and the value of your real estate seemed to double overnight. Even after the fed chairman warned you of irrational exuberance, you kept charging on those credit cards, continued lusting for that gas-guzzling SUV, that bigger house, that first-class jet trip to Fiji. But we all know what happens when you fly too close to the sun: a meltdown. Lehman Brothers disappeared, stock markets tumbled, and the housing bubble burst. The money pushers hid under TARP funds, and General Motors went bankrupt. Whether you're a soccer mom in Dallas, a new teacher in Chicago, a retired accountant in Los Angeles, or a Carrie Bradshaw wannabe swilling cosmos in your Soho loft, you now have a problem: How do you live a stylish life during the greatest economic downturn of your generation?

**THE ANSWER IS** right at your woefully unmanicured fingertips: *Bitches on a Budget: Sage Advice for Surviving Tough Times in Style* is the guide for women who want to look, feel, and live rich when the economy—and their pocketbook—is in the toilet. Face it, good times or bad, there are just some things a bitch shouldn't live without (stilettos, Prada, booze), and we're here with the inside scoop on how to get it all for less. We'll also show you how more is not always better, and how little can feel more satisfying than big—when used in just the right way.

Trust us, we know what ails you. You're not the first person to shred your credit card statements before opening them! Sure, these are scary times. What will life look like without our monthly cut and color, weekly nights out, and pricey health club? More important, what will *we* look like? All the rules are changing. These days you're not sure what to order at the bar, what to drive, or where to go for your escape (and, bitch, we all *need* to escape sometimes).

Don't give up. Don't hide your head (yes, we know the trailer-trash roots are showing—we'll help with that, too). It's time to come out and have fun again. Whatever your bank balance, *Bitches on a Budget* offers you the strategies you need to retain style dignity and avoid succumbing to soul-deadening bad taste. We'll help you cast out the excessive (say good-bye to big boob jobs and hand-rubbed Kobe beef) in order to make room for the chic and affordable clothing, food, destinations, decor, and entertainment of a modern era. We'll teach you the tricks of the trade so you can get the truly fabulous things every bitch lusts for—but at bargain prices. We'll guide you back to the simple things that once made a bitch happy—good sex, yummy food, fun with friends, and, of course, affordable, amazing shoes. Think of us as your fashion guru, grooming adviser, travel agent, home decorator, therapist, sommelier, and life coach all rolled into one.

## BUDGET IS NOT A DIRTY WORD

**FISCAL RESPONSIBILITY IS** like monogamy . . . if you think it's boring, you're doing it wrong. Since when has "budget" been a dirty word? After all, we're not talking chastity belts, abstinence rings, knee-jerk denial. Think of "budget" as just another way to say "edit." The key to good living is in using your limited resources wisely—we'll show you how to hitch your mind to that little lust engine that's driving you. The end result? You'll make smarter shopping decisions. Bargain buys will replace designer labels as your new badge of honor. Besides, since you want to be a good green citizen of the world, it's time to stop consuming everything in your path. (Nothing is less attractive than a bloated bitch.)

## BE A BITCH, BITCH

**"BITCH" ISN'T A** bad word, either. We're proud to be modern women. Women who know what we want and aren't afraid to get it; women with the sense to edit the good from the bad; women who choose to live with style and with conscience. Independent women who say what we think, are in touch with our femininity, and know how to enjoy our pleasures. Hell, we make less than men do by the hour, yet work harder and produce more value (just think about it: Can they have babies?). It's time to stand proud, bitch.

3

Remember, few things stay the same. Prices change, Web sites come and go, even big car companies fold. However different the world may look in six months or six years, the core of our advice remains simple and steadfast. A modern woman is an educated woman: She never stops learning, never stops loving, and never stops lusting. There are no sacred cows on our journey to living a better life for less. So sit back, relax, get ready to laugh, grab a scotch (if you've opened your IRA statement, you know a cosmo just isn't going to cut it anymore), and start reading.

# Chapter 1

# Shopping Out of the Apocalypse

YOUR STOCKBROKER IS out on his window ledge. Your banker doesn't return your calls. Worse yet, you've got to avoid Mike in human resources because you owe his daughter $15 for Girl Scout Cookies. It's bad out there. All you want to do is take an Ambien, crawl under a rock, and hope someone wakes you when it's over.

Bitches, we're going to let you in on a secret: Women might only make $.78 for every $1 men make, but *we're* the ones who drive the economy. We're the ones who decide what to buy and when to buy it. You think we're kidding? Just turn on the television. It's talking to you, bitch. And even when it's not—Rogaine and boner pills—it's still about you!

Forget free-market capitalism. Estrogen drives GDP. And, as with most things, only we can fix this mess. So it's time for us to stand up straight, toss our hair back, and do what we do best—stimulate this economy.

Stop fighting your God-given patriotic urges. Surrender to nature. That delicious surge you feel walking into a shopping temple is powered by female primordial matter itself. Embedded in your DNA is a fascination with the new and different—the urge to be the most desirable, sexiest woman you can be. This all-consuming need drives the economy.

Conquer your fear. Accept your birthright. Open your wallet. Never feel guilty for loving to shop. It's time to be an American and get spending again.

## BELIEVE IN LOOKS, NOT LABELS!

**WHILE IT'S YOUR** patriotic duty to keep the economy stimulated, it's your civic duty to cast off the outdated, more-is-better style of the nineties and aughts. No modern bitch wants a big footprint. Yes, it's time to get America moving. It's also time to throw out the ostentatious ($2,000 Chanel boots), the excessive ($20,000 Hermès Birkin), the ridiculous (Paris Hilton clothing). It's time to buy and spend wisely.

Remember, the smartest bitch understands *why* she shops, knows what she *needs*, and gets what she *wants*.

So shop around. Forget the elitist bullshit. The modern bitch knows that monogamy is dead—brand monogamy, that is. Long live your individuality. Curiosity, creativity, and art come together in your clothing and jewelry choices. The best-dressed woman harnesses all the resources at her disposal to find the perfect cashmere sweater, the hottest stilettos, and the most unique bling—all in service to her own style. So listen up. We'll give you the straight skinny on how to get shopping satisfaction without breaking the bank (or what's left of it).

# INTELLIGENT DESIGN:
## An Educational Primer

## PRAISE SONG FOR SHOPPING!

You shop to be covered. You shop to get naked. You shop for fun, entertainment, excitement. To stay current; to stay connected; to fit in. You buy to be in control. You buy to make the G-spot in your brain happy. You buy to be who you want to be.

Remember the good old days when you bought that unbelievable Miu Miu dress and those strappy Jimmy Choos (all at full price)? So hot! That bright, cherry red dress felt great, flattered; it was comfy. You wore it everywhere. You were the babe in the red dress. You walked with an extra swivel in your hips, felt gorgeous, desirable, transformed, your sexiest self.

That single Miu Miu dress is your model for the future. One piece, pricey to be sure, and certainly a relic of another era, but think of how much wear you got from it, how it made you feel—not to mention all the X-tra benefits you received! Your job today is to be an editor extraordinaire: to collect only those pieces that make you feel like the lady in red. This crisis is an opportunity to lead a better, fuller, and more streamlined life. So, no matter what the economy does, a modern woman lives by one creed: *Less is more*.

## THE POWER OF ONE: You Are What You Wear

*Fresh, sexy,* and *serious* are the building blocks of a modern bitch's closet. Whether you want to be the fresh-faced girl in blue blazer and khakis, the biker chick in leather jacket and motorcycle boots, or the power ranger in your little black dress and pumps, a good wardrobe allows you to play out all your fantasies.

7

Your goal is deep, long-lasting satisfaction. Invest in exquisite simplicity and get your down-and-dirty highs off cheap kitsch. In our current times, how, when, and where you buy are key.

Build your basic wardrobe by buying only on sale and buying only the best pieces you can afford—even if it means acquiring just one big item per season. Be patient—you're a grown-up! Each one of the building blocks should last forever—or as long as you keep your abs firm and your glutes tight.

Since you're such a thrifty and responsible bitch, you must have cash on hand or in the bank to pay for your purchases. You may use a credit card (accruing airline mileage) only if you pay promptly at the end of the month. This rule is *not* negotiable!

## BITCH'S BASICS

A great denim jacket. A leather motorcycle jacket. A navy blazer. An all-season trench. Blue jeans and black jeans with a perfect fit. Khaki trousers. Two white shirts: one button down, one ultrafeminine. A white cashmere cardigan. A bright-colored cashmere cardigan. A little black dress. A sexy party dress. A black suit-skirt and trousers. Black high heels. Metallic ballet flats. A great pair of black boots. Brown cowboy boots. A black hobo bag. A black clutch. A brown leather knapsack. Brown driving shoes. A set of X-rated lingerie. One hot chemise.

## HOLD ON TO HARD/PLAY WITH SOFT

Think of your wardrobe as a combination of hard and soft. Hard, well-made pieces, like outerwear, suiting, dresses, jeans, and trousers, last ages with proper care—of them *and* of your shape. Also in this "keeper" category are shoes, handbags, and jewelry.

Soft pieces, like shirts, socks, underwear, and lingerie, don't last forever. You wash and wear and sweat in them, so don't waste your money. The smart bitch mixes it all up: fancy suit from Saks, tees from Target. And, let's face it, we don't want everything to last forever—how boring would that be? A girl needs a little fun on the side. So thank God for Anthropologie to add a little decoration to our wardrobe.

## 0━━ *Thrifty Bitch*

### the staples every bitch needs

EXTEND THE life of your clothes and keep dry-cleaning bills to a minimum.

- Sweater de-piller. D-Fuzz It Sweater & Fabric Comb— $2.49.
- Lint roller. Evercare Magik Brush—$4.29.
- Leather and suede protector. Apply to shoes and bags *before* wearing.
- Antistatic spray. Don't cheapen a look with cling.

## ESSENTIALIST THINKING

The wily shopping bitch is an out-of-the box thinker, bold investor, and bargain hunter all wrapped up in one stylish package. Be a patient collector and, over time, gather the fundamental pieces of your wardrobe.

For starters, we're crazy for Brooks Brothers' single-breasted navy blazer with the shiny gold sheep buttons, made from world-famous Loro Piana Italian fabric. Really, you ask? Brooks Brothers? Yes, that misunderstood bastion of male boring has

9

a few fantastic basics in their ladies' department. At $348 this could be the most versatile piece in your entire wardrobe. You'll be so hip wearing this over a black tee shirt and black jeans with boots, or so preppy throwing it over your white button-down shirt with a pair of chinos and sockless loafers, or so businessy with it draped over a silk blouse with gray flannel trousers and black heels. The chameleonlike quality of this baby never ceases to amaze.

Our favorite black suit is ancient. To come clean: We bought it full-price at Armani fourteen years ago for a lot of money ($1,200—a lot of money now, even more in those days). It's so basic we can wear it to business meetings, black-tie dinners, and funerals. Stains are invisible. Outside of it getting a little snug, it could wear forever. In today's economy, you should be able to score a suit like this—with a little sharp intelligence—somewhere in a markdown cycle. This kind of buy may be your major purchase for the year, but it's a worthy investment.

## Thrifty Bitch

### basic black in all sizes

CHECK OUT Ann Taylor's basic black suiting. Great styling and available in regular and petite sizes. The perfect one-stop shop for your first business suit—or, more likely, your job-hunting interview suit. Retail prices begin at $330 and often go below $200 on sale.

The final hard piece to rave about (no, we're not going there) is a Piazza Sempione little black dress, bought this year on sale at Barneys for $320. Originally priced at more than $700, it required alterations to fit a less-than-perfect shape, but now it's a keeper. Perfect fabric, great simple lines. Worn with black Prada knockoff pumps and a white J.Crew cashmere cardigan—it rocks.

## Bitchin' Tip

### tailor-made

OFTEN A piece won't fit perfectly—it may come from the sale rack and be one size too big. Have faith, snap it up, and get it refitted. As you grow or shrink, clothes you love can be let out or taken in. Trust us, the best-dressed women are not perfect size fours or eights or twelves. They just have the best tailors! Go to the ritziest boutique in your area and ask which master they use—that's your new tailor.

## JEANS IDOLATRY

Perfect denim is every bitch's basic right. But should you spend $16 or $260 on yours? True Religion or Lee? Remember, "looks, not labels" is your new shopping mantra, so the correct answer is—it doesn't matter. What matters more than price is unadulterated love. If they're great-looking, make you feel truly fantastic, and are comfortable, you'll wear them constantly. Remember the power of one! A single great pair will cost you less than a bottom drawer crammed with unworthy losers.

Don't forget, a bitch should always go with her gut—don't suck it in. No lying down on the bed, legs in the air, just so you can pull up the zipper—save that position for more fun things.

What's feminism given you if not the right to be a belligerent bitch and freedom from uncomfortable pants?

## Splurgeworthy

### worth every penny

*WE LOVE* Earnest Sewn. So soft and comfy, and they wear like iron. Three real-life people oversee the production of each pair and they, along with the company president, *hand-stamp* the jeans. Hand-sewn wherever possible. Expensive. Available for sale periodically at earnestsewn.com, bluefly. com, and overstock.com.

## Thrifty Bitch

### save your assets, enhance your ass

- ◆ Don't be put off by cheesy labels. Five minutes with a seam ripper may remove that ugly emblem or tarty stitching on the ass of a low-rent pair. Think of this as a witness relocation program for your denim.
- ◆ Use the Internet to snag them from a reliable source (that accepts returns!). Just remember to factor in shipping charges and make sure you're really saving.
- ◆ Levi's, the most iconic of jeans, can be found at Walmart for as little as $16. ☺

# BE A BORN-AGAIN CONSUMER:
## How To Get What You Want
......................

**THE MOST SUCCESSFUL** shopper is the educated shopper. Understand the trends without falling victim to them; see how they're interpreted at all price points; learn the retail cycle and buy only the best value . . . these are your reeducation goals. Our one abiding shopping maxim: *Search and lust; wait and purchase.* Surrender to your fantasies—just don't get hustled.

Now that you know the lesson plan—it's time to go shopping!

## KEEP YOUR HANDS TO YOURSELF

Leave your house with only enough cash for a cup of coffee. Bring neither a credit card nor a license (stores are sneaky and will allow you to charge just by having a piece of ID). You're a fan of role-play, right? This time, instead of the naughty nurse, you're a tourist. Pretend each store you enter is in a foreign country. Not only are you far from home, but the stores are really museums. You can't speak the language and, since you're in a museum, you're strictly forbidden to touch anything.

You're now a shopping tourist discovering what's hot. Start big; aim high. Go to the stores you can no longer afford—Neiman's, Barneys, Bloomie's—and just cruise. Look. Do not touch. Remember, you're a museum visitor. No eye contact with salespeople. No big, "Hi, how are you?" Even if you're from the Midwest and warm and friendly by nature, control yourself. Put on your urban bitch face; pretend you don't understand and just keep moving. Do not get involved. Once you connect with a real person you're entering into an expensive committed relationship. If you let them get you undressed and in the fitting room—well, bitch, order the rice; wedding bells will be ringing.

As you move from department to department of these high-end stores, consider who would be wearing the clothes you see: urban hipster? suburban mama? society dowager? trust-fund brat? Fortune 500 CEO? nightwalker?

Indulge your fantasies—just don't open your wallet. Then leave the high temples of fashion and move into the mall. Here English is spoken and you can begin to touch again (bring the Purell). Work your way down the food chain: Bloomie's to J.Crew and Banana Republic. Neiman's to GapBody. Barneys to Zara and the Limited. See what repeats. Notice how Nine West has knocked off Prada; Banana has those hip new wide-legged trousers like Dolce & Gabbana; H&M has the cutest black-patent trench coats like Max Mara.

"Search and lust" will become your new motto. Once you find something you are mad for, walk away. Yes, walk away! Hell, you aren't the kind of slut who would go all the way on the first date anyway. Think about it, sleep on it, and if you wake up panting for that hot new blouse, wishing you'd made love to it, go back and make it your own.

The more you shop the less likely you'll want to buy anything. By roaming store after store, rack after rack, you'll find after a while that everything looks the same. A kind of somnolent, over-heated boredom washes over you, followed by a desperate urge to flee. You're overtaken by a fear you won't remember where you parked the car. Will you ever escape? Soon you're engulfed by a waking nightmare that you'll be locked in with the manne-quins who come alive when the stores shut down (okay, you saw that *Twilight Zone* episode, too). Snap out of it. Exit the mall.

The purpose of this exercise is to earn your PhD in shopping, leaving you with a trained eye for the truly fabulous.

*Green Style*

### recycle your clothes

ONE WAY to figure out what you need is to figure out what you *don't*—and today is a good time to dig out what doesn't fit and what you never wear. Edit those fashion faux pas from your wardrobe. Go straight to a charity near you. Who knows, that flaming tangerine tunic might look great on the right body—make another bitch's day!

You're exhausted by your first full-frontal shopping tour and fully aware of the latest trends. No need for embarrassment over last season's puffy-bottomed skirt. No regret knowing that if you'd done a bitch's recon last season it would never have sucked a single precious hard penny out of you. Put it behind you. Today is a new beginning. The next stop in your reeduca-tion: the retail cycle.

15

# A CULTURAL REVOLUTION:
## Out with the Old, In with the New
......................

## RETAILING LESSONS

Once upon time, before shopping became theater; before our identities were defined by what we wore; before we became alienated from our core values of family, friends, and charity; before we became the buy-buy-buy, need-it-now generation; before shopping became a substitute for other kinds of pleasure, life was lustier. Proof? Weren't families a whole lot bigger?

Sixty years ago Walmart didn't exist. Neiman Marcus was only in Texas. Victoria's Secret was just that—some horny guy's wet dream. There were few indoor malls, massive chains, or outlet centers. Hard to get your head around, huh? Like fashion itself, the business is in constant flux. It's hard for even the savviest bitch to keep up. How to deal? Learn the stores. Understand their strategies. Know when merchandise rolls in and when it must go out.

Take back the power!

## BRICK AND MORTAR FLOWS

Bloomie's, Target, Zara, Nordstom . . . all major stores start each new season with fresh inventories. Planning and buying of merchandise is done based on past season's sales. Depending on the business, fresh goods roll in at the start of each season and are replenished either monthly or bimonthly. To maintain a fresh feel and to finance future purchases, the merchandise must *flow*. New goods in—old goods out. This is critical shopping intelligence.

Couple this knowledge with the fact that, at most big chains, seasonal goods arriving on the floor are out of sync with real life.

For instance, you live in Chicago. It's February, zero degrees, and you're wearing a winter coat as you cruise through your favorite store freaking out at how small the bottoms are on the new bikinis. Hello, it's February! Months and months away from summer. Yet here's the summer stock, already beckoning.

Make this craziness work for you. Remember the goods keep flowing, and the merchants must make space for the new stuff by marking the old stuff down. So the winter jacket that arrived in August will be getting marked down just about the time you need it for winter, while the teeny-tiny bikini should be on its second markdown by the time you can go swimming in the lake. This is called clearance.

Don't be fooled, though. There's a difference between seasonal clearance and goods bought to be sold on promotion. When the latter happens, a big slug of goods are bought, marked too high, and put on the floor to establish a "regular" price (usually for four to six weeks, but this depends on laws state to state). Later they're marked down to trick all you budget-minded bitches into thinking you're getting a bargain.

Be suspicious. If there's a whole lot of one item on the floor, marked at, say, 20 percent off regular price, chances are it was jacked up and you're not getting a bargain. Be wary of circulars and catalogs "promoting" items—think about it; you're a smart B: They bought and planned to promote these goods at "sale" prices months in advance.

Recognize the difference between a clear-out-the-stuff-because-the-season-is-aging kind of sale and a general business-is-so-sucky-we-need-to-motivate-people sale. Normal bitches should respond to a one-day-only-everything-is-on-sale sale only if they *need* things.

Likewise, take a pass on the stores that offer $50 off a purchase three weeks from now if you spend $250 or more today.

17

See this for what it is—a sleazy seduction to get you into bed again. Succumb only knowing what they are doing to you and only if you have tremendous discipline. Plan precisely how you will spend that $50 three weeks hence—say on sorely needed underwear or bras. Better still, just say no. Since you're a normal person lacking discipline, you're likely to be a promotional victim and either miss your seven-day shopping window, or, if you get back in time, spend more than that $50 certificate.

Use the stores—don't let them use you. The best way is to know what you want (recon) and to keep an eye out for those magical days when clearance and promotions happen simultaneously. Only on these days do we allow ourselves to shop at the high temples of fashion. Say you have been watching a fabulous pair of Robert Clegerie shoes, a Jil Sander sweater, or a Marc Jacobs coat that arrived in August—all orgasmically gorgeous but also hideously expensive, so in this economy they're still hanging around. Now it's December/January (June/July for spring merch) and they're marked down for clearance. Wait. Keep watching. Soon the store needs to do a general promotion to make room for new goods (they just keep coming) and raise some cash. What happens? The waiting pays off. Now you get another 20 or 30 percent on top of the already marked-down price. Pounce. This is the absolute perfect storm of a smart-bitch buy.

In the end, if all else fails, stores still need to move the goods out. They need the space, and any cash in hand is better than an old schmatte sitting on a hanger in the stockroom. This brings us to the off-price part of our tutorial.


## STORES OF LAST RESORT

In the beginning, a few famous off-price stores like Filene's Basement and Loehmann's served as outlets for better boutiques and department stores, a place for high-end retailers to deposit the goods remaining at the end of the season. Great bargains flourished as they sold past seasons' designer ball gowns from I. Magnin and Chanel handbags from Marshall Field. Sadly, those days are done and gone.

As retailing grew, the off-price segment exploded. Marshalls, Ross, T.J. Maxx blossomed into big national chains. Manufacturers found that the off-pricers presented a great opportunity. Canceled orders and returned goods from big department stores could be sold through this channel. Eventually, brands started manufacturing *directly for* the off-pricers. The smart student asks: How, then, is it off-price anymore?

Generally, we're not inspired to shop in the big OP stores for apparel. The prices are not *that* great, and the product is dreary. That said, we admit to good luck buying name-brand lingerie and sleepwear at very reasonable prices. If you've got the time, hunt through the clearance racks, where the really expensive one-of-a-kind pieces end up languishing, lost among rows and rows of uninspired mediocrity. You can still find that needle in a haystack by listening. Indeed, the professional off-price shopper listens for the sound of hangers scraping—it's the sign of activity and may draw you to the true bargains.

We miss the real Basement.


## LITTLE CAN FEEL GOOD, TOO!

Small neighborhood boutiques offer unique looks, less widely distributed vendors, and convenience. Pleasures abound. The goods are carefully edited, the atmosphere cozy, and you're waited on hand and foot. Often you can find small, up-and-coming unique labels. In this economy, with everything else going bye-bye, places like these feel like a huge luxury. Still, the risk is high that you'll be pressured by an overly solicitous, probably desperate owner who'll tell you everything was made for you and looks just fabulous. (*Search and lust, search and lust.*)

In these places, inventory flow is slower than at the big guys. They're usually later to mark down, and don't offer big price reductions until the end of the season. Then they take big cuts if they need to raise cash or (and sadly this is happening all too often) if they're going out of business.

If it's a national brand you're considering—for example, a Vince sweater—check out a store like Nordstrom to see if it's on clearance before you take the plunge at a small store. Big manufacturers give big retailers "markdown money" (a credit to offset the cost of price reductions) to help cushion the stores' bottom line. Stores will then come back to buy more, knowing they're protected against loss. This is one reason for the deadening sameness of brands in big stores—the new little designer guy can't possibly guarantee the store's profit. Manufacturers typically don't give the little store the same break—as a result you may do better price-wise at a big department store.

O═══🔨 *Bitchin' Tip*

**beware!**

*S*MALL, WELL-CAPITALIZED (meaning they don't need hard cash to finance new goods) boutiques may put away basics and bring them back out next season—check that the merch is really fresh.

## PLACES OF WOR-SHOP: Everyday, Everywhere Emporiums to Meet Your Basic Needs

You don't need much these days.

How many black skirts are truly necessary? New $50 bras and $30 underwear are on hold until things pick up—trust us, he really doesn't care if it came from Walmart or La Perla. He'll get excited no matter what itty-bitty thing covers your ass. For the time at hand, when you need a little wardrobe filler, skip the middle guys (JCPenney, Macy's, Kohl's), those ho-hum places where everything looks the same.

If you want some shopping fun, be smart about it. Low-priced stores offer great, fashion-forward, inexpensive products. Sure, there are a few in the middle that we'll rave about. And, of course, if you play your cards right, the high temples offer wild possibilities on those certain magical days. So. Now that you know how to work the system, let's talk about how to get exactly what you want.

## QUICK HITS

Save time and energy by popping into reliable shops for filling in everyday wear. When you need a simple carton of milk, you go to the corner market—not Costco! Same with wardrobe tune-ups. Get in, out, on to better things.

Every bitch has a different body part that plagues her. If you're like us, shirts, sweaters, even shoes are relatively easy to fit. But pants! OMG! Let's not recount our pants agony. We've lived; we've learned. For a quick hit-and-run for basics or a fast little pick-me-up stop by:

**Banana Republic.** A great place for a working woman to quickly snag pants and skirts. Never too flashy, never too dowdy, these clothes are made for real women and designed to fit multiple body types. Reasonable prices, up-to-date looks, and a healthy inventory turnover means there's always something we want on sale.

**Limited and Express.** A little less pricey and filled with possibility. Pants for every shape in every style and color. These aren't "last a lifetime" quality, but they're perfect for when you need a little bottom filler for those five days of work outfits. Wait for their two-for-one sales and don't get too tricky. Go for basic black or khaki, maybe a navy with a pinstripe. Don't get sidetracked on anything but basics.

**Anthropologie and Urban Outfitters.** Anthropologie is *the* place to perk up a basic wardrobe! We use it to add color and sass to our usual basic black, white, and tan. Something is always on sale, and even if it's not, Anthro is the perfect place to splurge and brighten your day. Decorate yourself! Meanwhile, Urban Outfitters, owned by the same parent, shows the same sharp eye for cool-looking wares. Very fun looks, lower price points, and fashion forward. Go for cheapo, on-trend jeans (54 bucks).

**GapBody.** Reliable for loungewear, bathing suits, undergarments. Flattering, cute, won't make you look like a whore. If trashier lingerie is on the menu, head to Target. Skip Victoria's Secret. It originated as a store a guy could go into without being embarrassed to buy sexy duds for his wife—or so they say. Strikes us that it was his fantasy, not necessarily hers. The "bottom" line: very pricey, sensory overload, like a gross uncle selling sex to 'tweens.

# HEAD-TO-TOE NEEDS

## J.CREW: Perfect in the Middle

American royalty.

It didn't take Michelle O. shopping there for us to know that this place is a mainstay destination for any bitch, budget or not. Curie, Einstein, Mozart. Genius comes along only so often, and J.Crew is retailing genius. Once a mere hawker of basic preppy tops and bottoms, it's morphed into a specialty-store gem. Step through the front door to constantly rotating looks, simply luscious colors, and wearable, on-trend clothes.

These master merchants seem to read a bitch's every need. Take that soft salmon-colored ruffled-neck silk shirt, appropriate tucked into trousers with a light sweater for the office, or pulled

23

out over tight jeans with heels for a night on the town. Providing fresh, multitasking staples, while giving overpriced luxury retailers a knockout punch, J.Crew is synonymous with style and value.

The must-have in every woman's wardrobe is their basic cashmere cardigan, $158 at regular price and periodically on sale for just $99. Keep an eye out: Frequent shopping (in the store or online) pays off big for this one piece, which will add class and spice to your whole wardrobe. The colors are endless and yummy, from white (a bitch basic) to persimmon to dreamy aqua. The long-term investment goal of every bitch: Collect them all.

The Super 120s Jayne dress could be your little black basic in superfine 100 percent wool; get it for as little as $180 (it even comes in petites). A narrow red belt for around $29 changes any outfit. A girl could take care of her cradle-to-grave shopping needs here. Swimsuits, cover-ups, jewelry, perfectly priced wedding-party dresses, even basic black suits for interviews.

J.Crew does a brisk Internet business. But think twice! While online shopping is great for looking, we despise delivery fees. Beware of J.Crew selling sale merchandise as final sale on the Internet. Unless you are 100 percent absolutely certain that it's what you need, just say no. Keep the romance alive—don't get burned.

0━━ *Bitchin' Tip*

### feel it up

For CLOTHING that needs to be fresh-looking, try the squeeze test. Take a bunch of fabric. Wrap your fist around it. Then squeeze like you have that cheating guy's teeny-tiny

*(continued)*

balls in your hand. Okay, okay, you can let go now. Since fabric isn't Teflon, it'll show a little creasing—even some pricey Jil Sander or Prada types. But you want fabric that when wrinkled springs back and looks like it'll speak normally again. Nothing's more annoying than the skirt that needs to go back to the cleaner after you've worn it once. (We assume you don't do the ironing—really now, that's too much to ask of any bitch.)

## ZARA AND H&M: Two Hot Europeans

Nobody turns tricks like Zara and H&M. It's just like a European hottie to keep you coming back for more. These mass fashion merchants roll the goods in and out in the blink of an eye. The more the turn, the fresher the look; the faster the turn, with as few markdowns as possible, the more moola the retailer makes. These style mavens turn their stuff constantly. They design, source, and retail, giving them control of their own destinies, and they're always fun to walk through. Carefully. Hold on to your wallet! The price points will make you feel like they're doing you the favor—it's hard to find an item at Zara for over $249.

We love Zara for lots, although, in full-frontal disclosure, we almost always walk out empty-handed. It's so tempting, but we keep reminding ourselves we don't really want to look like a whore (well, most days) in those fringed suede stiletto boots, even though they fit and are comfy and only $99. Shop here with a quick-handed friend who can give you a loving bitch slap.

Their outerwear, often made in Spain (where they're based), is impressive. Leather jackets open at $99.99, and, if you hit the

25

right design, could fill your biker jacket needs (just make sure it's simple; Zara can sometimes add an unneeded flourish).

This past week, because it's subzero where we live and there was no way we could imagine getting naked again, ever, for anyone, we passed on the perfect summer-weight navy cotton blazer—unconstructed, white pinstripes, the subtlest touch of Lurex. For $99, it would have been ideal for jeans or white linen trousers, and would pair nicely with their gauzy floral hippie-inspired shirt, complete with belt, for only $39.90. If Zara's high-fashion European design matches your style, you'll find reasonably priced disposable basics for work, play, and weekend wear. Just remember the goods don't stay long.

Same with H&M. Get it while it's hot! This smart Swedish retailer takes a position on a look and color and it will repeat and repeat. If orange is the color, you'd better like orange, because handbags, shoes, blouses, lingerie will be showing you orange. We like someone that takes a stand.

While Zara stays focused on apparel, H&M sells lots and lots of shoes, hair accessories, hats, scarves, and bras, in addition to their ready-to-wear. Über-up-to-date fashionistas, they offer fun pieces seemingly for pennies. We like hunting for little flats and fun scarves for under $10. Every so often a hot raglan-sleeve Parisian knockoff jersey dress, in a great color like dark aubergine, can be had for less than $15.

We love H&M because they believe in design for the masses. And any store that gets the two greatest living fashion designers in the whole world to do collections for them belongs front and center on the shopping list. They've featured amazing collections from Karl Lagerfeld (Chanel) and Rei Kawakubo's Comme Des Garcons, so they're doing something right. Yes, they can be a little tacky, but the investment risk is low and they take returns.

## BIG IS GOOD

Freedom and impulse buying come together for one blessed moment at big-box discount stores. Stop being a complete shopping brat! When you're broke and need to buy something, *anything*, new to wear, here's your strategy: Drive to the box store closest to the priciest zip code in town, where you'll find the best selections and hottest looks.

Yes, this is a rare moment when you have permission to go without a plan. You'll be the chicest and cleverest bitch when you preen and say, "Thanks, don't you just love it? I bought it at Walmart/Target/insert box store here," and impress all with your impeccable eye and bargain-hunting prowess. Your grandmother knew to stretch hamburger with flour; you know how to stretch your budget—by mixing box-store finds with high-end classics.

## THE BIGGEST COMPANY IN THE WHOLE WIDE WORLD

True, at times Walmart is dowdy. But think of it as that really nice boyfriend—you know, the one who's so "good" for you! Yes, he's a little boring and thick around the middle. And okay, you're right, it's maybe a bit odd that he's balding on only one side. But he's so thoughtful about how hard you work. He always asks how you're doing when you walk in the door. He tries to save you time and money. He has a good overview and vast resources. You're in control of the relationship, so you pick and choose when you go to see him. And remember, unlike that handsome bespoke Italian, he's always there for you.

At the risk of being obvious, let's say it: Walmart has the most terrific everyday prices. No high/low fake promotional strategy for this behemoth—they beat it out of their vendors to pass the savings on to you. L.e.i. tee-shirts, soft to the touch, well made, in good colors: a whopping $5. Fantastic Danskin Now activewear: $9.99 for bottoms and only $14.99 for one of the best silhouetted jackets out there. Iconic designer and mother of the puffy coat Norma Kamali has an NK for Walmart line that rocks. Best of all, because they seem to sell lots of extra-jumbo sizes, you'll feel skinnier just hunting for your size.

Our proudest shopping bargain on a recent visit was a To the Max sheer, short-sleeved, silver-netted shirt for $12.99. We paired it with a $5 gray cami and the compliments flew at a very fancy dinner. Despair overwhelmed us when we found a pair of black patent-leather high-heeled boots for twenty bucks—way more comfy than the ones we paid ten times as much for at a really fancy specialty store (think purple dinosaur).

So, bitches, don't dis Walmart. It should be part of your shopping arsenal—but it's not your main discount-store destination for high-fashion clothing and accessories.

That would be Target.


## RIGHT ON! TARGET

Each season, across all categories, Target invites guest designers to do collections. The bull's-eye people are totally committed to being at the forefront of hip design. Whether it's featuring up-and-comers like Proenza Shouler and Thakoon, or collaborating with hot, established designers, like Alexander McQueen, Target delivers fabulous merch that is totally up-to-date, and priced for action. The smartest shoppers scour the Net for their latest designer catch, then get to the stores early in the delivery cycle. Hot goods run out and aren't often replenished. So let your fingers cruise the keyboard, take notes about impressive pieces, and motor over to claim your booty.

Jewelry is an awesome spectacle. Want to sport the baubles of red-carpet celebs? Acclaimed jeweler Erickson Beamon, a favorite of the stars, designed a special collection just for Target. These rocks shine! Seriously. We're talking the most unbelievably gorgeous jewelry at a fraction of the price of the real stuff. Look like you just walked out of their high-end London boutique. From $30 to $50, the EB collection is dripping with huge faux jewels on cool rose-gold and gold-colored chains. Even Target's Xhilaration brand is loaded with secret gems. We spotted an oversized, articulated wooden bracelet that spelled safari elegance—for around 5 bucks.

All Target's accessories kick ass. Don't forget the shoe aisle (as if you could). For only $24.99 we found the most divine pair of Marc Jacobs's knockoff peep toes in stunning navy and beige patent leather. Plus, the handbag assortment will have you jumping with joy. And wander through their Gilligan & O'Malley (another bull's-eye-owned line) for fabulously priced, gorgeous lingerie.

Other steals? For half of J.Crew's retail price, Merona (Target's house brand) tee shirts are a great buy: fashion cuts and cool colors from $9.99 to $14.99. Shorts and khakis from $12.99 to $19.99 are great kick-arounds (and throwaways!). Explore swimwear separates from $14.99 to $19.99. Can't you see yourself lounging poolside in a Pucci-inspired pattern?

But beware, bitch. There's a definite Disney quality to Target—after all, they modeled their customer service formula after Mickey. They call customers "guests," are quick to offer help, and aim to give off a cool-earthy-crunchy-glammy-Hollywood-charity-driven vibe. Trust us: No one is all that. Yes, Target is the most seductive of all the mass retailers—just don't go all the way. While you've got permission to impulse buy, you need to look yourself in the mirror in the morning. Remember, this is just a store trying to sell you stuff you probably don't need anyway.

## ACCESSORIZE YOUR WAY OUT OF RECESSION BLUES

**THE LITTLE EXTRAS** are the way a girl survives a recession. Yes, your clothing is all black and white with an occasional festive gray; accessories are an opportunity to express yourself, to get that desperately needed fresh and sexy boost.

We love color in accessories. Stuff your hands into luscious amethyst-colored gloves. Don a red plaid cap or straw panama. Wrap vibrant scarves around your neck. Go color crazy; light up your face with deep purples, gorgeous aquamarines, cool corals. Handbags can take a wardrobe to a whole new height. Whether they all come from Forever 21, the street guy at Seventy-seventh and Broadway, or on sale at Lord & Taylor, they're the perfect perk. Of course, jewelry rocks—and if there was ever a time for a girl to fake it, this is it!

And what is a woman without shoes?

### A BITCH'S ACHILLES' HEEL

It had to be a male press corps that jumped all over those thousands of shoes in Imelda Marcos's closet. This was news? *Every* woman loves shoes. As always, shop high, buy low. Sometimes we slip our little feet into the latest from Manolo and rejoice that they're just not cut for us and are so uncomfortable we'd never buy them anyway. Then we go on our bargain-hunting way and find a similar pair at Nine West.

## TAKE BACK YOUR FEET

Never be a silent fashion victim. Do not buy uncomfortable shoes. Try shoes on at the end of your shopping trip, when your feet are at their most bloated. Despite what the salesman says, most of the time shoes do not stretch with your foot. (Men are always exaggerating when it comes to size!) If shoes feel bad in the store, they'll feel bad when you walk to work. Be honest: Those pumps tossed in the back of your closet . . . they never felt good and never will. Besides, you spent more on Dr. Scholl's pads to protect your feet from crippling blisters than you spent on the shoes! Vow right now never to do this again. When in doubt, pass on them.

For normal, everyday, comfy high-fashion shoes, check out Nine West. It's like these babies walked off the catwalk and straight into their shops. Whether online, at the mall, or in their outlet stores, Nine West is a surefire bet. If your basics are covered and you need a shoe fix to zing up your wardrobe, grab a bright-colored peep toe. Don't let yourself look like a Dorothea Lange photograph! Shoes are the place to add charm and color, and Nine West makes it easy.

*Green Style*

### recycle and save your shoes

MEET YOUR neighborhood cobbler. No, not the pie man, the shoemaker. Bring new shoes in for taps and heel guards. Bring worn shoes in for makeovers—have them professionally polished and protected. Replace heels, soles, and zippers (when possible) to extend wear. Give your shoes a second life!

31

## A BAG JOB

Nope, we're not talking about a cover-up of any sort. How is it that you think $1,800 for a handbag is normal, so when it goes on sale for $900 you end up raving about what a bargain it is? Well, bitch, it isn't. Too much unreality television has crept into your life. Buying a Fendi bag is not going to make you into one of those *Sex and the City* gals downing martinis at lunch and screwing hot new guys every weekend. Sorry, we don't think so—it's time to get real.

That doesn't mean we're complete killjoys. You can look the part of the *Sex and the City* gal without blowing the wad. Buy knockoffs and great bargains to see you through. This is the easiest part of the bitch's job: Go to the top department stores; walk through to see the latest looks. Little clutches, hobos, satchels, totes—whatever. The latest and greatest handbags are so large that our toy poodle would get lost inside, forget about that ringing cell phone. But we take note and look for the big trends. Then we go to all our secret haunts to find really good knockoffs.

0╍━ *Splurgeworthy*

### two-faced bitch

REMEMBER WE said one great black hobo is a required basic for all women? We lust after the Balenciaga Arena bag. Sophisticated, with updated styling, and it comes in lots of sizes. Our dream starts at (we blush) $1,095. Start saving.

## *Utterly Splurgeworthy*

EVERY STYLISH bitch now and then passes through New York City, fashion capital of America. When you're there next, go to Worth & Worth, hatmakers. Meet with Orlando Palacios, tour the back room, absorb the old-world charm. While this master milliner stocks ready-made hats for men, he's learned that women are far more discerning, so he opts to create the exact hat the lady wants. For less than $300! Picture it: a fabulous Milan straw with a brim wider than a city block, custom-fitted, so you look and feel ready to recline in the lavender fields of Provence. This splurge lasts a lifetime. Nurture those glamorous fantasies! Embrace a lost art and a lost way of shopping! Head to the sixth floor of a commercial building in Midtown . . . take the elevator up . . . open the door . . . expect Johnny Depp or Justin Timberlake to pop out in one of their hipster toppers.

## NEW DAY, NEW WAY:
### Be a Guerrilla Girl

**PLUGGING IN/UNPLUGGING**

Online shopping is the devil. Online shopping is an angel. A modern bitch knows how to accept a paradox. Yes, online shopping has it rewards, but it's a dangerous game. Poking in the wrong spots can get a girl into big trouble. Develop standards for how, when, and what you buy online. Use the Internet to gather intelligence, to save time, to buy basics, and to dig out real bargains.

33

Let your fingers do the walking for a start—but trust us, unless you're a fashionista par excellence, you're going to get overwhelmed and confused in virtual reality. The Internet is like an infinite universe: You don't know where it begins and ends. You can spend forever looking and end up in a black hole. So let the brick-and-mortar people edit out the good from the bad. They're professionals—*use them*. Do an in-person shopping tour in real reality to get a true lay of the land.

The number one reason you cannot meet all your wardrobe needs online is that every article of clothing *must* be felt up before purchase. In the business it's called feeling the "hand" of the fabric. This tells you more than anything about what you buy. You know the story: he looked hot online in that Facebook picture, but you see him in real life and, uh, how could you know he needed his own zip code? If you buy online, pay for shipping, and then need to pay to return it, you've made a very poor investment. In fact, it's worse than that date; at least he paid for dinner. (Thank God—you couldn't afford to bankroll that appetite.)

0— *At Your Fingertips*

### online recon

- www.vogue.com. *Vogue* online—need we say more?
- www.luckymag.com. Careful, this is one big, whorey, glam ad mag, but *soo* on-trend.
- www.thebudgetfashionista.com. Find sales, offers, product reviews.
- www.frugal-fashionistas.com. Budget re-creations of celebrity wardrobes. Lots of fun.

*(continued)*

34

Use the Internet as an add-on tool. Say you're out shopping and find the perfect basic white Theory blouse. It's pricey, not yet on sale in the store. Type in the style number, or Google "Theory blouses on sale," and it pops up at a store in Miami. Since no one has any money left to spend in Miami, it's listed at 40 percent off, a huge bargain for a necessary bitch's basic. No matter the shipping fee, it's still cheaper than the full-priced one in front of you.

Or you found the perfect Frye boots . . . you know, black, outside zipper, great heel, good toe, perfect for under jeans or with a hip skirt. But every store is sold out in your size. Go online; if it exists someplace in the world, you'll find it.

## At Your Fingertips

### control yourself

THE INTERNET offers such convenience—it's so easy to just push the send button, and before you know it Mr. FedEx is at your door. We all know how hard it is to return things once you own them. You're out of packing tape; calling for a pick up is confusing; the lines at the post office on Saturday are impossible; FedEx is twenty miles away and the cost of gas rivals the cost of the item. So get a grip on yourself—and be careful.

You are allowed to shop online for known quantities when you find them at great prices. For example:

- True basics. Like, you live in Hanky Panky. They cost $18 everywhere, but you find them online for 25 percent off, at a retailer that doesn't charge for delivery. Go ahead, bitch, order up a dozen and extend time between trips to the laundry.
- You've felt it up. You've tried it on. You're lusting. Take that Etro dress you saw at the unaffordable boutique at the beginning of the season. You know it fits and you're simply smitten. You just found it online for 75 percent off. Go for it!

## I REFUSE TO JOIN ANY CLUB THAT WOULD HAVE ME AS A MEMBER

Think about Groucho Marx's sage advice when considering what to make of the invitation-only Web sites selling merch for a limited time only. They had us wondering: Do we really want to be invited in?

These sites are the hottest thing going. They create demand, making you think you're oh-so-special because you were invited. We joined one simply by saying we were a reader of a newspaper . . . meaning they'll let anyone in. What they want is to boost their customer base by having you invite others. How else to get noticed? They build lists, grab information from you, and pump you up to feel special and therefore lucky to get the big things that being a member of their club entails.

We were set to totally hate them. But, truth be told, we got so overstimulated browsing their sites we actually bought something. Even though we're shoppers extraordinaire, we found ourselves looking at some brands we'd never heard of. At first this made us suspicious . . . after all, just ask us: No one knows more than we do! But, after some research, it seemed some of the products were the real deal. Use discretion at these places—make sure what they're hawking deserves the hype.

Could these sites be the ultimate sample-sale destination? The new Filene's Basement? The places where manufacturers can preserve the sanctity of their brands, protect prices, and avoid pissing off full retail customers, yet sell their overstock (or dogs) at a fraction of retail? Yes.

Our bottom line: Look, don't touch, unless there is a really *huge* bargain for something you're already familiar with and deeply covet. (There are some pretty good buys lurking—75 percent off in many instances.) You may *not* buy from one of those sites unless you've actually touched the goods and tried them on in real life. Period.

This doesn't mean we aren't now addicted to *looking* at the daily e-mail offerings from ideeli, Gilt Groupe, Rue La La, and HauteLook. Just be smart: if you do find something you must have, before *each* purchase read the return rules for that specific item. Be careful you don't get stuck with stuff you don't want. The temptations are great, so act with extreme caution.

## ZAPPOS WINS THE ONLINE JACKPOT!

We love Zappos—let us count the ways:

1. They're based in Las Vegas—how kitschy is that? (Okay, not a good reason, but really, now, a world-class, über-cool company in Flamingo Land, completing the holy trinity of sins: gambling, sex, shopping . . . Who wouldn't love it?)
2. Great selection of shoes.
3. They send purchases immediately, no shipping fees in either direction, so if we don't like them we put them back in the box and—zap-o!—they're gone-zo.

4. The site is *so* easy to navigate. You can sort by size, which prevents you from falling in love with a shoe you can't have.
5. They offer really helpful customer reviews about fit.
6. They're branching into women's clothing with the same Astroglide shipping and return policy.

## UNPLUG THE TELEVISION

Never buy anything on television. First of all, how would you ever explain that's what you were doing with your spare time? No, you do not need another ring, another flattering wrap jersey dress, or another Velvet tee-shirt. Do not allow yourself to be bullied by the fast-talking celebrity huckstress with the ticking clock and the dwindling countdown of embossed green faux-lizard belts. Ignore that saleswoman with the white tiles for teeth whose job it is to drum up panic, to remind you in a variety of unsubtle ways that if you don't own one of three remaining cubic zirconia lapel pins your life may never, ever be complete. The only panic you're entitled to these days is panic over falling real estate and 401(k) plans.

You need nothing from television but pure adult escapism—*House, Nurse Jackie, Entourage, Weeds. . . .*

## POWER TO THE PEOPLE!

### JOYS OF CONSIGNMENT

Listen up if you're a prissy bitch and don't know how consignment stores work. Or if you're a prissy bitch and know how consignment stores work and won't step inside with your dainty little Chanel-clad foot. If your greedy little heart keeps pounding "gimme, gimme" and your empty bankbook answers back, "No way, no way," then it's high time you got your ass through the door of the coolest little money saver near you.

Consignment stores go both ways. (Recall spring semester, junior year?) Consignment lets you *buy* and *sell*. Take that skirt that fit ten pounds ago sitting in the back of the closet. Despite too many years of good intentions, you still can't pull it over your hips. March through the door of Next Time Around, Second Hand Rose, the Finer Consigner, or whatever original name your neighborhood reseller has chosen. Together set a price, and sign an agreement giving them 50 percent (more or less) of the take when the item is sold. If, after a certain number of days, your skirt hasn't sold (yes, it was Prada, but who wears chartreuse skirts?), you must return to pick it up. If you forget to collect it, the shop takes ownership (this is how they make their big money). Be a thrifty bitch and mark your calendar, go back, grab the skirt, take it directly to a local charity, and get the tax deduction.

For some of you, the thought of buying a possibly lice-infested hat or another bitch's stinky shoes is sure to inspire a gag reflex. Get over yourself. Higher-end consignment stores are fantastic places for accessories—bags, belts, shoes (bring the Lysol). The best of the stores are stocked full of cool vintage clothing like old Gucci pieces and Stephen Sprouse dresses. Just be smart. Don't fall prey to the "almost good enough" or "OMG, it's a real Dior dress" classic mistake. Even if it seems so cheap or so famous, the same "search and lust" rules apply wherever you shop.

Our proudest consignment kill: a flirty yellow silk number for fifty bucks. Oh-so-smugly we smiled as everyone at the big society wedding kept asking, "Where did you find that dress? It's fabulous!" Best of all, we brought it straight back to the store (we could never wear it again after all that high praise) where another equally tasteful bitch snapped it right up. The net cost for our evening wear—twenty-five bucks. Such a thrifty bitch.

## PLUG INTO AN AC/DC FLEA FEST

Call yourself Calliope and find a flea market in your local paper, or go online to find the ones in your area. We suggest going first as a buyer. If it's a really good, high-traffic, regularly scheduled flea market, look into renting a table. Do this with a group of friends, bring the stuff you want to get rid of, hang out and have fun. Stay strong. If you go as a seller you're not allowed to buy anything that day. Hold on to your hard-earned profits.

## THE END OF DAYS

The final breakdown of our modern economy: Host a swap party—no, not a spouse swap; that's so sixties! We're talking clothing swap. Once a month, to freshen up your wardrobes, invite everyone for a potluck supper and potluck clothing swap. Get the pleasure of newness without spending a dime!

# Chapter 2

·····················

# Grooming
## MAINTAINING A BASELINE
## OF MAINTENANCE

IME TO COME clean about why you spend so much time and money grooming.

It's not because having Olga (the former Russian weight lifter) squeezing out the blackheads around your nose feels good. It's not because Pierre's peroxide concoctions burning your scalp feels good. And it's certainly not because Dr. Richboobs sucking the fat out of your thighs feels good.

Face it: You groom to be dirty—to be the hottest, sexiest bitch you can be. You groom to be rich—to attract the strongest caveman out there. You groom to live forever—to look in that mirror and count the smooth decades ahead.

But just like hunting for that big Neanderthal or rich investment banker are passé vestiges of a primitive drive, so too is succumbing to product marketers and service providers preying on a

41

girl's God-given insecurities. It's time to wake up and be a modern grooming slut. It's time for *you* to define the rules of the game.

Remember, products are just cosmetic enhancements, not magic wands. Beyond sleek packaging and good marketing, little differentiates them. Remember that service providers work for you; like all relationships, they need adjustments now and then—price adjustments. Remember that there's nothing sexier than experience and no greater pleasure than knowing what you want.

Every bitch's grooming goal should be simple: gorgeous, graceful aging. We don't want to look seventeen again (ugh!). And we don't want to squander our savings—what little we've got left. What we want is to look and feel sexy, to make the most of what we've got, and to not get screwed (well . . .) along the way.

## NICE 'N' EASY HAIR RELIEF:
### Love, Cut, Color, Care

### HAIR OBSESSED

You hate your hair. It's too thin, too thick, too curly, too straight. The color is dark, it's mousy, it's oxidized, it's gray. The ends are split; the strands are fried. It looks different every morning; it looks the same every morning. How neurotic!

It's what drives you to that oh-so-swishy salon where a visit sets you back more than a month's pay. In the minute between swiveling in the chair with the handheld mirror and standing at the pay station, you feel transformed. But you know the feeling that comes next. Your stomach tightens and your esophagus fills with bile, as the girl with goth hair and tattoos running up both arms looks out from under her heavily armored eyes, hands back your bill, and patronizingly informs you that the gratuities cannot be added to the charge. Already in a panic over the cost, now you calculate how much cash you have and realize you owe the assistant who washed you out more than a month's worth of coffee at Starbucks. It is bitter, that feeling.

But take heart! You're not alone: just as most women think they're too fat, most women hate their hair. Yes, you're just a normal bitch with low hair-esteem. This makes you easy prey for all those overrated, snippy stylists with more attitude than talent, for those glammy mags whoring goods masked as "tips," for those nauseating cure-all shampoos and dyes pitched by overprocessed starlets. Baby, it's time for some serious hair behavior therapy.

## LOVE THE HAIR YOU'RE IN

First, tell yourself that there is nothing wrong with your hair. That five-hundred-dollar salon visit is not going to part the Red Sea. It will not restore your portfolio to 2007. And, it most certainly will not make your mother love you more than she loves your sister. Once you wash out the shampoo, conditioner, and hair-enhancing products they sold you (yes, you were allowed to put those on the charge), you find that it is still just your hair—and you are still you.

### Five Easy Steps to Loving Your Hair

- Accept the weight and texture you were born with.
- Accept the color nature intended.
- Accept that it won't grow beyond your shoulders.
- Accept that you are not Jennifer Aniston or Beyoncé.

43

- Accept that no one has those swinging, long, flat-ironed-to-shit, shellacked-for-television and magazines 'dos.

Good for you! Finally you've come to peace with your hair as nature intended.

Yes, you're feeling better. But that's no excuse to go all earth mother. Your goals haven't changed. What do you want to be? That's right, a drop-dead-gorgeous sexy bitch. In fact, in these depressing times, when everything seems out of reach, when you aren't treating yourself to half of what you deserve, taking control of your tresses is downright empowering. The questions for today are as follows: How often should you cut? What style works? Who should do the cutting? How should you handle the color and care conundrums?

## ESCAPE FROM EDWARD SCISSORHANDS!

Do all hairdressers think we are just dumb lemming bitches or what? Telling us to trim our hair every six weeks to keep it healthy? Like it's going to get the flu or measles? Right. Do they think our hair uses a calendar? Do they think we believe hair breaks precisely on the microscopic one-half-inch end they clip? These days, with money short, you're not allowed to get a haircut every six weeks. Sorry, eight weeks minimum between clippings.

## CUT IT UP!

History shows that in bad economic times hemlines come down and hair gets shorter. It's counterintuitive, since shorter hair requires more maintenance. But, as anyone who's ever gone short will tell you, it is uplifting. Nothing like a rising new 'do to distract from the falling Dow! Think about it: Since hair remains one of the few free, renewable resources, it's time to get creative. You have a living canvas to play with. If you don't like a cut, it'll always grow back—unlike your portfolio. So: Flat-ironed hair is out. Soft looks and modern geometrics are in. Fringed hair is a budget bitch's dream—no straight lines to go all shaggy on you between groomings. Have fun! You certainly have more spare time at home to play with yourself now.

## Bitchin' Tip

### no lab rats allowed

THROWING YOURSELF at the mercy of a swanky, expensive stylist will *not* lead to hair salvation. If you're paying the big bucks for a new 'do, then do your homework. Know what you want before you sit in the salon chair. Don't become a hapless victim of your stylist's *Access Hollywood* hair fantasies.

## WHO GETS TO DO THE DEED?

If you're happy with your hairdresser, if you think the prices are reasonable, hold up your hand. If you've got your hand in the air, then you're a devoted fan. In fact, since you're such a devoted fan, demand a frequent-user discount!

Now, for those of you who didn't raise your hands. If you're unhappy with your stylist, or just unhappy in a general cosmic and broke kind of way, there's nothing like a fresh new relationship to perk you up. Keep an eye out for haircuts you love on friends, on fellow commuters, and on people lined up at the coffee shop. Approach them and ask who does their hair.

45

Whatever salon you end up at, be a ballsy bitch. See if there's a difference in price between a little trim and a major styling—if there isn't, ask for one. Make certain they'll trim your bangs for free between cuts. Some salons offer lower prices in off hours—you may save yourself big bucks by going in for a Tuesday-morning quickie.

## Bitchin' Tip

### keep blow jobs where they belong

Unless you're going to a prom, bar mitzvah, wedding, or are being honored for winning the Nobel Peace Prize, save *big* bucks at the beauty parlor by blowing your own hair dry. Yes! Dogs are not the only animals who can blow themselves.

## MORE WAYS TO CUT

Do a little research. Call those few snooty salons still left on the highest-rent street in town and find out when their training nights are. Play out your modeling fantasy by volunteering your locks. Everyone needs to learn somehow, and these super-expensive places periodically train their staff on live human specimens. Master cutters and colorists will supervise a fledgling stylist. You may walk out with a different look from what you expected, but you can rest assured it will be masterfully done. (Yes, you are a guinea pig—but what do you expect for free?)

Let's say it's the end of the month. You've already splurged, oversplurged, and—yes—over-oversplurged, and now you're in desperate dollar straits. There's still Supercuts and Great Clips. Yes, they do train their stylists, and yes, they are really, really cheap. Go in smart. Go in careful. Go for a straight-across trim; keep your fingers crossed, and you should be okay!

---

O━🔑 *Splurgeworthy*

### two-faced bitch

$W$E'RE ALLOWED to contradict ourselves—we're women, after all. In every city there are some stylists who are in fact hair *artists*, those who deserve the hype, whose work is transcendent and priced to match. If you find yourself down in the dumps and truly desperate, rather than jumping or calling the Samaritans, track down one of these masters and go for a major hair redo. Just remember this is an emergency visit; afterward, you're back to regular appointments with your mainstay, who can follow the genius's lines for a fraction of the price.

---

## DON'T CURL UP AND DYE!

The hardest habit to break? *Color addiction.* Think hard before you begin. Trust us, this habit is bad for you, bad for your hair, and bad for your budget. The hellacious smell of the stuff should be a tip that the color soaking through your scalp every three or four weeks can't be good for you. Ever notice how your stylist wears rubber gloves? She's protecting her skin—and not just from red fingers. This stuff gets absorbed into the body. Who knows what havoc it causes over the long term? Admittedly, hair dyes are safer now than they've ever been, but any true-blue "greenie" reading the ingredient labels will run the other way.

Still not convinced? Then remember processing is bad for

47

your hair. The biggest single source of damage to glorious, natural-sheen hair is chemical processing, followed by blow-drying, flat-ironing, and shampooing.

As for cost, once you go the full-coverage route, you're hooked. There's nothing less attractive than the creeping skunk line of color as your hair grows in. Once you start, every four to six weeks you're back in the salon in need of another color session.

$0\!\!-\!\!\longrightarrow$ *Splurgeworthy*

### balayage—true artistry

$\mathcal{F}$OR STUNNING highlights, find a salon that offers the French technique of balayage for gorgeous, natural-looking color. Using a brush, your stylist applies color from bottom to top of the strand. More dye saturates the base, less saturates the root, producing a natural, sun-drenched effect. Fabulous!

Unbelievably, most women who color their hair stay close to their own color range. Unless you're covering gray, do not even consider doing this. *Hello!* What is the point? Why waste precious cash and equally precious time? There are oh-so-many better things to do with both!

If you feel you *must* color, go crazy-wild and do something fun and different. Brunette? Go platinum. Why not? Blond? Consider going goth—just like the trendy receptionist at the salon (take a pass on the face armor, though). Or if you aren't that adventurous, try some well-placed foils around your face to brighten and change your look. These partial foils subtly highlight without creating that dreaded skunk line, and are relatively painless to grow out. They'll be a fun color pop every time you look in the mirror.

Be savvy—don't be a color slave.

## Bitchin' Tip

### hair mascara

*Y*OU JUST can't control yourself. Despite our advice, you keep processing in that one-shade block of all-over color. Trailer trash peers back at you in the mirror. It's been just three weeks since your last color fix, but that root line is coming in fast. What's a girl to do? Check out Masc-A-Gray ($7.99), and Nice 'n Easy Root Touch-Up ($7.29).

## SILVER IS AS GOOD AS GOLD

In the early stages a few stray grays are not noteworthy. Do not let a stylist hook you into color slavery as they "helpfully" point out two or three little threads and promise you salvation. Wait. Wait. And then wait some more. Only as it verges on mousy flat should you begin to color. Start with partial foils. Find a colorist who can help you develop a strategy that doesn't cover the gray, but instead eases you into an overall natural-looking change that requires only occasional touch-ups. You'll be on a journey toward lighter hair, which is nature's way of softening your overall look as you age. Remember Meryl Streep in *The Devil Wears Prada*? If you're lucky you'll end up with the most sophisticated, sexy, stunning silver. Trust us, the worst skunk line of all is the gray one.

49

## home solutions

*L*ET'S NOT forget the drugstore option. If you're in need of a change but want to scrimp like a good bitch, a box from CVS may be the ticket. Remember, everything can be fixed, even that screaming lime green nightmare we once found in the mirror . . . oh, but we won't scare you. Give it a whirl. The company Web sites are totally fun to cruise, and our favorite is Christopher Robin for L'Oréal Paris—www.lorealparisusa.com. With his sexy French accent and cute friend-of-Winnie name, he walks you through product after product in their hair color line.

*At Your Fingertips*

## color for the hair down there

*N*OTHING BEATS Betty—"color for the hair down there." We love Betty. It makes us laugh. It makes us smile. We forget we're broke every time we think about Betty. Check out www.bettybeauty.com. For $14 it's the most amusing hair color solution on the market. Available in the expected colors and also red, lavender, yellow, and pink. Surprise him and yourself!

## SMART CARE FOR YOUR HAIR

If there were a nice 'n' easy solution to all our hair-care needs, one perfect, fail-safe product, everyone would be going gaga over it. Instead, you've got thousands upon thousands of choices, each making wild and competing claims. Don't succumb to the temptation! The bitches' mantra "less is more" is especially true when it comes to hair care.

## KEEP IT BASIC

The less you shampoo, the better it is for you and your hair. Like dyeing, flat-ironing, and blowing (hair), shampooing every day damages the strand by taking out all those lovely lubricants your hair needs. Particularly if you have very curly and kinky hair, it's hard for the natural oils to do their magic all the way to the ends. Sudsing bubbles don't help!

The first ingredient listed on the shampoo label is the major one—it's usually water, although some swishy salon brands call it aqua (love it). The next most likely ingredient you'll find are the suds-makers: ammonium laureth sulfate and ammonium lauryl sulfate—doesn't sound so yummy, does it? Often you'll find DMDM Hydantoin, methylchloroisothiazolinone—preservatives. Nice. Ammonium chloride and sodium chloride. Should we keep it up? You get the point. These are not what nature intended for our manes. So, yes, there's nasty stuff in most shampoos and conditioners. The good news is that you rinse it out.

## BE A SHAMPOO AND CONDITIONER SLUT

Given the toxic cocktail of ingredients in most products, we like to mix up our shampoo and conditioning product routine. Many beauty experts say that's the way to achieve maximum product efficacy. We aren't sure we totally buy this, but sometimes we're just lazy bitches—out of shampoo and roaming the aisles of

51

Costco, CVS, or Whole Foods, we'll grab something new. For basic cleansing needs, the cheapest of the cheap will get out dirt, oil, and trace metals. Often, though, we don't like the way they smell or the way they leave our hair feeling. But this is a personal choice. You may love apricot and banana essences and they may make someone else want to throw up.

Find a cheap everyday product that you like, filled with all the evil ingredients that you can't pronounce or read without a 10x magnifier, but try mixing it up with a less chemically enhanced alternate.

O━━ *Thriftiest Bitch*

## beauty supply stores

FIND YOUR local beauty supply store. Not only do they sell jumbo, salon-size shampoo and conditioners; they also carry everything from flat irons to boar-bristle brushes. Make friends; see if they'll give you a bigger discount than what's marked on the bottles. Often they distribute to local beauty shops and give them better prices. These days, business is not all that red-hot, and they may be willing to pass on the same savings to you.

## THE SALON BRANDS

Yes, you can charge these at the shop (and these days even CVS and Target carry the big salon brands), but should you? *Probably* not. After all, you can find less expensive products that work just as well. Sometimes, though, a bitch needs an irrational treat. Case in point: How many pairs of black shoes do you really need? Being a bitch does not go hand in hand with being rational. On occasion we've been suckered into a long-standing affair with a salon product or two. This is okay, so long as you use them wisely. No blind dates these days! Buy only a product you've already been introduced to and know you adore, no experimenting on the recommendation of your stylist pusher.

Let's say you've already played around with a pricey product. Maybe your fancy shampoo's aromatherapy eliminates the need for pricier relaxing agents (Ativan, blood pressure medication, alcohol, analyst). Maybe it's one of the few remaining little life luxuries. In this case, go for it. Just remember: Shampoo less often and mix it up with other products.

## Splurgeworthy

### phyto products

OUR LONG-STANDING affair is with Phyto products. Originally we were seduced when they were available only in Paris, and we couldn't get enough. For years we'd risk mayhem by stuffing breakable glass bottles of mallow shampoo and conditioner into our luggage. While they are way pricey and we no longer buy the shampoo and conditioner, our one absolute must-have everyday product is Phytodefrisant Botanical Hair Relaxing Balm for when we blow-dry (a three-ounce tube costs $26 and seems to lasts forever). Now available in the U.S., this is one of our indulgences.

## CUTTING CORNERS

53

Lest we forget, time is money. Your morning routine should be simple and cheap. Easy for us to say, right? We haven't seen your unruly mane when the alarm goes off. Listen, we know how bad it can be. . . . Maybe you're a girl who wakes up looking like that weird alien from *SNL*—the character with those grotesque appendages sticking out of her head at all angles? Lovely. You roll out of bed, steal a glimpse in the mirror, are tempted to wash the horror away. Hold up. Have you been paying attention? Women are *compulsive* shampooers. Daily washing is a no-no. Just wet it! Radical idea, right? Blow-dry if need be. Tame the beast, by all means, and get on with your day.

Or maybe you've got a gorgeous 'do that holds up well, or you've been blessed with naturally beauteous bed head, but oil weighs it down after a day. Invest in a dry shampoo. These powder sprays absorb oil, add volume, and save time and effort. Bumble and Bumble makes a popular and reputable product. Our money's on Bastiste Dry Shampoo—for a mere seven bucks, it does the trick and earns raves.

## KISS AND TELL RULES

### A GUIDE FOR MAKEUP SANITY

When it comes to all things makeup, always bear in mind the KISS rule: Keep It Simple, Stupid. Don't fall victim to $25 mascaras or $250 firming cleansing lotions. You need only a few basic products to keep your skin clean, hydrated, and adorned. It's time to prune your overgrown makeup basket right down to the bare necessities. A good wash, a single all-purpose moisturizer, and a great base are the foundations of any smart bitch's wardrobe.

Simple doesn't mean you should grow underarm hair and

54

toss out your deodorant. Simple doesn't mean that even though we are becoming a socialist state it's time to go all Soviet-era drab. We all need a little bright face candy, and now more than ever is the time for fun colors that change with the occasion and the season. Every girl needs a cheap thrill. What bigger thrill is there (okay, we can think of a few) than going into Sephora for a little prime-time pick-me-up? New makeup gives a girl a quick, affordable buzz. So, yes, you *do* have permission for an occasional impulse buy.

## BE STRONG

Invest your dollars wisely; everything in life starts with a great foundation. This is the one place you should never skimp. Some skin does best with a cream foundation, some with powdered minerals. Other skin needs just a simple tinted moisturizer. Whichever works best for you, foundation is the best place to put your precious cosmetic dollars.

Finding the right foundation to invest in is a purpose-filled mission. Since drugstores and mass-market stores don't let you open and try foundations, this is the time to brave the department-store counter. Use those cosmetic hustlers to your advantage. You know the types: They shanghai you onto their makeup stool, cake on too much product, and under hot lights do the heavy sell. Each is employed by the brand they are pushing—not by the store. It is in the Laura Mercier lady's interest to sell you Laura Mercier and the Lancôme guy's interest to sell you Lancôme. Be a whore; sample their wares. Listen to their stories about why theirs is the most technologically advanced, micro-bursting-derma-bubble-filled product that through innovative, cutting-edge, soon-to-be-patented, time-release technology massages to orgasm your tired skin, leaving you with that "just after" glow. If only!

55

Bring a friend. Not only do you need a bodyguard, but buying foundation is like buying eyeglasses—you can't really see yourself clearly. Trust another bitch—not the salesperson—to give you the straight story. Remember, both color and viscosity are key. Too pink on yellow skin, too light on dark skin, too dark on light skin—well, it's all too horrible to contemplate. Worse still, as you age, too much makeup filling in those itty-bitty wrinkles only accentuates them. As with all things modern, less is always more.

O━━ *Bitchin' Tip*

### turn, turn, turn

Unless you're little Miss Perfect Sunscreen Bitch, change your tone and tint as the seasons change. In warmer weather a darker color and lighter coverage are timely. In the dead of winter a richer formula and lighter color might be just the ticket. No need for a major overhaul, so do not fall victim to the salesperson's spiel and come home with a whole armload of new "seasonal" products. Tiny tweaks will do the trick.

## SEPHORA: Makeup Mecca

Who doesn't love, love, love Sephora? Well, maybe "lust" is more accurate. After all, entering this glossy black-and-white palace fills us with that overwhelming, blind, thinking-with-the-wrong-part-of-our-body kind of love. You know, the hunger-to-acquire kind of love. The this-will-make-everything-better kind of love. The no-one-can-walk-in-and-have-none kind of love. In this bleak and deprived time you deserve nothing less than requited love. Here's how to get it.

Enter this beauty mecca with your heart, but spend with your head. Know your strategy before you set foot inside. Do not enter the skin or hair-care aisles. Look askance at the $75 lip plumpers and the $100 fragrances. Instead, zero in on the $14 Sephora-brand lipsticks, the $16 Stila eyeliner, and the $17 Make Up For Ever blush. These affordable, quality products will give you a happy glow without the guilt. If only all lust could be satisfied so easily.

O═──▄ *Thriftiest Bitch*

### lash out!

MAYBELLINE'S MASCARAS rule. Smart women know that mascaras should be changed every three months. With over thirty different mascara products, Maybelline knows their stuff. And starting at $4.40, Maybelline mascara is the biggest beauty bargain going.

While a smart splurge may seem like an oxymoron—after all, what fun would a splurge be if it were smart?—buy that new lilac shadow and matching lip color, that yellow-slicker nail polish and magenta eyeliner. Oh-so-much less expensive than a pair of new Ted Muehling or Gabriella Kiss earrings—now sadly dead to you. Submitting now and then to cheap thrills provides a surge of joy and squelches the craving for deep-pocket expenditures.

## At Your Fingertips

**two ways to love**

WE CAN'T get enough of Sephora—after all, it feels so good to touch things, to sample colors, to run our fingers through bins of lip glosses. But we also love checking out sephora.com for sale items. Yes, S-A-L-E. It's a four-letter word and it's not a dirty one. We found a Stila lip six-pack, originally $48, on sale for just $22. Need we say more?

## Thriftiest Bitch

**go down on . . . prices**

WHILE YOU get your rocks off at Sephora 'cause it's so damn stimulating to be there, remember that most makeup is made of the same old stuff. So the drugstore and mass-market brands will give you the same splashes of color at half the price (though, sadly, half the fun). For under ten bucks, check out Revlon's ColorStay lipsticks; for under five bucks, see Cover Girl's endless array of eye shadows.

## SKIN CARE REGIMENTED

**ENOUGH'S ENOUGH**

For too long you've been sold overpriced skin-care regimens and you're not going to take it anymore.

You know how it happened. In a vulnerable moment a pushy

salesperson got under your skin; with alarm she noticed those whiteheads and blackheads, the flakes, the pooling oil, the nascent wrinkles and frown lines. Promising the answer to all your woes, she smoothed onto your hand a series of lovely-smelling products, then slyly drew your well-massaged wrist under a pink-hued cosmetic light. Since you stopped attending religious services and needed something to believe in, you surrendered to the possibility of the all-over glow that could be yours if only you bought into their twelve-step skin-recovery program. Before you knew it you were on your knees, signing on the dotted credit card line.

○━━ *At Your Fingertips*

## www = bff

*Y*OU CAN'T help it. You've decided to splurge on the newest beauty craze. Wait. Before you lunge for that hot new lip stain or succumb to that supposedly sublime smoothing serum, do some research. Check out makeupalley.com, where you'll discover endless customer reviews of practically everything on the market. Don't hand over your credit card until you know how many people would repurchase, how well the product wears, how it compares to others of its kind. Think of MakeupAlley as the biggest high school bitch, the one who's got the inside track on everything, whispering her juicy gossip straight into your ear.

Stand up and kiss good-bye all those pricey lotions and potions, the department-store counter, and Sephora. It's time to meet and greet your new destination for skin-care needs: Walmart, CVS, Target, and Walgreens. We're in a really bad recession. Remember?

## WHAT YOU NEED AND NOTHING MORE

To keep it simple, here's your shopping list:

- **Skin cleanser.** Soap and water are too drying, removing essential oils that your skin needs. Opt for soap-free cleansers. Our faves are Cetaphil and Neutrogena— just $7.99 for eight ounces, easily a six-month supply.
- **Moisturizer.** Check and find the right Neutrogena, Skin Effects, or Oil of Olay product for your skin type. In the $8.99-to-$20.99 price range, these brands are reasonably priced and offer good quality.
- **Exfoliation.** St. Ives Apricot Wash ($4.29) or Skin Effects Purifying Effects Deep-Cleansing Enzyme Scrub ($6.99) clear away dead cells. Plus, they briefly offer that prepubescent softness, so you feel like a virgin again (ha!).
- **Toner.** Dickinson's Original Witch Hazel ($5.99). If you tone, this is the old-fashioned soother for you. We love its cleansing and healing properties. There's a reason it's been around since before the radio.
- **Peels.** If you're pining for your lost monthly facials, try an over-the-counter peel from either Skin Effects or Neutrogena. Priced in the $25 range, to be used monthly.

## know the skin you're in

MASS-MARKET MANUFACTURERS offer products for every skin type. Their Web sites are sophisticated, easy to navigate, and will help you target the right product for you. No human interaction, no chances of anyone preying on your insecurities and selling you schlock you do not need. Check out oilofolay.com and neutrogena.com.

*Bitchin' Tip*

## give me the drugs!

RETIN-A MICRO and Renova are two of the better-known brand names of tretinoin, a drug developed from vitamin A and used primarily to treat acne. These have been proven effective in reducing the appearance of wrinkles, since one of the by-products of vitamin A is increased production of collagen. They're available only by prescription and do have side effects, including redness and skin irritation; use only under a doctor's supervision. Your skin will be more susceptible to damage while using these products, so avoid sunbathing or waxing.

61

## CHANGE WE CAN (SORT OF) BELIEVE IN

In the go-go Bush days you waltzed into the posh spa for your regularly scheduled afternoon of delight. The cedar walls and eucalyptus trees radiated health. Soothing New Age music played in the background. Just stepping in, receiving the receptionist's calm smile, you felt relaxed, rich, privileged. In the oversized changing room you slid your feet into fresh white terry thongs. A helper dropped a warmed white robe over your shoulders. You held a mug of steaming green tea while waiting in the massaging lounger for your weekly mani-pedi and monthly waxing . . . all right, all right, enough already. Yes, it was good. Yes, you miss it. No need to wallow.

Listen, it's okay to admit you miss aspects of Dubya, and this is one of them. We all have our dirty little secrets, and certainly few are as all-over satisfying as that afternoon tryst at the spa. Alas, one of today's little sacrifices is your spa delight.

But the question remains: In this economy, where do you go to keep your little piggies looking kosher, your eyebrows arched, and your "hair down there" trimmed? Lovely spa afternoons are done and bankruptcy may loom, but that's no excuse to go all cavewoman. The compromise? Go to your local corner mani-pedi place, find an eyebrow threader, and sneak back for an occasional afternoon quickie with your old stripper.

## MAKE AMENDS

First, say hello to your neighborhood down-and-dirty manicurist. You know the place. It's had the same sign in its window for a decade: OPENING SPECIAL: MANI-PEDI $24.99! You passed it by for years, just like the boy you wouldn't give the time of day to until you were desperate for a date to the senior prom. Now you need him, and you must make amends. But you've got to have a strategy. Don't turn your precious digits over to just anyone. Listen up before you dip your feet into those whirlpool baths or get your cuticles clipped, because there is nothing nastier than the fungus and bacterial infections lurking inside grooming joints.

## Clear-cut Rules

1. Bring your own tools. Go to a local beauty supply store and buy your own clippers, cuticle cutters, emery boards, push tools, even water bowls for your hands. Take them home to sterilize them after each use.
2. Be a demanding bitch and ask to see not only the shop's license, but also the license of the aesthetician working for you. Make sure the pictures match!
3. Consider carefully if you want to have your cuticles clipped. This often leads to breaks in the skin, which are an easy entry point for bacterial infection. If you opt for this procedure, make sure your manicurist uses the clippers from your own kit.
4. Be an even *bigger bitch* and make sure the manicurist has gloves on or has really scrubbed her own hands.
5. Buy and bring your own nail polish. You'll be happy to have it on hand at home for touchups.
6. *Never* put your feet in a whirlpool bath. Yes, you watch them quickly spray it clean, but the filters and hoses the water passes through never really get clean. Better go to a shop with an old-fashioned basin for your feet that you can watch get scrubbed. Consider bringing your own disinfectant. Embrace your OCD.

*63*

## THE HAIR DOWN THERE . . . AND OTHER PLACES

This is painful stuff. You loved the $90 Brazilian you were getting at the old place. It was pristine. They never double-dipped. Each time wax was applied a new stick was used, and the sheets on the table were crisp and freshly changed. The aesthetician was charming; even in the "position" you discussed the hot spot for vacations, compared the price of cucumbers at Whole Foods versus the farmer's market, and vented about your latest man trouble. Cheaper than any therapist was she. . . . Well, maybe you can't quite give her up.

It's okay.

You just need to think differently about how you use her, that's all.

Like all other service providers, business is not that robust in the "hair down there" removal market. So:

Negotiate. See if she'll reduce the price by 20 to 25 percent if you agree to a package. Honey, 10 percent is not motivational these days.

If your love life and the weather are both frigid, take a pass until things heat up again.

Skip the full-out Brazilian; a regular bikini wax is cheaper.

Stretch time between waxings. This is one spot where very few people should notice the change.

## SAVING FACE

While you can skimp on "hair down there" treatments, your face should never reflect sacrifice. Maintain your eyebrows, girls, but do it smart: Skip the waxing. Instead find a spot that does threading. Originally from India, this procedure is now all the rage in the States. The technician uses two pieces of thread, grabs the hair, and out it comes, follicle and all. No red patches. It's a cheaper, less painful, and faster alternative for facial hair removal.

**use your tweezers and a razor**

*J*UST LIKE pen and paper still write, landline telephones still connect, and the burners still work on your stove, tweezers still pluck and razors still shave.

## UPLIFT YOUR ASSETS

IT'S BAD ENOUGH that you hear the echo of your mom's voice every time you yell at your kids, but if every time you look in the mirror you see her face staring back at you, those overpriced creams you schmear on morning, noon, and night are just not cutting it. You're ready for a full-frontal assault. If in the boom times you had your friendly neighborhood plastic surgeon's number on speed dial, then, honey, this is no time to delete it. A little tune-up is just what the doctor ordered. No, bitch, *not* a full overhaul: No full lifts allowed. And, for heaven's sake, nothing brand-new. Remember it's in bad taste to flaunt big ones in depressed times. Sorry, no new titties this year!

Like everything else, today's cosmetic surgery has a whole new face. Remember the bitches' mantra: Less is more. Full face-lifts are like buying a Hummer when a Prius will get you around. Besides, even in the best of times, the most natural and enhancing cosmetic remedies are peels, lasers, and teensy-weensy injections of toxins and plumping agents. So now, with money scarce, a girl needs to be extra choosy about how to smooth and tighten, where to lift, and whom she gets into bed with to make her feel better.

Before you do anything you must meet the criteria for spending money on cosmetic procedures.

65

# PLASTIC SURGERY RULES DISSECTED

## BELOW THE NECK

You are allowed to consider work below your neck only if:

- You had gastric bypass and now have oodles of unwanted flapping skin.
- You have a huge trust fund not invested with Bernie Madoff.

## ABOVE THE NECK

You may consider tiny work if:

- On a daily basis your friends and colleagues ask you who died, why you haven't been sleeping, or if you have a life-threatening disease.
- You are recently divorced, over fifty, in the dating market, and need to be competitive with twenty-five-year-olds.
- You are out of work (and who isn't these days?) and need to look younger to land a job.
- You have bad genes and look at least ten years older than your actual age.

 *Thriftiest Bitch*

### the real fountain of youth

$\mathcal{E}$VER NOTICE all those older women with beautiful porcelain skin, no age spots, and no wrinkles? Wonder what their secret

*(continued)*

is? Sunscreen. Or rather, sun avoidance. Whether they used an umbrella, wore a huge hat, or religiously applied SPF 30+, they've limited their exposure to the leading source of damage to the skin. The sun. Don't get all smug because your daily moisturizer already has SPF 15—all sunscreens are not created equal. Make certain yours protects against both UVA and UVB rays. Slather it on every two hours and after each swim. Sunscreen is the cheapest fountain of youth we know.

## GET INTO BED ONLY WITH THE RIGHT TOOL

So you qualify for surgery and are wondering what to do next. First, find the *best* plastic surgeon or dermatologist in your area. Since this is a cash business (no insurance reimbursements), everyone you know is pushing cosmetic enhancements. Medispas are springing up on every corner, friends stage Botox parties in their homes, even your internist has morphed into a service station offering "a freeze and fill-up" at your annual checkup.

Do not be a dumb bitch! Unless you want to look like a frozen zombie with a drooping eye and blowfish lips, allow no one but an expert cosmetic surgeon or dermatologist to inject potentially lethal toxins and fillers into, pour acid on, or wield a scalpel on your face. Check around, ask around. While no one will admit to having had work done (yeah, right!), everyone will know someone else who has. Walk in armed:

Know your budget before you begin. Don't get talked into doing more than you can afford.

Visit at least three potential doctors.

Interview and ask: How long they have been in practice? How many procedures like the one they are recommending have they done? What is their rate of success? Have they ever

67

paid out a malpractice claim? Most states publish lists of doctors, their credentials, and whether they have been subject to board discipline. Check them out.

Aim a critical eye at their face book (no, not that Facebook!) photos. Examine before and after pictures of other patients.

Bring a friend with you. Debrief after each visit. Trust a fellow bitch to give you the candor and perspective you need.

Walk out if they try to upsell you. Walk out if they're impatient or won't reveal malpractice information. Walk out if the face book looks fishy.

0——🗝 *Bitchin' Tip*

### let's make a deal

♦ *Negotiate.* Face it, bitches: These times suck. During lean days, nipping and tucking applies to our budgets. But if you're shrewd you may find yourself at an advantage. Particularly hard hit by this economic downturn are elective cosmetic procedures, so this is your opportunity to get a deal.

♦ *Negotiate.* Ask the right questions. Make the right demands. Does your doctor offer a sliding scale? Tell them you want a discount if you do a series of peels or injections. Remember you're talking with several doctors, so if you receive a better deal from one, ask the others if they can beat it. Everyone selling something gets a whole lot nicer in desperate times.

♦ *Negotiate.* Botox, Restylane, Perlane, and Juvederm often offer rebates to the doctor. Just like when you

*(continued)*

redeem a supermarket rebate coupon, your doc takes a label off the used box and sends it back for cash. Pharmaceutical companies often offer two-for-the-price-of-one syringes. Make sure the savings and syringes are passed on to you.

## NIP AND TUCK OR PRICK AND PEEL?

Remember, this is war. The cosmetic-physician industrial complex has fueled a beauty-enhancement arms race. So what does this mean for you? First, stop thinking of yourself as a piece of meat waiting to be sliced and diced. That is so last decade. Neat little pinpricks—a little toxin here and a little filler there—go a long way. This is the modern age of lasers and peels, so old-fashioned knife-wielding remedies should be the last resort. The new euphemism for cosmetic surgery is "facial rejuvenation." Your goal is not to have your chin pulled upward to your eyebrows. Find the right ammunition to make you look fresh, rested, and relaxed.

## OH! WHAT A LITTLE TOXIN WILL DO

Botox is a miracle cure inside a tiny vial. Derived from toxic bacteria, when ingested or injected in noncosmetic form it can lead to paralysis and death. Or worse, when injected in the wrong spot or overused, it can leave you looking like a stroke victim or one of those frightening, frozen-faced mannequins. Every Tom, Dick, and Mary is offering injections. Trust us, and go only to a board-certified MD for your work. Most treatments last three to four months and can run anywhere from $250 to $1,000, depending on how many injections and what kind of deal you cut. For maximum benefit, focus on frown lines between the eyes, forehead furrows, crow's feet, and wrinkles around the lips.

These days, Botox has some competition. Ask your doc about Dysport, recently FDA approved, reputedly faster, and long-lasting.

## IS FILLER FINER?

The most popular fillers are Restylane, Perlane, and Juvederm, all brand-name products derived from hyaluronic acid—a naturally occurring substance in our skin. Unlike Botox, which actually paralyzes those wrinkly places, these products fill in and plump out your wrinkles, while stimulating new collagen growth. Think like an addict as you plan, because you will be buying "syringes" when you go for filler. So if you can afford only one "do up," go for the nasolabial folds, the creases that start at your nostril and run down to your mouth.

A fill-up starts at $500. In an effort to promote business and hook new customers, manufacturers of these products are offering two-for-one pricing on syringes, so if you end up with extra, plump up around the cheeks.

O—— *Splurgeworthy*

### the bitch's choice

*A* COMBINATION OF Botox and filler is your best buy for a totally rejuvenated look. For $800 to $1,600 you can buy six months of the fountain of youth. A pretty penny, sure, but the results are like ripples in a pond. Pump up your self-esteem, save on pricey product, and savor the yearning stares. How does she do it?

## no dollar footprint

*A*ND DON'T underestimate the importance of putting on a good front. Most physicians recommend diet, exercise, rest, and—yes—smiling as a way to uplift your mood and your look. It's been a long time, bitch, but give it a try.

## BEAUTY IS ONLY SKIN-DEEP—WHAT A RELIEF!

Once you've decided it's time to pull out the more invasive big guns, the first procedures you might consider are chemical peels and laser treatments. Both treatments are effective at reducing brown spots, smoothing out imperfections, and stimulating collagen that plumps up the skin, filling out those nasty wrinkles.

## THE PEELS

Peels are divided into three main categories: AHA, TCA, and Phenol types. AHA (alphahydroxy acid) is the least intense and can restore a healthful glow to your skin. Irina at your local spa can give you a cheap AHA thrill for under $100. Your skin will feel smooth and glow for a few days. TCA (trichloroacetic) acid peels are the choice for women who want more serious work. The active agents in these peels are high-test and need to be applied in your doctor's office under controlled conditions. Sometimes more than one is needed for long-term benefit. TCA peels can be had for as little as $500, and they'll have a more dramatic and longer-lasting result than an AHA peel. Pass on the Phenol peel—it is the very strongest, has a very long recovery time, and is mucho pricey (in the thousands).

71

## BEAM ME UP

Lasers are exploding as a cosmetic tool. Your choice will be between lasers that remove skin and lasers that just penetrate the skin. Ablative laser treatments work by removing the outer layer of the skin. As the skin heals, new skin is formed and new collagen growth has been stimulated. Recovery time from these treatments can be several weeks. Nonablative treatments do not remove the outer dermis but focus light under the skin, leading to improved texture, less wrinkling, and elimination of fine veins and age spots. These may take several visits.

## NIPS AND TUCKS

The only surgical intervention you are allowed until the Dow tops 10,000 again and your house is worth what it was in 2006 is a blepharoplasty. Never heard of it? It's the procedure that takes the excess skin out of the upper eyelid and the fat out of the lower eyelid, and it's the one surgical intervention that makes the biggest difference on most faces. More permanent than toxins and fillers, removing that unsightly sag from the upper eyelid can reduce the appearance of aging dramatically. A reputable plastic surgeon's fee should start at $1,200.

*Thriftiest Bitch*

### night work

STOW THOSE bags under your eyes. Treat yourself to the ultimate luxury—a full eight hours of sleep. After all, nothing important ever happens before ten a.m. Your inner bitch needs her zzz's.

*Chapter 3*

......................

# No Money Is No Excuse

## BE A HEALTHY (AND THRIFTY) BITCH

*J*UST BECAUSE YOUR purse strings are tight, your anxiety level elevated, and the future of the free world uncertain, there are no excuses for sitting on the couch swilling martinis chased by boxes of Double Stuf Oreos and chocolate orgasm ice cream. While every normal bitch needs a little medication now and then, enough is enough. If ever you needed a "natural" high, now is the time, and there's simply no better way to do it than by getting your house in order. Yes, that temple you live in—your body.

Follow our advice and clean up your food act, get your ass in gear, and spend a little more time on the best free pleasures life has to offer. We guarantee hard times will never have looked—or felt—so good!

Let's begin by deconstructing the holy trinity of exercise, nutrition, and body image.

73

1. **Exercise to stay healthy and feel good.** Find activities, new and old, that you love doing—no, not because you're chasing Gisele Bundschen's physique, but because you're just having fun. *Fun,* yes. Didn't expect that word to appear in a chapter about fitness, did you? Think about it: As a kid playing tag in the backyard or hopscotch in the street, did you call that "exercising"? Of course not. You couldn't wait to get out the door. The joy was the game—not the caloric burn. How, then, have you managed to turn play into another scheduled, flavorless activity?

2. **Eat well.** Eat foods that provide essential nutrients. Eat foods you love for the sheer delicious pleasure of yummy, good cooking. Remember when a plate of fresh pasta with homemade tomato sauce was just supper, not a nasty bowl of carbohydrates? Return to basics. Stop teasing your palate! Find healthy ways to give it what it wants. The explosive sensory satisfaction of robust food makes life worth living!

3. **Accept yourself.** Wake up, look around—in this multi-culti world we live in there's no longer a single icon of beauty. A woman with a hip modern aesthetic doesn't settle for just loving her inner bitch; she knows the outer one is fine too, whatever her shape! After all, how many of us are six-foot Nordic beauties or African princesses? And if you need more proof: Tyra Banks cast a whole season of models under five-seven. It's about time you learned to be happy in your own skin— you'll live smarter, better, happier, and longer.

# BE LIKE GOLDILOCKS:
## Step Up to the Balance Beam
......................

**NO, THIS IS** not an inspirational self-help book for all you insecure bitches out there. This is a flat-out lecture.

Take care of your body. Accept the good, the bad, and the
ugly—love it for what it is. Contrary to the continued visual
harangue of the media, there's no ideal body type. You've been
given one body, and every bitch's goal is to find what works for it.
Your job is to keep it in the best shape you can for a long, healthy,
and fun life. Think Goldilocks—obsessing is too much, doing
nothing is too little, taking care of yourself is just right. . . .

So:

You do not have permission to be morbidly obese. Stuffing
your face to escape reality and find comfort may work temporarily, but those serotonin highs from all that processed junk
are a short-lasting and ugly fix. Being overweight is not okay for
you, and it is certainly not okay for the polis—after all, since
we're becoming a communist state, should we all be paying for
your insulin?

Don't get all smug, you superskinny bitches—just as (if not
more) dangerous to your health is starving yourself. Destroying
your muscles in a misguided quest for control and perfection?
Enough. Being the thinnest bitch out there is not going to make
you a hot, happy babe. It's just going to make you look like the
starving, unemployed refugee that you just might be.

Stop, take a deep breath, and consider the words of the mother
of American cooking, the rock star of food, the Amazonian queen
of the kitchen, our Lady of Lovin' What You Eat—Julia Child.
Her famous words, "everything in moderation, including moderation," are your new mantra. Take it from her. She lived with a
zest for food and life till the ripe old age of ninety-one.

75

# EVERYTHING IN MODERATION

**HOW MANY STORIES** have you heard of the grandma or great-aunt who, despite her two-pack-a-day cigarette habit, wine imbibing, and sedentary ways, lived to a hundred? And how many stories have you heard of the elite marathon runner who, despite an excellent diet free of saturated fat, alcohol, and junk food, collapsed at fifty doing a low-key 10K? No, don't start drinking, smoking, and sitting, and don't stop running—the point is that there are no guarantees.

Experts agree that eating a healthy diet low in saturated fat, loaded with fresh fruits, nuts, whole grains, and vegetables, keeps your body performing optimally. Eat fresh fish high in omega-3s—like bluefish (check out the yummy recipe on page 276), sardines, mackerel, and salmon. Throw away the processed foods—that shit is killing you. Snack smart. Have a great piece of fruit or try skinny cucumbers (really) with a pinch of fleur de sel. Buy dried apricots. Nibble nuts. A few chocolate-covered raisins aren't going to kill you, either. Pigging out does that!

"Low-fat," "low-carb," "low-sugar," "low-calorie" emblazoned across cookie cartons are *not* erasing the essential junk ingredients most are made with. Look closer. Trans fats abound, and calorie content is only marginally less on most of these boxes. A calorie is a calorie. Garbage in is garbage worn.

Instead, make your own chocolate-chip cookies. Use whole-wheat flour, reduce the sugar, use high-quality butter, organic eggs, and killer chocolate. Feel like that kid again. Cook, mess, clean. Pour a big glass of milk. Dip 'em. A few won't hurt you. And if you make them yourself, they'll taste so much better. That's right—satisfy yourself with your own two hands. You've been doing this all your life—why stop now?

Balance is the game.

Be smart about how you eat—constantly denying yourself the stuff you crave only leads to obsessing about how much you want those brownies and can't have them. The end result: You want them more. The more you crave, the more likely you are to wake up in the pantry with crumbs all over your face. Snickers lover? Who doesn't adore those caramel-covered peanuts in gooey chocolate? You have permission, now and then, to slowly, sinfully consume a candy bar. Are you dying for ribs slathered in sweet sauce, rich, mayonnaisey coleslaw, collard greens cooked in bacon fat? Have a plate of authentic BBQ on that now-rare night when you eat out. Since trips to restaurants happen so infrequently now, make the most of them—let yourself order decadent foods that are hard to prepare yourself.

on the environment and the economy—not to mention our bodies. When the prices are right, when you can swing it, buy local. Support the community, reduce your carbon footprint, and enjoy fresher, more nutritious produce and meat. Check out locavores.com to find people in your own community dedicated to eating locally grown and harvested food. Do everyone a favor and be a healthy, homegrown bitch.

And good God—every bitch in these times needs a drink. Just remember your mantra: moderation. But hold on; in case you're starting to get all loose and excited about your vices— absolutely *no* smoking. Not in moderation, not ever. Besides cancer, heart attack, and the five-bucks-plus-a-pack price tag, unless you live in a vacuum-packed trailer in the park, second-hand smoke is killing everyone around you.

Not to be Debbie Downer, but no one lives forever. Hyper-focusing on whether something is "good for you" (usually a euphemism for calorie count rather than an assessment of vita-min/mineral content) will drive you insane, just as mindlessly stuffing your mouth will wreck your body. Chances are that a lifetime of denial or guilt about food will lead to weight and mental-health problems. It's all about making balanced choices so you can enjoy the ups and downs of the ride.

## TRUST A PROFESSIONAL (AND BALANCE THE BUDGET WHILE YOU'RE AT IT)

**MAKING REASONABLE CHOICES** about nutrition and exercise requires guidance. Start with your physician at your annual checkup. Yes, we know you're hustled in and hustled out, but hold your ground and demand time to talk about the most important ingredient in health care, one that would save our country a shitload of money, one that's a linchpin in saving our economy, possibly the single biggest ingredient on the way to a balanced national budget: preventive care. Go to your doc armed with a list of questions about what your ideal weight should be and what a balanced diet given your medical history would look like. Together, set a direction for an exercise and food regimen that makes sense for your physical condition.

A smart bitch knows her BMI (body mass index), a rough measure of fat to overall body mass, and keeps it in check. She also has an ideal weight range specific to her body type that she's comfortable with and tries to maintain. Remember, everyone is different! Looking like a dissolute catwalk freak or Anna Nicole Smith (you know how that ended) is not the goal. Every bitch has different bone structure and metabolic rates—work with your doctor and find your own zone.

⊙━━ *At Your Fingertips*

### just the numbers

To CHECK your BMI, use the National Institute of Health's simple calculator at www.nhlbisupport.com/bmi/.

- BMI less than 18.5? You're too skinny, bitch. Do you really want people whispering, "Skeletor," behind your back? This isn't a good kind of attention. Confer with your doc.
- BMI 18.5 to 24.9? You're a healthy bitch. Congrats! Look in the mirror. Do you resemble a bug-eyed twig

*(continued)*

79

strutting the runway after a breakfast of coffee and half a pack of cigarettes? No? Good. This is what you're aiming for. Admire what you see; keep it in shape.

- BMI 25.0 to 29.9? You're an overweight bitch. Wake up, shut your mouth, and get to work. No sugarcoating it.
- BMI 30.0 or up? You're officially an obese bitch. But don't lose hope. You're not alone. Find some support, confer with your doc. Be the Biggest Loser. Get started. *Now*.

Now, to determine what you need to work on—weight loss, weight gain, cardio, flexibility, strength training, etc.—your next stop and smartest investment will be the absolute best trainer your budget allows. It may feel like an extravagance, but, hey, this is your temple we're talking about. Find a trainer who'll devise a program *just for you*. Unless you're a rich bitch, *this is strictly a short-term arrangement*. We're talking just a quickie, the ol' in-and-out. (Get your head out of the gutter, girl—this is strictly a fitness assessment, so no illicit activities on the StairMaster, no matter how many calories you think you'll burn.) You'll want a program tailored for your body mechanics. Look into whether your health insurance pays for a visit to an exercise physiologist, nutritionist, physical therapist, whomever. . . . This is your first stop in this marathon.

Be reasonable in your expectations. You're at the beginning of a long, slow build to a healthy lifestyle, not a faddish sprint. And, since life is not a dress rehearsal, be sure you actually take pleasure in the food you eat and the exercise you do.

Speaking of pleasure, it's high time to find activities that you love to keep your body toned and well lubed.

# A BITCH IN MOTION

**START WITH THE** premise that any movement is better than no movement.

Experts recommend thirty minutes of moderate physical activity five days a week for a healthy body and healthy heart. Ideally you should alternate among a variety of routines. You want to work on endurance and conditioning (hiking, running, and swimming); building muscle (free weights, bands, lifting the baby); and stretching/range-of-motion exercises (yoga, creative sex, dance). Heart disease is the leading cause of death among women in the U.S., so conditioning and aerobic activity are vital. Weight-bearing exercises are also key, since they guard against osteoporosis. And keeping yourself limber as you age is essential for overall flexibility and joint health.

## ⚷ *At Your Fingertips*

### what goes in?

*You* PAY good money for the government to do this work. Now use it!

- First off, learn how to read a food label: www.cfsan. fda.gov/~dms/foodlab.html.

- Do not be a gullible bitch. Get the straight story on fat free versus regular calories in so-called "good for you" foods: www.nhlbi.nih.gov/health/public/heart/ obesity/lose_wt/fat_free.htm.

- And, while you're at it, demand your local town or city pass a law that requires restaurants to post calorie and nutrition values on menus. Now that you know how to read labels, put it to good use.

# WHICH BITCH?

**WE ALL KNOW** the hardest part of exercising is getting off your ass. Remember, any motion is better than no motion! You're more likely to get moving if you know *what moves you.* So, who are you? What drives you? What are your weaknesses? You could spend months in therapy figuring this out, or you could glance below. Chances are you fit one of these types. Accept it and get on with things.

## THE LAZY BITCH

She just can't get it together to do anything. Every day in every way she means to get going. Tomorrow she's going to start jogging, riding her bicycle, walking two blocks to the store instead of driving. The next day arrives but it's too cold out, she has a headache (the same one she had the night before when her husband wanted to have sex), the laces are broken on her sneakers. It's gotten so bad she's moved her pillow and blanket to the couch on the main floor so she doesn't have to climb the stairs to her bedroom.

## THE EVER-HOPEFUL BITCH

With unflagging hope she buys gear for each of her new, fabulous sports and activities. She begins each with the fervent belief that being properly outfitted will catapult her into the Boston Marathon, onto the LPGA tour or the cover of *Sports Illustrated.* (You don't have the heart to tell her the *SI* swimsuit edition has nothing to do with women or sports—it's all about men's fantasies.) But she talks about working out way more than she works out. Clearly she is not an exercising bitch. Friends detect her good but impotent intent and label her wimpy.

## THE PEPPY BITCH

She is just *so* happy to go and work out, she just *can't* get enough! So cheerful. Whether in her little tennis whites (racket in hand), Speedo swimsuit (goggles in hand), or pressed Bermuda shorts (nine iron in hand), she keeps to a routine. Coming back from her morning six miles, before getting the kids out the door and running off to her job, she gushes about her endorphin high, practically climaxing when she describes her squat thrusts. She is such a good sport. Face it, she annoys the shit out of just about everybody.

## THE CHILL BITCH

You remember her from college. She was the modern-dance minor. Tall, willowy body. Talks in long, slow, deliberate sentences, heavily modified and amended. Now she's into power yoga, Pilates, cross-country skiing, and long day hikes. Most likely a vegetarian, cultivating her own farm because it's the only way she can trust that her sacred body ingests truly organic and ethical foods.

## THE KILLER BITCH

And then there's the beat-the-crap-out-of-everyone Killer Bitch. She never plays nice, and needs to win it all. She has no opinion about the Lazy Bitch, the Ever-hopeful Bitch, the Chill Bitch, or the Peppy Bitch—in her quest to flatten them, she never even sees them. Gear is professional grade, never pretty, never clean.

Lazy Bitches, you have a problem. You need help, and you can't do it alone. But who to turn to? Peppy and Killer Bitches can't begin to understand your ennui. Chill Bitch, her brow knitted with concern, is way too evolved in her self-realization to feel responsible for another bitch. Your best bet? Befriend an Ever-hopeful Bitch, come clean to her about your little problem (not the sex one), and enlist her aid in getting you off your fat ass. If this fails, inquire whether your health insurance covers therapy.

If you're like us you fall into the second category: the Ever-hopeful Bitch—well-intentioned, verbal, neurotic, and not naturally good at sports. Yet if accompanied by a chatty friend, we'll do almost anything for hours.

If you're that Peppy Bitch, a true endorphin junkie, team sport player, skilled athletic goddesses—go for it! More power to you. (If we sound snarky, it's just because we're jealous, so jealous.)

Chill Bitches, you really are cool, and we all have something to learn from your flexible physical state (if not your rigid PC views).

Killer Bitches . . . well, you're not reading this book.


## MAKE THE MOST OF YOUR TYPE

**FIRST, ALL YOU** Ever-hopeful and Lazy Bitches: Get started and don't quit. Find your friend(s) and partner up. You just haven't found the right exercise, mates, or mind-set. We'll give you some new ideas and a kick in the butt.

Peppy preppies. Yes, you're lucky as hell, and have found your niche, but times are tough and those pricey sports clubs are killing you. Plus you probably need to add a little Zen to your package—if for no other reason than to stop irritating everyone around you.

Chill ladies—you're probably doing just fine. Relax. Skip ahead. *Namaste.*

And you Killer babes (who of course aren't reading this because you're too busy kickboxing or knocking the wind out of everyone on the opposing volleyball team)—well, we all need to take a page out of your book. What can we glean from your sweating, clench-jawed ways? To never pay attention to what others think about how you look and how you play. To lose yourself in the game. To stay focused on the prize. Yes, the prize! Not winning the game— that's *so* Bush-era. The prize today is better health, more fun, and a fuller life. *This* mission can actually be accomplished.

## WORK IT OUT

### GYM DANDY

The American strip mall landscape is littered with health clubs, swim clubs, and tennis clubs of every shape, size, and stripe. You know, the one you joined with incredible enthusiasm, seduced by the super-duper introductory special offer just for you on the day you visited. Instead of $150 to join, the pleasure could be yours for just $100 and a low $75 monthly fee. With great energy and determination you worked out on your way home from work for several months, or, even more righteously, set the alarm one hour earlier in the morning.

Then you got a cold, your kid got a cold, maybe even the dog got a cold, and you missed a morning, then another, and pretty soon you fell off the wagon. Yes, on occasion you dragged your ass in on the weekend to a complete mob scene, and oh, how oppressive it felt! By now the bloom was off the rose. Not only were the locker rooms stinky, but you felt your skin crawling, and were sure some pervert had wired the showers for video of your privates. It just wasn't fun. The dues were automatically deducted from your checking account for the year of that contract (yes, those sleazy suckers figured out how to mainline your cash when you signed up), and every time you thought about it you soothed your guilty conscience with a SnackWell's cookie.

It's okay.

For some of you, that whole hermetically sealed, generically equipped exercise scene is just not the right venue. Live and learn, go outside and play. Others may just have tumbled into the wrong joint. The rule of thumb when it comes to exercise machines, routines, equipment, and venues is this: Keep it simple. You *do not* need fancy. You need clean and you need reasonable. That's why our very favorite spots nationwide are the YM/YWCA, JCC, or local town and city rec departments. Check out their rate structures, which vary by city and town. Unlike chain clubs that are perfectly content to suck you dry, these places may offer a sliding-scale fee or waiver of initiation charges for those needing financial assistance.

But some bitches just like for-profit clubs. They can't live without those extra perks (expensive juice bar, gossipy sauna, hot instructors). If this is you, and you choose a for-profit club, take advantage of free trial packages to really see how it feels. Also, in an ideal universe, opt for a month-to-month plan until you're sure you're going to commit long-term to the facilities. No initiation fees, period. As always, remember that all of these clubs are in deep doo-doo. Negotiate! And never, ever let anyone dip directly into your precious checking account again for payment—walk first.

## FREE WALKING ROCKS!
## NO APPOINTMENT REQUIRED

Ladies, strut your stuff. Step outside and *go*. No fancy gear, no lessons, no bullshit. According to WebMD (www.webmd.com/

fitness-exercise/benefits-of-exercise), "if you walk 4 miles a day, four times a week, you can burn 1,600 calories, or nearly half a pound a week." Over the course of a year that's twenty-four pounds. Four miles may sound like a lot but it isn't—a healthy adult can do a mile in fifteen minutes at a fast clip.

What more could a bitch want in life than a healthy walk with a hyperchatty friend? Start slow if you aren't in shape, and step it up as you get stronger. Let your arms swing free and quicken the pace. Ideally you want to walk fast enough that you can talk, but be winded enough that you can't break out into song (save it for the shower). Your goal is to elevate your heart rate and work up a sweat.

Invest in good shoes and consider hand weights. But skip the fancy exercise duds! You're supposed to get sweaty and look rugged—otherwise you aren't really moving your buns the way they need to move. (Remember, Walmart has really inexpensive Danskin warm-ups if you feel you must look the part.) Otherwise, reject the gear and gratuitous accoutrement. You don't need magazine subscriptions or odometers or sleek water bottles that double as shoulder massagers. Just walk, bitch! Walk and talk. Keep it simple.

0━━━ *Splurgeworthy*

### footloose

You've only got those two little tootsies, and they've got a long way to go and an important load to bear. Once you're into a consistent exercise routine, get fitted for a pair of all-purpose training shoes that suit walking and all the other fun sports you're now learning. Locate the best running store in your area; let an expert foot fetishist—uh, salesperson—

*(continued)*

examine your feet and recommend a pair based on your arch, width, toe box, etc. It may be one-size-for-all when it comes to your pashmina shawls, but your kicks need to be specialized. No bargain-basement stops here! Protect your knees, hips, and back in the long term by wearing the right sneaks now.

As for walking companions, make sure they entertain. What better time to get filled in on the neighborhood gossip, catch up on the latest installment of the *Real Housewives*, fret about the prospect of your three-year-old entering kindergarten in diapers, discuss the hot new guy in IT, obsess about the right paint color for the kitchen. An hour won't seem long enough! But you'll skip the walk if you find your partner dull or grating.

Put your organizing skills to good use. Invite a group of people you want to get to know. Create a Saturday-morning walking club or add a Sunday-evening walk to the movie group. Merge walking with other hobbies—tell yourself you can go to Target only if you walk there and home again with your purchases. Make it fun! Organize urban walks to check out the new cupcake shops or adult toy emporiums.

Say you're a single bitch on the prowl. Take little Maxie, or borrow your friend's cute little Bichon, Chihuahua, or Labradoodle. Think like a streetwalker trying to attract attention, but dress the pooch (not you) in a hot outfit. Head out the door with confidence. As long as little Fido is friendly, it's insane how many people you'll pick up on the street. Use the canines to get crazy, ladies.

88

ROSALYN HOFFMAN

## ELEVATE YOURSELF

Once you have a good walking routine going, don't plateau. Expand your vistas and degree of difficulty. It's time to take the walking show on the road.

Check out local reservoirs, which often feature paved paths and pristine and lovely views. Next, get maps of your local area and look for walking trails. Lace up your sneakers and visit the nearest bird sanctuary (see chapter 5). Bring your friend(s) and a picnic. Make a game of it and see how many different birds you can identify. Count and walk. Walk and talk. Count and talk. Or forget the birds and gossip about who's doing who.

Getting stronger? Start going up. Nothing beats an ascent for good heart-pumping exercise. Get out the old khaki shorts and matching shirt, buy a cheap canteen from an army-navy surplus, borrow your friend's Patagonia wool socks. Gear up and climb. Start small, with little local hills, and work your way up to a nearby small mountain. Keep going. Soon you'll find that just by walking out the door with your chatty friend, you're on your way to conquering Everest. Walking and talking . . . we were born to do these things.

Just keep moving.

## Thrifty & Green Bitch

### how we roll

You BOUGHT a cruiser bike (see page 195); you got a free bike tour of the Florida Keys by organizing the trip yourself and getting all your friends to sign on the dotted line (see

*(continued)*

page 170). Now you're ready for a cheap, eco-friendly adventure that'll get you in amazing shape. Just two hours of leisurely cycling burns around five hundred calories, and faster or uphill cycling burns more than that. Plus, cycling puts no pressure on your joints, and is a low-impact way to tone abs, get your heart rate up, improve mood, and commune with nature and friends. Whether you're in the Florida Keys or at your local reservoir, get rolling.

## WORKOUT TRIAD: Stretch It Out

### PILATES, YOGA, AND TAI CHI CHUAN

While we weren't modern-dance minors, we *are* spiritually in tune with the energy of yoga, Pilates, and tai chi. Nothing is more soothing (short of drugs and alcohol, let's be honest) to calm your spirits in good times or bad.

Based on the principles of centering, concentration, precision, breath, and flow, Pilates helps enhance a strong mind-body connection and offers a keen focus on breathing and core strengthening. Few exercise programs work as well at buttressing your back and abs. Originally developed by Joseph Pilates to rehabilitate soldiers after WWI, this exercise is great for women sixteen to eighty. We're not big fans of mat classes, but love using the machines—there's something so sexy about working out on beds called Reformers and Cadillacs!

Yes, yoga can be intimidating. There's just something paradoxical about such a hip, cool, hey-man, groovy activity that makes us feel so klutzy. You know, you get to the class and the instructor—after a slow, ambiguously profound morning meditation—snaps up and tells you to go into Downward-facing Dog. For a moment you think you're in some new sex-position class, until you look left at the woman's butt in your face. You hurry to copy her, but before you know it, Plank, Child's Pose, and Triangle have all been intoned and you're still trying to stand up straight from the Rover position. Trust us, we've been there. But for feeling refreshed, relaxed, and really flexible, nothing beats a great yoga class.

The trick is to find the right kind of yoga, a style that works for you, and a good instructor. Shop around, check out different styles and different teachers. Once you've mastered the positions (in yoga class), consider doing it at home; but, at the beginning, we're more comfortable having corrections made to our posture by a professional. While yoga seems benign, you really can injure yourself—never, ever, ever get yourself into positions that hurt. Do not allow anyone to intimidate you into pushing beyond what your body can comfortably do.

While every girl may not be flexible enough for yoga, every girl should be able to master the forms of tai chi chuan. There are many branches and styles of this martial art. Get out to the park, find a class that you like, and get in line. Reassemble your body. Experience yourself in a new place and time. This is the single best mind-body connecting exercise we have ever done. Open up your life force through carefully crafted motion handed down through generations. Forget the fads—thousands and thousands of years of teaching and practice mean something. Excellent for blood flow, balance, posture, and general movement; plus, studies show it helps reduce blood pressure and offers relief for chronic illness. This is the single best stress-reducing exercising we have ever done! Okay, okay, we know . . . *reassemble yourself, life force, new place and time*—we sound like that *om*-ing modern-dance minor. But we're willing to take that risk: This stuff is so good.

91

## ENDURE/RESIST: Box and Lift

Just getting through most days now seems like an endurance test. While it may feel counterintuitive, adding more physical punch actually relieves the mental anguish. Our advice? Go down to the local gym and check out boxing. No joke. Few activities will give you as much aerobic workout, coordination work, and strength development. Be like Muhammad Ali, a butterfly, light on your feet, quick with your hands. Talk in rhyme. Borrow boxing gloves, don a face mask, and get to work. Splurge—hire a sparring partner. That's right, screw talk therapy and release your aggression the old-fashioned way: Smash someone's face. Trust us, you can let yourself get aggressive—your partner will wear gloves and a mask, won't get hurt, and won't hit back. Where else can you experience this?

Once you have the one-two punch down, start beating the shit out of a punching bag. Picture your boss, your stockbroker, your ex, the bus driver who closed the door in your face, perfect senior class president Patty who always got As, was head of the cheerleading squad, wouldn't give you the time of day, and stole your boyfriend. . . . Stop. Get over it all by punching it out. You have no idea how good it'll feel to release all your pent-up aggression and angst. You'll leave schvitzing.

When you're finished, head over to meet Olga in the weight room to start training for London 2012 by learning to lift a barbell. Yup, a barbell. It's time to try out Olympic weight lifting. C'mon, don't be a wimp; how else will you be able to tell everyone that you've mastered the "snatch" and the "clean and jerk" lifts? Besides, every bitch needs resistance training, and nothing beats lifting for muscle strengthening and bone building. No do-it-yourself-ing allowed here! You need guidance and a slow progression with an outstanding teacher. This is one sport you can hurt yourself doing: only lift under supervision. Work at progressively increasing your load—you'll actually be changing the metabolic balance in your body. The breaking down and building up of muscle burns calories not only while you lift, but as the day continues, since your body is working to repair and rebuild. And don't forget, the more muscle mass you have (no Ms. Worlds, please!) the more calories you burn at rest. Recreational Olympic lifting has another major benefit for today's busy bitches: it takes only forty-five minutes per session. Lower your resting heart rate and blood pressure. Reduce body fat. Save time. Feel sexy and strong as She-Ra.

## BE A STAR!
## DANCE DANCE REVOLUTION

Shut the television off. There's just something too pathetic about being slumped on your sofa, longing to feel better about yourself, while *other* people dance to a cheering crowd on TV. Enough already with all the voyeurism. Stop pleasuring the networks who produce the shows, the advertisers selling you disgusting food. Stop giving them your ratings and money. Pleasure *yourself*!

For an average-size woman, vigorous dancing can burn four hundred calories an hour. It's fun. It's sexy. It'll make you laugh. Start by finding a good ballroom dance studio in your town or city. National chains like Fred Astaire Dance Studios or Arthur Murray Dance Studio offer a wide range of classes. Of course, like everything else, they're only as good as the instructors. Usually classes meet one night a week, so you can't claim you're too busy. Plus, there's nothing better to reignite a tired relationship

93

or bond a new one than holding a partner close, feeling the heat of his body, and getting in touch with the moves he makes. Go with other couples. Dance the night away. (Then, after this foreplay, go home and keep burning calories with other forms of dance.)

Ballroom dancing not high on your list? Check out tap classes. Really, when was the last time you got to stamp your feet and make lots and lots of noise? (We're pretending that tantrum last week didn't happen.) Not into tap? Consider line dancing. Square dancing. Do-si-do around the town hall, swirl your skirt. Hip-hop, break dancing—you name it, you can do it. There's a dance form for everyone—even modern.

Or just push the coffee table aside, pump up the volume on your stereo, put the baby on your hip, and treat yourself to a private dance party. Be silly, get your blood moving, imagine a crowd of envious bitches.

## BUDGET SUBSTITUTIONS

### NO MORE SWEET'N LOW!
### GET HIGH ON THE REAL THING

Look, Aspen's no longer an option. You can't afford the lift tickets, the swanky lodges, never mind the hot toddies. Gorsuch's shearling après-ski jackets? We don't think so. Wait, don't head in just yet. You aren't a quitter. The joy of the slopes—er, hills— can still be yours. Pick yourself up and go—*sledding*. Free, wickedly fun, and all that uphill trudging makes for an amazing workout. Remember the snow-day ecstasy of childhood? The flushed cheeks, wind in your hair, snow up your nose? (No, not at the club in South Beach.) Feel the rush again. Pile four friends on a toboggan. Steal cafeteria trays like you did in high school. Get sexy and straddle your beau—face-to-face—on a flying saucer, and scream as you slip and slide together. Then come home and warm each other up in the same position. Keep your heart young in more ways than one.

Identity crisis now that you can't hang with your starchy friends at the golf club? Try croquet. That's right, channel your inner Victorian bitch. Grab some friends, a parasol, and set up your wickets in the local park. Stroll, chitchat, take in the sun (this is, of course, the perfect moment to wear your custom-made straw-brimmed hat—see page 33). Such a civilized sport, and so much better than boring golf. Plus, croquet lets you banish those diva bitches—you know, the ones who have to win everything—by knocking their balls into the poison ivy!

No, you can't afford polo or horseback riding. Mount your bike and take to the streets. Tone those gams, enjoy the scenery—and be glad you don't need to feed a bike or clean up its shit.

Stop lusting over a yacht; join a community sailing club or buy a secondhand kayak. You used to Jet Ski. Now you surf or—simpler still—do like the leader of the free world and boogie board. Squeal in the waves, embrace your inner teenage boy, strengthen your bod . . . without washing your savings away. Twenty bucks at Target will get you a rad boogie board.

Old-fashioned fun and games are staging a comeback, and it's time to join in. Reprise college years with a game of ultimate Frisbee on the quad. Pretend you're in high school, find a date, and go Rollerblading in the park. Be an elementary school kid again and buy a new jump rope. Roll back to a time before play became work and exercise a drudge.

Get in touch with the child in you—no special handshake or bloated bankbook required. These alternatives are way cheaper,

95

more social, and remind you that fitness can be fun. Getting in shape should be a *by-product of pleasure,* rather than a solitary, dull, status- or body-obsessed labor. If those hours alone at the gym aren't making you happy, find something that does. Say *arrivederci* to those snotty clubs draining you dry. Renew your soul, your portfolio, and your shape. Play.

⊙━━ *Bitchin' Tip*

**public displays of athleticism**

$\mathcal{C}$ALL YOUR local parks and rec department and ask about adult recreational leagues. Kickball is big again, really. Adult ice-hockey leagues are flourishing—it's not just the kids that get to knock the crap out of one another. Play round-robin tennis on town courts. Field hockey and soccer teams abound. Put a whole new spin on the term "soccer mom."

## SKIP THE KNOCKOFFS

These days, you're passing on processed junk food and opting for the real thing. Aged Vermont cheddar (from Costco) versus Cheez Whiz; homemade cookies versus Chips Ahoy; Berkshire pork chops versus SPAM.

In the same spirit, get your ass out of the gym now and then, back to the activities that inspired the workout machines. Have you forgotten those gym exercises are based on real-life stuff? Feel the wind in your hair as you skate on a pond . . . hear the sound of water slapping as you paddle the river . . . experience the *thump-bump* of your heart and the crunch of your feet as you run a country path. Escape the blare of the television, the generic crowds, the acrid odor of electricity, the soul-draining

96

sameness. Go cold turkey, quit the club, and save big bucks. Besides, outside of new boobs, this may be one of the few times the real stuff will cost you less than the fake.

**Out of touch with real life? Here are some hints.**

| FAKE & EXPENSIVE | REAL & FREE/CHEAPER |
| --- | --- |
| Exercise bike | Real bike |
| NordicTrack | Cross-country ski |
| Treadmill | Your own two feet; the road |
| StairMaster | Staircase |
| Rowing machine | Kayak or canoe |
| Indoor rinks | Skate a pond; Rollerblade on a path |

*Thrifty Bitch*

### secondhand jobs

WHEN GEAR is required, don't get suckered in by the shiny and new. It'll stay shiny for all of five minutes. Instead, visit school clothing/sports exchanges to find used cross-country skis, tennis rackets for the town courts, golf clubs for the public course, old croquet sets, badminton sets, ice skates for the ponds, etc. Play It Again Sports offers a good selection—find one near you at www.playitagainsports.com.

## SEX IS SPORT, TOO!

Sex is a value proposition. As we all know, women experience so much more than mere carnal lust. For us, romance, intimacy, and exercise are all packaged inside one flexible box—like you needed more proof that we really are the best when it comes to multitasking! Why not make sex part of your exercise routine? After all, we've been going on and on about play and fun . . . what free activity could better embody this lesson? Forty-five minutes of energetic intercourse burns a couple hundred calories, keeps you limber, and releases soothing chemicals good for your whole body. This said, you are not a slut. Your goal should be any activity that gets you moving—*not* having sex with anything that moves.

You'll find that the sexual experience is enhanced by being in top-notch shape. Since you're becoming such a thrifty bitch, think of this as just another two-for-the-price-of-one opportunity: Exercise increases blood circulation, and blood rushing to your privates is what you need for great sex. What do you think all those boner pills are doing? Moving the blood. Since you're a smart woman who thinks with her head, you can achieve the same effect without becoming a drug addict. Not having a penis is so liberating!

Another easy way to enhance sex and stay trim? Stretch. Regular hip, pelvic, and inner-thigh exercises increase flexibility and rouse your blood (and maybe arouse your partner, too). To do a pelvic lift, lay flat on your back and bend your knees. Slowly raise and lower your pelvis—lift the tailbone enough so you feel the contraction of your abdominal muscles. Equally simple are butterfly stretches—just sit on the floor with the soles of your feet pressed together. Tighten your abs, keep your back straight, and lean forward until you feel a gentle stretch. As you stretch, focus on taking deep, cleansing breaths. Notice all the sensations in your body; focus on every little pulse and tingle and shiver. This kind of mindful attention pays great dividends in bed.

## GOOD SPOTS HUNTING

Dr. Freud said that the only real female orgasm was vaginal, but we all know better. Most women reach climax through direct clitoral stimulation. It works, no complaints here, but . . . what if Dr. Freud was onto something and there is a special orgasm you haven't discovered? The idea was famously professed by Ernst Grafenberg, after whom the mysterious and controversial "G-spot"—you know, that Bermuda triangle of the vagina—is named. Who knows whether these male doctors were right; today's bitch is skeptical when men tell her how her body works. Still, you owe it to yourself to spend some quality time, alone or with your partner, and go hunting. Happily, this will cost you not a dime, will fill those evenings you used to spend at fancy restaurants, and may enhance your bod and self-esteem. Try different positions. Keep at it. Oh, the sacrifices we make for thriftiness . . .

*Splurgeworthy*

### what's all the buzz?

STIMULATE THE economy as you stimulate yourself. That's right, invest in sex toys. Remember, exercise is play—how can you be expected to really play without a few toys? Check out www.goodvibes.com for a wide assortment of playthings, customer reviews, staff picks, even eco-friendly choices. Or buy local. All modern bitches should feel comfortable strutting into their local sex shop, handling the merchandise, and asking questions. Think of it as a rite of passage. Good sex toys can be pricey, but they're long-lasting and offer way more entertainment value than a video rental and a tub of popcorn.

## STUCK AT HOME?

No partner to share fun and games with. You're inside. The weather's frightful, the baby's asleep, or it's the end of another hideous workday and you can't possibly leave the house for anything or anyone. Buy a few toys (the kid kind), turn on your television, boot up your computer, slide in a few DVDs. No worries. No excuses.

■ **Get a jump rope.** Yes, anyone can do this. Find a spot where you can swing the rope without upending vases and knocking pictures off the walls. If you live in an apartment, find a spot where you aren't jumping on someone's head—not only do you want to be a good neighbor, but you're not allowed to quit with the excuse that the people downstairs bitched. They complained? Sorry, you're not off the hook. Get a hula hoop—it's silent as an electric car.

- **Turn on the television.** True, we said to shut it off for home shopping and the dance competitions that breed passivity, but for exercise entertainment it's a real tune-up. If you've got premium cable or a dish, check out ExerciseTV. Everything from yoga to Pilates to dance to striptease and pole dancing is there for the grinding. Word of warning: If you find yourself glued to a walking show (yes, there really is such a thing), turn it off! When it's so bad you find yourself standing in front of the television watching people walking, it's high time to leave the house and run—*do not walk*—to your therapist.

- **If you don't have cable, you'll find a glut of free exercise videos online.** Check out www.exercisetv.tv for cardio, yoga, stretching, and strength-training workouts. These should augment your exercise routine, of course, not be its heart. There's just something deadening about being stuck in front of your computer, assaulted by the extreme perkiness of some instructor. Free is free, yes—but life is short.

- **We'd be remiss if we didn't mention the vast world of DVDs.** Pick your favorite exercise, go online and do a little research to find the most highly recommended DVD, and get to work. Collagevideo.com is a big help, letting you browse by price, experience level, and user satisfaction.

For sculpting abs and connecting with your slinkiest, sexiest selves, check out Kathy Smith's *Flex Appeal: A Belly Dance Workout.* Burn fat, tone muscle, feel all worldly and exotic without leaving your living room—then show off your moves in the bedroom. We're also big fans of the Gaiam series of yoga DVDs, which offer a range of options and aren't grotesquely New Agey. (Plus, you get to gaze at superhot Rodney Yee, which adds to the yogic bliss.) Their *AM and PM Yoga* is a fave for short, simple, soothing routines to add easily to your day.

Borrow a DVD from the library or a friend before purchasing—don't order blindly off the Internet. And even if you do start strong with a DVD, without the socialization aspect it's wickedly easy to fall off the wagon. Invite a neighbor to join you at a regular time a couple days a week. You'll save big bucks over a gym *and* get a good laugh watching each other grunt and shimmy.

O━━━ *Bitchin' Tip*

### wii fit = we silly?

WHAT IS it about our culture that reveres activities that *resemble* other activities? It's like if we're not doing it in front of a glowing screen, it's worth less. Growing more ubiquitous every day is the Wii Fit. Nintendo says it "combines fun and fitness"—maybe so, but we remain skeptical. One, it ain't cheap. Two, we're not convinced how many calories you're actually burning. Three, we can't help feel a little silly using a video game as our workout guru. Still, any motion is better than none, and fun is fun. If it gets you off, enjoy. Just don't forget the real world outside your door . . . a video game may be a nice change of pace, but if you're using it instead of living in reality, breathing fresh air, playing with friends—press "off" pronto.

.....................

# Chapter 4

# Home Remedies to Get You Out of Recession Depression

*I*T'S ALL A matter of perspective.

Just think. Ten pounds ago you thought you were heavy. Five years ago you thought no person of color could ever be elected president. Two years ago you thought your job sucked. Fifteen rooms would be just right for your dream house. Twelve place settings of Christofle's silver flatware would make you complete.

Today you know better.

You really weren't all that heavy ten pounds ago. Thank God you underestimated the voters' intelligence. While your job may still suck, don't you feel grateful to be working? Aren't you glad you're still in that cozy house or apartment? And imagine you polishing that pricey Christofle silver? We don't think so.

Perspective, bitch—it's the look of the future.

Any serious architect or designer will tell you that great

103

design is all a matter of perspective. How you look at something, what aspects you choose to examine, your angle of approach—all this will influence your experience of any space and object. And trust us, this new modern era is *all about* perspective. It's time to adjust your view, narrow your focus, and reconsider the lens through which you see everything.

Feeling bad for yourself because you can't have the new house, new kitchen, all new furniture for the family room? Feeling bad because you can't take an exotic sun or ski vacation, eat in those fancy restaurants, attend pricey rock concerts? Sorry—you don't have permission to curl up in a ball surrounded by years of excess clutter, watching television and drinking bad chardonnay.

Get a grip, bitch!

Snap out of it and get to work. This is an opportunity to have fun, to focus on the fine points, and to enjoy being at home. First, clear the clutter and cast a fresh eye. Your goal? Recycle, reuse, and restore what you already own. Then play with color, hang new art, hunt for vintage, obsess over table settings.

Learn new skills. Develop a fetish. Become a collector. No paying someone to tell you what to like (except us, of course!).

Be your own expert, bitch.

Open your eyes. It's time to get modern.

## FREE YOUR MIND, FILL YOUR WALLET

**PURGE THE LUST** in your heart for all those meaningless, out-size status pieces you've been mindlessly pursuing and thinking indispensable to your happiness. You know, the La Cornue stove, the Noguchi Freeform Sofa, the set of original Fornasetti wall plates—they won't make you happy. Well, at least not *that* happy.

We're going to focus on finding just the right, bright, and totally chic things every bitch should covet. Think of household decorating like you managed your wardrobe: Buy clean basic pieces and freshen the interior with new accessories. Rotate pieces in and out.

But first, just like those overpriced colonics of a bygone age cleansed your system, it's time to empty the crap from your home. Every bitch deserves a fresh start. Should you have to live with all the mistakes you've brought to your bedroom? Absolutely *not*. Throw them out. Now. Feel like a virgin again.


## OCD, YEAH, YOU KNOW ME

**OKAY, WE'VE ALL** been there. The piles and piles of stuff filling the corners, tabletops, bookcases, closets. The cute little souvenir snow globe from the Big Apple, the three-inch Degas ballerina you bought your daughter the one time you were able to drag her to the museum, the porcelain bulldog from your mother-in-law. How about those stacks of magazines (the well-read *People* with newlyweds Brad and Jen on the cover, the last edition of *Domino* you purchased to give you inspiration for a home makeover)?

Toss the crap.

Beyond the psychic pain of giving up on what is sure to be the Brad and Jen collector's edition, once you know the rules, this is simple stuff. Hard to parse out what should go and stay? Stuck in the "what if I may need it/it was a gift/I do love it, really I do" quandary? Just apply these simple rules to every item in your path:

# #1 Last-time-used Rule:

If you haven't used an item in over a year . . .

Like that avocado green Crock-Pot your mom gave you. No, it's never seen food—but, hey, Crock-Pots are *so* in now, aren't they? Sure, it's been five years, but you never know, maybe you'll get the urge. . . . **Toss it.**

# #2 Always-hated-it Rule:

**A) Self-purchased:** Remember the expensive art piece you bought in Tucson? Once you got home you realized it wasn't abstract but a very bad still life of a very aroused obese man. Funny, yeah, but the pain outweighs the humor every time you think of how much you spent. There's nothing abstract about it anymore, and no use pretending. **Toss it.**

**B) Gift:** Your fiancé's mother gave you a painting from her beginners' oil class. You hung it up; what else could you do? But it's a hideous figure that suspiciously echoes your Tucson error. A poke in the eye each time you glance at it. Stealthily move it to a less conspicuous corner on its way toward the part of the house due for a major flood. Or end things with your fiancé and return the painting. **Toss it.**

# #3 Could-be-worth-something-besides-it-was-my-great-aunt-Tilly's Rule:

Keep it, as long as you have a place to put it away. While there are lots of things in your history you would like to forget (we won't enumerate), one day you might be happy to have that gravy boat or Czech red glass candy dish.

## #4 Sentimental-objects Rule:

The movie ticket stub from your first date, receipt from the dinner that ended with a mind-blowing kiss, Hallmark card decreeing puppy love, condom wrapper commemorating the first time you had sex . . . Come on, trash is trash.

You are allowed only one memento from each love affair (if you're a slut, one from every other love affair). This junk should occupy no more than a shoe box. All right, you sluts: a boot box. **Toss it.**

## #5 I-love-it-and-the-chip/crack/tear-is-very-small Rule:

Don't kid yourself—it's broken and you ain't gonna fix it. Don't cling to imperfection. It's time to euthanize. **Toss it.**

## #6 But-it's-a-book Rule:

We too love books. Handsome hardcovers, key advice and how-to guides, well-thumbed stories from childhood, novels that decades later send shivers through our bodies. But not every Danielle Steele, Nora Roberts, and James Patterson paperback ever printed is a worthy space stealer. Say good-bye to pulp paperbacks. **Toss it.**

If there are other people around with opinions, you get our condolences. The job becomes all the more complicated when you have to negotiate with their pack-rat craziness. It sucks. Be tough. Give family members one chance as you become the

107

mad tosser. Buy them each a good-quality plastic box with a cover at your local hardware or housewares store. Then get to work. If, suddenly, your daughter is attached to the ballerina that she never saw before, put it in her box. The snow globe, unless it's vintage, goes bye-bye. Your mother-in-law's porcelain dog? Shit, you're the bitch and it's your house, isn't it? Walk it to Goodwill.

## ⊶ Bitchin' Tip

### contain yourself!

WE'RE WILD devotees of the Container Store. Since we're not naturally organized, this is like entering a wondrous foreign country. They've got ways to contain things we didn't even know *needed* containing—like, who knew you needed special organizers for bras, underwear, and socks? We love their paper-goods area, houseware jars, and file boxes. Start in the back, where there's a sale room. Just don't get carried away. Some things simply *don't* need a container . . . be careful you don't get caught in the container-for-a-container-for-a-container trap. Next thing you know, your home is one big Russian nesting doll.

## GREENBUCKS ENERGY

LIKE THE GARBAGE that burns and runs power plants, make good use of your junk. Turn it into sorely needed hard cash. That said, everyone else is in the same bad economic place, equally anxious to auction off Aunt Tilly's candy dish. So be realistic. Chances are you don't have an *Antiques Roadshow* item lurking in your attic or in plain sight on the coffee table. If you think that rose glass pitcher, *Titanic* etching, or god-awful little green leprechaun may be the ticket to retirement (or paying off the Visa bill), do your homework. Start researching Depression glass (how timely), deco art posters, and Hummels. Cruise the Net looking for similar items. Click on eBay and watch, watch, and watch some more. *No buying.* Your goal is to set a benchmark price so you know what the object is worth.

If you still think you've got a treasure, take a digital photo and send it to a reputable local auction house. Even if they're interested, don't get all excited; this is not exactly the most robust auction market.

Now separate your stash. Auctionable items. Craigslist listings. Consignment-store assignees. Yard-sale orphans. Charity objects.

Selling on eBay is a snap. It just takes a little time to set up the account, monitor, and then ship items. We're partial to consignment stores because they're local, but the market they reach is smaller. A sharp bitch will skip the middleman and their commissions and go straight to Craigslist, or set up shop in her own backyard.

We particularly like Craigslist for unloading bigger items like furniture and appliances—it's local and the buyer will come to you to pick it up. Yard sales aren't what they used to be, but in this economy people are looking for cheap thrills, and yard sales—whether you're a shopper or a seller—are as American a thrill as apple pie. (Aren't you proud to be a part of a nation of such environmentally friendly, recycling consumers?) Charity donations will make you feel good and, depending on your financial state and the tax code du jour, could provide a nice deduction.

Make a chart. Determine where each object should go. Stay organized—otherwise you may end up dumping valuable stuff.

Starting this kind of cleaning is tough, but once that OCD kicks in you won't quit until everything is "spic and span."

Now that you've scaled down, it's time to monitor the intake. Same mantra applies to decor as to your diet (see page 75): everything in moderation. Allow back in only what you truly adore. If you haven't searched and lusted for it, it's not getting inside.

## HOMESCHOOLING:
### Decor in Depression

**ENVIRONMENTS IMPACT HOW** we feel. Actually, *everything* impacts how we feel—we are girls, aren't we? Living among relics, your home full of questionable style from long-gone decades, hijacked by objects once belonging to relatives you didn't know or didn't like—how can you feel anything but confused? Surrounded solely by metal and glass—hard concrete underfoot, recessed lighting overhead, a single Ansel Adams photograph—how can you ever feel warm and cozy? Hunter green walls, ebonized floors, ruby damask curtains—how can you feel anything but claustrophobic?

Try this angle: Decorating your home is like getting yourself dressed. Would you put on a skirt and blouse, add boots and a sweater, your best pearls, your grandmother's diamonds, then throw on a fur coat to go to the store on a hot summer day? No. So think like a modern bitch. It's time to streamline your look. Form, function, and a little whimsy are all you need to create an environment that gives you peace.

*Om!*

# REVIEW AND CORRECT

**FEW OF US** are lucky enough to live free of encumbrances. No, we're not talking about your husband, kids, pet turtles. We don't mean your collection of obsessions and neuroses, either. Think other kinds of baggage.

Like your first sofa purchase—you know, the one you fell for before you knew better. That Las Vegas wedding of a sleeper sofa with roll arms and loose cushions covered in a now-faded royal blue floral chintz. Shall we continue? The old brass lamp with the pea green shade, the dark red faux-Oriental carpet, the hand-me-down French provincial dining table with the cherry stain. Yes, we're all in favor of mixing up styles, and don't recommend being a slave to minimalism—but keeping this old baggage weighs you down.

Still, until you get a new job or win the lottery, you can't just get rid of *everything*, and certainly not all at once. Learn what to dump, what to keep, and how to improve the keepers.

Let's take the faux Oriental. It's hideous. It's big and dark, which is why your roommate's cat liked it. It smells bad. Get rid of it. Buy a new carpet.

Florals are making a comeback, but that original sin of a sofa either needs to be born again in a new fabric or be put out of its misery and sent on to sofa heaven.

The brass lamp is blah, yet all it needs for a chance at happiness is a little loving cover—a great new shade.

The French provincial table from Great-uncle Dick's dining room set? Well, it has potential. Its legs aren't square and sleek, the top is beveled, it has funky edges. Still, with a little vision it could be the one really cool outré piece in your living/dining area. But *not* in stained cherry.

# REGRADE THE TABLE

**WHO HASN'T BEEN** stuck with a piece of furniture that is so ugly, so the wrong color, so not a reflection of the hip, stylish bitch that you want to be? Take that big cherry table (or oak chair, or mahogany side table, or birch bench . . .) and fix it.

This is your first big DIY project. No bitching.

You're home now; what else are you going to do?

Consider this free exercise and entertainment. Need inspiration? Think glossy white or glossy black. They're unexpected, fun, and give a nice edginess to too-tame traditional pieces. Get as high a sheen on the finish as your two little paws can sand and paint. Trust us, you'll be amazed.

Once you've got Uncle Dick's table painted, update the whole look by checking out Philippe Starck's Victoria Ghost Chairs, incredibly sexy Plexi chairs that come in many colors, made by Kartell. We love the clear—they're just so, so . . . invisible! The original will run in the $330 range, so haunt the Web to see what comes up in knockoffs.

*Thrifty Bitch*

## help! i need somebody!

*L*EARN HOW to restore, refresh, refinish—skills you'll use again and again. With some basic know-how, you'll have the balls to snag dirt-cheap yard-sale pieces and do the refinishing work yourself. No idea where to begin? Go to Lowe's—or, better yet, your local hardware store—and plead stupidity. Take advantage of these rental husbands or sisters—they'll be more than happy to help you out. Or visit Lowe's extensive online how-to library.

## SOFA SPARKNOTES

**IT'S TIME TO** meet your maker regarding the sofa.

If it was well made to begin with and is in A+ structural shape, make a 911 call to the upholsterer. If it's in grade B or C condition and you don't want to spring for the upholstery, think about slipcovers. Yes, they can be fucking annoying—why do you think they're called *slip*covers? Certainly not because they're sexy like lingerie. If it's in failing shape and no reasonable slipcovers exist to disguise its ugliness—expel the damn thing. Look, this is the biggest piece in your room, and if it reads as a tattered, failed loser, it'll make you miserable. You've had your fun, made your mistakes; now move on. It's not like you have a child by it or anything.

Your new couch (re-covered or bought) will be neutral. It's the biggest upholstered piece you own. The little black dress of the living room. The key ingredient, just waiting to be all tricked out with amazing pillows. So go gaudy or garish, refined or intricate, whimsical or silly—with the pillows. Change them with your mood, the season; keep a different set for each boyfriend. You can find playful graphic pillows for $1.29 at IKEA, or order luscious, soft, fit-for-your-precious-noggin cashmere pillows for $99 at Overstock.com.

## CLEVER ILLUMINATION

**WE ALL HAVE** our fetishes.

Fabulous lamps and fixtures are ours. We're working out an angsty, existential need for illumination, and the happy by-product is an array of brilliant lighting pieces.

For great visual impact nothing outshines a stunning chandelier. Yes, a chandelier, those crystal dangly things that were once the iconic fixture of great wealth. Picture the maids in their naughty little uniforms, climbing ladders with feather dusters while the chauffeurs, butlers, and dissolute scions of inherited wealth looked on (or up).

Oh, what fun you could have with yours!

Today ceiling chandeliers come in all shapes and sizes. The design market has exploded, and is filled with so many options that the pursuit of ceiling-fixture perfection can be a hobby in itself. And hey, if you're not buying (yet), that makes you an even more frugal bitch, right? Go into search-and-lust mode, hot on the trail of a new big thingamajig. Whether you take off with a vintage or new Sputnik, swing from an antique lead crystal or new Murano glass chandelier, or dream of world peace and want a simple unified globe, proceed slowly and carefully.

Big things hanging from your ceiling make a big statement. Do it right. Start by looking at the best resources for clean, modern home design to get a feel for the market. Keep it big, make a splash, but not so outsized you need to move out to make room for it. We're suckers for the Murano chandelier in red at Design Within Reach, or the chrome Mod 2097 from Flos, or an authentic old leaded-glass-crystal job. We love the juxtaposition of all that flourish in an entirely clean space.

All are pricey, but if they're the main focal point in a living or dining room they may be worth the investment; build around them with IKEA and Craigslist finds, or use these pricey fixtures as your models as you hunt for knockoffs.

Lighting can also help you bridge styles. No matter what style or period your house or apartment, the Murano chandelier *will* work in your dining room. Google the hot Bourgie lamp. It's got traditional-looking curlicues and flourishes, but it's made completely of Plexiglas. It can sit on any end table next to almost any couch in a room with a neutral carpet and simple floor-to-ceiling curtains. Or consider using an Artemide Tolomeo floor lamp next to a traditional club chair.

Remember that brass lamp? If you want to keep it, get a new shade. Aged pea green is simply unattractive. Believe it or not, you'll probably need a professional's advice. We recommend finding a lighting store and bringing in the poor makeover candidate for consultation. Trust us, when you go to look for new shades there will be all kinds of issues you had no idea about.

Like: How big is the harp? Should you get a spider clip on? Do you need a new fitter to attach the shade to the lamp? Does it have a finial and, if so, how will that relate to the new shade?

Or, if it's a simple size-for-size transfer, bring the shade to your local Target. We trust you to do this alone, but don't get tricky. You'll find a glut of heinous, overly flourished shades out there. Do *not* come home with patterns, flowers, odd colors, or teeny pleats.

115

## KEEP CARPET PRICES IN THE BASEMENT

Underfoot can be hard or soft.

We like soft in the bedroom (yes, we just said that!) and hard in the main living spaces. Actually, we're wood-floor nuts in kitchens, living spaces, and hallways. Tiles and stones rock too (sorry), and we can certainly get behind a single plane of gorgeous terra cotta or limestone. Whatever you choose, keep it to one material to make your space feel bigger, more unified, less cluttered. Area rugs in the living spaces can be sent out to be cleaned and are simple to replace, so if you have kids, pets, slobs for boyfriends, or drink lots of red wine, this is your best carpet solution.

Geometrics, graphic florals, and Mondrian-style blocks of color on area carpets are good-looking. West Elm, Pottery Barn, and Crate & Barrel all offer fabulous fashion carpets. If you find a bargain and fall for it, this is a terrific way to update your old space. Since these stylized floor coverings have a strong presence, we don't recommend a major investment unless you're one of those design savants or have pro help.

*Splurgeworthy*

### get felt up

FELT IS *hot*. Check out the designs of Melina Raissnia of Peace Industry (peaceindustry.com). These soft, durable rugs are fairly traded, free of nasty chemicals, and so beautiful it's silly. For other sustainable and fun felt accessories, don't miss LoooLo Textiles (looolo.ca). They make a simple pillow a work of art.

For best value and a clean, timeless solution to area carpets, hunt around neighborhood carpet stores for a high-quality wool remnant rug. Oftentimes, when swaths of carpeting are laid, large pieces are left over. Sometimes they're *big, big* pieces. Before you look through the pricey custom-carpet books, ask the salesperson about remnants. Usually they'll have a bin filled with cuttings, or you may find yourself poking through the big rolls in the back room, searching for carpets of interest.

Your goal is to find high-quality, neutral wool pieces that you can have custom-cut to your room dimensions (again, we like them big) and then have the edges bound. Beige, off-white, and taupe wool sisal looks are easy on the eye, and work in both modern and traditional spaces. Sometimes the remnants are even big enough for you to do wall-to-wall for your bedroom. This is win-win for everyone—stores get rid of their ends; you save a ton of money.

## ⚊ Thrifty Bitch

### sisals, grasscloths, and cotton rugs

FOR DOWN-AND-DIRTY coverings check out the naturals. Inexpensive and disposable.

## ⚊ Bitchin' Tip

### a borrower be

DON'T BE shy. Ask to take things out on loan. You name it—the floor lamp, gilt-edged mirror, pair of bookends. While

*(continued)*

your neighborhood Pottery Barn or West Elm won't be happy with the concept, local antique and specialty high-end stores will be only too delighted to work with you. This will save you big on impulse-purchase hangovers. Hell, an unscrupulous bitch could rotate great art for years without spending a penny. We definitely do not endorse this. Everyone needs to eat.

## GET THE COLOR RIGHT

These days, we're reborn color purists. Meaning we go for white. Bridal, virginal, new-beginning, fresh-start white . . . punctuated, of course, by a stray color pop or even a random wallpapered plane. We aren't *that* pure.

Don't worry—we're not color bullies, either. We've lived and we've learned. Hunter green, khaki, mustard yellow, red, even colonial blue above the chair rail and Hepplewhite cream below—they all *can* work. So you do have permission to play with color. After all, we supported your trip to Sephora for the quick, cheap rush of a new lipstick. In these spare times, a date with Benjamin Moore may be just the lift you need. Yes, Big Ben knows how to get us all wet—with paint, that is.

If you're a crafty DIYer, he's your man—no commitments, just a little fun and a big mess. If you're not used to painting your own walls . . . well, now's the time to learn.

You may be tempted to make a major color change. Think carefully—just like chopping off your hair can shake things up, you'll have to live with the consequences for a while, or work hard to correct errors. You're allowed to be impulsive, but run your ideas by at least one trusted friend.

We warn you: Nothing can scare or perplex a bitch as much as selecting the right shade. On that teeny-tiny swatch at Home Depot it says, "Love me; I'm the perfect buttercup!" But get it home, climb the ladder, paint the moldings, and little buttercups start pulsing back down at you in glowing neon yellow.

Or, seductive magazine after magazine features rosy walls and promise eternal feng shui happiness. They lure you in with a warm and loving glow. When you discover the color is called "Better than Prozac Red," you hunt down the manufacturer and race to buy two gallons to paint the living room. Only one wall is complete and self-doubt sets in. You ignore the feeling. You tell yourself you'll experience Nirvana when the job is done. Except they neglected to warn you that a dark color on white requires three or four coats—so two weekends and four gallons later, you finally finish. You owe the husky neighbor a big favor for moving Aunt Gert's glass hutch in and out, but you put that debt away, along with the gnawing sense that this is all wrong.

You try dimming the room lights, adding a lamp, hanging a mirror, removing throws, adding cushions—all in an effort to be at peace. But instead of a warm and happy glow, it's like Freddy arrived on Friday the thirteenth with his paintbrush and you're living in a bloody nightmare.

Yes, color is very tricky. Next time get a small sample, bring it home, paint a big swatch, and examine the color in the morning, afternoon, and night. How fickle those pigments are.

So you still have the itch for jewel, earth, or pastel tones? Go for a small bathroom, back hall, mudroom, cozy den, closet interior, library, or a stray wall. Everywhere else, take our advice and be a color purist. You'll thank us in the morning.

## favorite shades of white

*Y*OU'LL BE shocked at just how many shades of white and off-white there are. Spend a little time comparing whites in a store and you'll see they are not all created equal. Bring home samples and do swatch tests on the wall. Even though they're white, the pigments change in your space and in relation to your furnishings. We recommend Benjamin Moore Superwhite (BM-1-02) on ceilings in a flat finish mixed with 25 percent of whatever "color" white you choose for your walls: 75-to-25-percent ratio. We've recently successfully used Big Ben's: China White (BM-1-74), White Dove (BM1-06), Soft Chamois (BM OC-13), Seashell (BM OC-120). Use flat on the ceilings, eggshell on the walls, semigloss on ceiling trim and floor moldings. We love shiny things and use high gloss only on doors, casings, and built-ins. (Go to www.benjaminmoore.com for an excellent color guide and paint tutorial.)

## marmorino venetian plaster

*Y*OU NEVER heard of balayage either, and look what it did for your hair. This is another place to throw some extra cash if you happen to have it on hand. (Yeah, ha, ha, we know.) Marmorino Venetian Plaster, a mix of slaked limestone, ground marble, and pigments—applied with remarkable skill—turns a wall into a work of art. It's at once smooth as

*(continued)*

glass and shiny as a mirror, with a depth of color and texture that's astonishing. The process is painstaking and laborious. Check out www.videojug.com/film/venetian-plaster-step-by-step-with-firenze-marmorino, but unless you're one handy bitch, splurge and get a good-looking Italian to come by and do the job—to your walls. Very expensive.

## ACCESSORIES :
### When Little Feels Good
......................

**ACCESSORIES ARE THE** way a bitch survives decor depression (yes, we already told you). This may seem like basic, even obvious advice, but so few people do it. We've got dozens of friends who utterly fail to realize the power of accent pieces. Countless bitches, wanting a new look or longing for more dazzle, opt for a whole new set of furniture in an entirely new color scheme. Don't make this mistake. Be thrifty. Be smart. Keep your lens narrow.

## JUST THE RIGHT HANG-UPS!
......................

### DOUBLE THE FUN

Mirrors rock. Think Grandma's place in Miami: the walls of mirror, the gold furnishings, the plastic cover on the sofa . . . We can do without the plastic, but those mirrors? Love 'em. They're a perfect, simple, and cheap way to enhance any room. We're not talking Poconos ceiling mirrors (although we like your thinking), but well-placed, space-enhancing, light-reflecting

121

mirrors. We love decorative ones too, though this leads us to another tricky discussion.

Frames. When you bring a mirror into your house, you're inevitably bringing in a frame too.

Here's the thing about frames, girls. Listen well. A frame is meant to *enhance the object* it is surrounding. It is *not* meant to scream out at you, unless it's that particularly spectacular Miami gold. And at the price points we're talking, it cannot possibly be spectacular gold, or one of those custom-made, serious wood jobs with luscious rococo edgings. To put it bluntly, we're telling you to buy cheap mirrors, which means anything too fancy frame-wise is going to look like shit.

Think of your sunglasses. You wouldn't be caught dead in those screaming red metal ones with the cute bee adornment in the upper right lens. Don't put anything tacky on your walls either.

You know all those stores and Web sites selling wall hangings and decorative art? Use caution. Resist anything but the simplest, most elegant looks. Don't get tricky—absolutely *no* wrought iron or ugly brown wooden frames. Very simple metal frames can work. Simple black frames, red frames, even bright yellow frames with pencil-size moldings, yes, we like those. Rimless can work, too. We do have a thing about dazzling gold frames (and we didn't even have a grandma in Florida), but we warn that these are high-risk adornments. If you can't afford to do it right, don't do it at all.

If you can't find the perfect mirror, switch your search to empty frames. Find fabulous frames and then head over to your neighborhood mirror maker or glass store and have them cut mirrors to fit. A single big frame filled with a mirror is awesome. A cluster of unusually shaped frames filled with mirrors on a wall are awesome, too. And, if you can afford it, consider having a professional come in to mirror a wall. This will double the size of your room and may, uh, double your pleasure in other ways, too.

---

---

## ART XENOPHOBIA

### BE A GOOD NEIGHBOR: Keep Art Local

Today is the day you begin to collect art.

Yes, in this down-in-the-dumps misery, you are becoming an art connoisseur. From now on, nothing goes on those walls that's a copy of anything.

Start slow and small. Blank wall space is better than junked-up wall space.

Art should make you happy, sad, calm, enraged. Like

*123*

everything else that goes into your sensory surroundings, it should evoke something.

In good times, the galleries around you were flourishing. Art prices were skyrocketing and almost anything that was hung had a buyer. Those days are over. Your pocketbook cannot support Damian Hirst. He's doing fine without you. And the old masters are dead. They don't need your money.

We believe in supporting living artists who need to eat, creative types who add beauty, who provoke discussion, and who stretch limits—they need our support now more than ever. Find emerging artists and support their work. Go to your local artists' association. They often offer classes (maybe you can paint your own wall art?) and provide a venue for emerging artists to show their work.

What's more fun than finding a piece, talking to the woman or man who created it, falling in love with it, and then being able to afford it and take it home? It'll always have a story and a memory. Oh-so-much better than a framed Monet water-lily print.

*Thrifty Bitch*

### children's art

WE ALL have it.

Take selected pieces, frame them, display them. You'll be amazed how Sally's crudest line drawing, framed in simple aluminum, rivals the work at that hipper-than-thou gallery. Frame the art you love the most. Put the rest in the box from the Container Store. We have a papier-mâché dog (a second-grade project) front and center on the most expensive piece of furniture we own. A ceramic pop art Coke can props up

*(continued)*

the cookbooks, and a simple graphic PigBeePhant (pig, bee, and elephant mutant) hangs proudly in a bright red pencil-thin frame.

## At Your Fingertips

### etsy!

ETSY ONLINE (www.etsy.com) is amazing—a site where artists and craftspeople sell their wares, no middleman. Search by object, location, color. We entered our town name and were amazed at the number of artists selling cool stuff. Our eye landed on the sweetest blue bud vase—handmade, fresh color, ten bucks. (And, since we agreed to meet the artist at a local coffee shop to pick it up, no shipping fees.) Later we searched for any object in the particular shade of bright blue we're lusting after. What popped up? A hip, whimsical, limited-edition screen print of a peacock. Support independent artisans and outfit your pad with original pieces.

## SENSUOUS TOUCH

### PLUSH PLEASURE IN BED AND BATH

When you go to bed, you should be met by a smooth, sensuous touch. A delicious soak in a hot bubble bath should conclude with a soft, deep embrace.

But when was the last time you bought new sheets for your bed? Ages ago.

Towels? Right after college.

Bitch, you spend more time in the bed and bath than any-where else. Outside of your toothbrush, which objects get more up close and personal?

Do you need reminding of a few basic facts? Okay, here goes. Things suck. Life is short, wars rage, money's tight, jobs are sparse. You've been forced to deny yourself most daily pleasures. But this is one place to indulge. These days, the only legitimate way to pamper yourself is with everyday objects—the things you use constantly. The things that know your skin and curves better than any man ever could.

Buying new linens and towels is a sensory experience. Touch. Remember you have five senses? Nope, they didn't disappear with your retirement account. Here's an opportunity to reclaim the senses.

Plus, sheets and towels offer yet another chance to come into the modern era. A modern woman's bedding should reflect her clean taste (not clean living, don't get nervous). Remember the color rules—no outlandish primary blast here, please. Keep it simple. Personally, we think there's nothing crisper than an all-white bed. We love the paradox.

Only organic, bitch? We support you. A lovely unbleached ecru muslin will work, too. In any event, don't try to be an original decorating genius or very clever making your bed. (Clever-ness belongs *in* bed).

Our best bedding investment has been in Charisma sheets. We've bought more and less pricey kinds and, over the course of time, these have held up best to heavy use. Sheets are a personal preference, though, and can be confusing to buy. Just get what you like. Your fingers know what feels good.

## linen lowdown

*W*TF *is* thread count? It's simply the number of threads per square inch. Higher should mean softer. Still, thread count alone isn't all that matters. For best quality cotton sheets look for Egyptian and Pima (Supima), both made from long staple cotton—the best. Yarn size and finish are important, too. The finer the yarn the finer the fabric, and a mercerized finish will mean a stronger fabric. Check also the ply of the sheets. The softest sheets are made with one-ply fine yarn. Buyer beware: Unscrupulous makers may label a package as "1,000 thread count" but it may really be a 250 thread count woven with a four-ply thread. Tricky, huh? Trust your fingertips, not the package. As far as texture goes, this is entirely a personal choice. Cotton percale offers a crisper, cooler feel. Sateen's softer. Flannel's . . . well, flannel. Dive into whatever you like.

## send them to the laundry!

*Y*OU HAVEN'T been on vacation since Dubya was president. Oh, but the memories linger. Remember how the best part of the trip was getting into the bed that *someone else* made? That *someone else* turned down? Upon whose pillow *someone else* placed a little chocolate? No, it's not the chocolate that was the luxury. It was the break from doing

*(continued)*

127

the work yourself. It was the freshly laundered and *pressed*
sheets you slid into, so smooth and silky you skipped the night-
gown. Want that same feeling? Send the sheets out to be laundered and pressed. A splurge, yes, but it'll save you the time
and trouble of washing and folding, and you'll feel like you're
on vacation. Okay, you'll have to make the bed yourself and
there will be no chocolate on your pillow. But the simple thrill
of sliding naked into clean, fresh, pressed sheets . . . the other
thrills likely to follow . . . This occasional splurge is worth it.

## TOWEL ME DRY—BUT WHICH TO BUY?

**YET AGAIN, KEEP** it simple and trust your ever-exploring fingers.

For years little confused us more than buying towels. You
walk into the linen department desperate to replace the old
towels with the bleach marks, holes, and fraying ends.

But they all look alike. As you pull one off the shelf a clerk
spies you and makes a beeline over—before the other loafing
salesperson notices there might be a live one. She starts to tell
you how the low-twist yarn is special in the towel you're holding
because it makes the towel lighter and oh-so-fluffy. Instead of
absorbing the water off your freshly showered body it will wick
it away, and the towel dries faster. You're still wondering where
the water goes when it's "wicked" when she starts selling you
on the heavier, denser, more absorbent high-twist number that
will leave your body dry as the desert sand.

Egyptian. Supima. Pima. Turkish. Microcotton. Cotton. Microfiber. Bamboo. Modal. You'll find all these "ingredients" and
more on towel labels. Just like you've become a savvy food-label
reader, apply your skills to the towel tags. While we're purists and

generally favor the most luxuriant 100 percent cotton Egyptian, Supima, or Turkish fabrications, more important to us is the hand, the size, and the thickness of the towel (sounds dirty, doesn't it?). There's nothing more sensuous than the embrace of a huge, plush bath sheet when we emerge dripping from a hot soak. While we don't mind that it takes our towels time to dry, if you're obsessively clean, shower twice a day, and never do your laundry (although that would be a bit weird for such a neatnik), you might be happier with a blend or a microfiber.

Organic cotton is readily available, too, and gives you a break from pesticides used on cotton crops. Bamboo towels, another hot, eco-friendly choice, are supersoft, durable, and good for people with allergies or sensitive skin.

Pure, clean white holds up longer (colors fade) in the wash. If you have an all-white bathroom, you're allowed a dalliance with bold, popping jewel tones.

Above all, no gross embellishments, garish florals, gold trim, or anything that's trying too hard. It's a fucking towel, not a piece of art.

## OBSESSABLE COLLECTABLES

### COLOR CORRECTIONS

And you thought we were anticolor. Wrong, bitch. Color *accent pieces* rock. The brighter, the bolder, the odder, the goofier, the more we love them. If you can be a controlling, self-disciplined bitch and keep your room cool and serene, then adding a tomato red chair or violet leather bench into that sea of calm will launch you to the head of the class.

129

By keeping the boldness of color to your accessory choices,
you'll be able to change the look of your room for next to nothing. Coral was so last year. You know, all those rooms painted
coral, all the faux-coral napkin rings, appliqués on pillows, table
trays. They were small investments and now you're sick of them.
No big deal—eBay them! What about stunning sage velour pillows and lavender vases for the fall? Next spring think floral
(yes, we just said that)—it'll be hot again.

Remember the lady going out in too much clothing on a summer day? Don't fill the room with everything at once. Rotate the
pillows like necklaces, the vases like earrings, the throws like
coats. Keep them working together (you wouldn't wear a plastic
bangle, Tiffany diamond clusters, and an L.L. Bean raincoat as a
normal costume). It's amazing how you can change the way the
place looks and feels by keeping your eye focused on the small
items. And, if everything else is neutral, those small (think
cheap) items look really big.

# BECOME AN ODDBALL:
## Show Your Genius
......................

**OKAY, YOU PURGED.** Now it's time to think about what you want to add back in. No, not big, expensive things, but odd little vanities you can while away your leisure searching like mad for—things like baby booties, matchbooks, even old cloth tape measures. Imagine hanging old yellow cloth tapes, separated by two inches, side by side by side on a wall or from your ceiling. Unravel them to different lengths: five feet, then four feet, six inches, then four feet, then three feet, six inches. You'll look like a genius installation artist. Or consider developing a color-related, shape-related, product-related shopping compulsion. All things turquoise, cylinders, even dinner bells.

Think impact. Think in OCD fashion: Lust for just one kind of thing. Revel in being odd.

One thing about collections is that if you find a passion for a period or a kind of object, the possibilities are endless. Start small; start cheap. Build your knowledge base. Research online, get books. Become an expert. Not only will you spend your time hunting and discovering new places, but you may develop a real passion that will enrich you. Literally.

We have an acquaintance who fell for textiles. It became her life. Everywhere she traveled she bought the best examples of local fabrics she could afford. She learned about ancient dyes and weaving. She began to buy older and more esoteric pieces. Her collections are now so vast and impressive museums exhibit them. She's considered a world authority and is invited (they pay her way!) all over the world to speak about her stash. She religiously takes out pieces packed away in trunks in her house, rotating her collection so she always has some new, colorful, interesting conversation piece hanging on her wall.

Our current collectibles are not as awe-inspiring for dinner conversations, but are totally random and fun. Round things. Weird, odd round things. Once we decided on round things, our first stop was to buy round Styrofoam balls and cover them with moss. Then, while waiting for a friend to finish her job pricing donated objects at the hospital thrift store, we found a ball covered in tiny, shiny white conch shells. It was pretty cool and only $.50. We snapped it up and could not wait for her to finish her shift to share our glee. Before we could chortle, she emerged complaining about how hard it was to price things, and she had just put a $.50 tag on some god-awful ball of shells. She looked around the store to show it to us and was astonished someone had actually bought it. Grinning ear to ear, we took our treasure out of the bag. Imagine her chagrin. Target supplied our next orb for just $4.99—a perfect red lacquer ball. Then we found a black carved wooden ball from Africa in a head shop. Followed by a serious white onyx ball from an antiques store.

Other collectibles we are in love with are midcentury vases, saltshakers and -cellars, candlesticks, and erotic netsuke carved figures.

## COOL KITSCH OR TACKY GARBAGE?

**NO ONE CAN** say for sure.

The one rule is that in any tableau, one seriously kitschy or tacky garbage object can survive under severe scrutiny. (We have a pink poodle ceramic saltshaker on our table.) More than one and you'd better have the coolest person you've ever met pass judgment and give you the thumbs-up.

Or you could be a ballsy bitch. Let's say you still have your childhood collection of My Little Ponys. Make it your mission to collect them in every color ever made; display them on a glass table in a completely white room—*Met Home* will be right over.

## FRIPPERY AND FINERY!
....................

**WITH THOSE CHEESY** floral chintz sofas and shabby-chic faded blossoms surrounding you, it's no wonder the thought of more flowers in your home makes you gag like Alex listening to his once-beloved Ninth Symphony in *A Clockwork Orange*. But toss the roses out with the water? No, you just need to pick the right flowers and plant them in the right places.

Fresh florals are making a design comeback. Just a little differently. If you've got a nubby-textured couch, buy a white wool pillow with a huge red flower appliqué to freshen things up. Do the unexpected. Cover a traditional wing chair in a plain fabric that has a single photo-transferred geranium winding up the back. Or take out Grandma's china with the floral pattern and use it on your modern Parsons table.

Great style is all about contrast.

## THE PLEASURE OF FRESH FLOWERS
....................

**THIS IS NOT** a splurge but a necessity—always have fresh flowers in your life. Always. This is not a negotiable rule. They are a guaranteed prescription for happiness. (Bitch, you *can* be happy, if only for a moment, true?)

Treat yourself once a week.

We prefer flowers that look and smell pretty: Rubrum lilies. Tulips. Freesia. Lilies of the valley. Hyacinth. But we're equally in love with red anemones, yellow gerbera daisies, and white Stars of Bethlehem (they last forever).

*133*

Nothing livens up a room more than flowers. Clean up the house, put away the homework, file the *paid* bills, clear the bread bags off the counter. It will be so nice. But add in a vase filled with red or yellow tulips and the room will be transformed. Your eye will go directly to the pop of color—this is the least expensive, quickest room pick-me-up we know.

A single perfect flower in a stunning ceramic vase beats a dozen fresh roses. Besides, you know about buying those roses—kind of like buying tomatoes in the winter—something plastic and waxy about them. You spring for a bunch, follow the directions, cut the stems in hot water, add the chemicals. They sort of open, but within a day or two it's like you're looking at a dozen limp dicks hanging in your vase. Like you need that!

Buy only flowers just about to open, place them out of direct sunlight, keep water fresh, and they should last a long time (longer than those limp dicks). Trader Joe's has the best-priced flower assortment short of the wholesale flower market. We've been gathering tulips and freesia for just $4.99 a bunch!

## HOP, SKIP, JUMP

MIDCENTURY MODERN BECAME hot by skipping a generation. No one wanted the old furniture from those fifties ranch houses, so it was cheap, cheap, cheap. All the very cool, creative hipster types who couldn't afford pricey antiques bought it because they could afford it. Some of them actually bought it because they believed in modernism. (Remember the modern movement was about reducing form and function to its essence and creating fine, affordable style for the masses—how timely then and now!)

Be a contrarian and think of the rush to modern as your opportunity to get back in touch (a little) with the frippery and finery of another era. A bitch is nothing if not in touch with her paradoxes. So as necessity forces us to pare down, it's inevitable that we'll begin to lust again for curlicues and lace. These days, designer boutiques offer their chichi customers brown paper bags to keep those ostentatious initials like LV and CD under wraps. Will they always be like the scarlet letter? Not likely. Maybe we'll even find corpulent beauty iconic once again.

In the meantime, be trend-forward and on the lookout for out-of-favor objects. Remember, it's *not* labels you're lusting after (we're over that for good!), but rather excellent craftsmanship, beautiful objects that *happen* to be discounted because demand is temporarily down. French silver rococo saltcellars. Gorgeous satin-glass vases. Campy, utterly impractical Toby Jugs by Royal Doulton. Intricate toile trays depicting scenes of aristocratic splendor.

Keep an eye out for big things, too. A nineteenth-century divan with a carved back and flourished arms and legs. Reupholster it. You don't want a replica of the original toile or some pretty stripe, oh, no. Go for a deranged take—toile with hands popping up in repeat, or sedate stripes with strange daisies winding through them. Make this the focal point of your room.

Mix these finds into your clean, modern home and—presto change-o—you're back to the future.

## Green Style

### reupholster this

- Reprodepot.com offers an amazing array of funky, vintage-inspired fabrics that'll knock some sense into any fuddy-duddy piece.

*(continued)*

135

## SHOPPING FOR HOME GOODS

### KEEP AN EAR TO THE CHATTER

Never heard of Fornasetti? Where have you been? You thought
Ted Muehling only did jewelry? Well, we'll have you know he
partnered with Nymphenburg for some of the most elegant china
pieces being made today. It's time to get over your ignorance.

The best way to get smart? Sit on your ass and cruise the Net.
Nothing will stimulate your decorating genius as much as explor-
ing blogs like Apartment Therapy, Stylehive, Design*Sponge,
Cool Hunting, or whatever's hot at the moment.

Enter the blog world and find intelligent life obsessing right
along with you. Tap into a community of bitches just like you, people trying to figure it all out and happy to share their knowledge.

We were interested in the Karlstad sofa from IKEA. Great
price, good colors. But what did the world think? How did it
hold up? Was it comfy? We polled our friends at Apartment
Therapy and found, yes, it was a big winner.

While hunting down the sofa we stumbled onto an image of
random flea-market glasses—they'd all been etched in exactly
the same place, an inch below the rim on the goblets, and
stained blue on their base. Gorgeous. While we've collected

glasses forever and ever (and naturally thought we knew everything), this image led us to a site that teaches you how to etch and stain glasses yourself. How did we even get there?

We were then led to another crafty site (www.craftster.org) and found all these cool projects a bitch can brew at home. We aren't crafty, at least like that, but we have friends. . . .

⚿ ━ *Bitchin' Tip*

### martha, martha, martha

$\mathcal{M}$ARTHA STEWART was onto being a clever, crafty bitch a long time ago. Cooking, crafting, recycling, thinking outside the box. (A bit of perspective: If she were a man do you think she would have gone to jail? *No*.) If you can weed through her product empire, she still offers pretty shrewd home style tips. We like watching her show and thumbing through her magazine.

⚿ ━ *Bitchin' Tip*

### blog fog

$\mathcal{B}$ITCH BEWARE. There are blogs and there are blogs. Of course, they're all hoping to make a buck by setting up *the* definitive site so they can whore to the advertisers. As you cruise, make sure the skank is not skanky. If they're plugging the sidebar products and they're butt-ugly (we found a few blogs promoting hideous lamps and noted that the sidebar advertisers matched each product recommendation item by item), move on.

137

## OUT IN THE WORLD: The Big Boxes

You already know how the stores do the dirty (see pages 16–18). While seasonality for home furnishings is different, the idea of making money is the same. That means in order for the stores to profit on their investment, goods must turn. The old in-and-out applies to most things in life—pots, rugs, couches, and place mats are no exception. Wait for items to go on sale. Search and lust before you turn your hard-earned cash into a new lamp. Search and lust before you spring for that outdoor patio set. Search and lust, even for that new pillow.

## GET ROOTED AT CRATE & BARREL AND WEST ELM

Know the go-tos. No need to reinvent the wheel.

When basics are in order, head to Crate & Barrel. Awesome home merchants. Okay, maybe not as awesome as they used to be—a result of more competition (isn't free enterprise the best?). Still, for furniture, tabletop, small electronics, vases, big glass bowls, they should be among your first stops.

We like Crate & Barrel because they are hip and *dependable*. They've had the same basic white plate for $9.95 in stock forever. And every bitch needs a set of basic white dinner plates. Period. Dishes are always chipping and breaking. You start off with a dozen or more, but within a few years find yourself with an odd number of seven or nine. You won't have to keep replacing the whole set when one breaks, making these a truly thrifty buy. Good basics let us get tricky in our table settings—mixing eBay, flea market, and hand-me-down dishes—while the clean white keeps unity on the table. CB2, Crate's newer, more modern, slightly more affordable line, holds lots of pleasures too.

We also love West Elm. A little hipper and more modern, with a narrower product offering than Crate, they're an incredibly well-priced alternative. Bed frames from $229, Parson side tables for $169, amazing sectionals. Add in über-hip, up-to-the-minute wall ware, like mirrors and kitschy accessories, along with the best bedding assortment around . . . you're an instant home fashionista.

## DESIGN WITHIN REACH

Every modern bitch must cruise through a DWR store. If you can't get there in person, go online. This is like wandering around a museum, but you get to bring the stuff home! Find fully licensed classic designs from such luminaries as Saarinen, Eames, and Nelson, along with new modern designers. This is our dream store. Pricier than Crate and West Elm, but way less expensive than the design center stores and fancy department stores, they are without doubt the best single resource for fantastic lighting, unbelievable chair and table assortments, chic modern rug selections, and clever, functional accessories. Get your ass over there. Start drooling. It'll make you want to sell your house or apartment and move into a loft just so you can really be a modern bitch. Maybe one day.

*Splurgeworthy*

### design center sales

ONCE OR twice a year the design center near you clears out floor samples and returns. This is the time to snag a great make for 70 percent off retail. Our advice is to befriend a decorator. You're a layman, after all, and really don't know Baker from Holly Hunt from Starck. A great decorator will.

*(continued)*

139

Some centers will let "visitors" in with a pass to cruise through their showrooms, but, in most showrooms, vendors will not sell directly to you (and, even in this bad economy, will still be mean as vipers). If you have courage and your feelings aren't easily hurt, go by yourself in advance of the sale days. Walk and walk and walk some more. Go home, research the companies, see who has the best stuff, identify items you may want. Determine your needs before you go. If you're after a new couch, stick to couches on the day of the sale. Killer bargains can be had—just make sure it's really what you need and want. Otherwise it's not a bargain but an albatross.

## THE LITTLER THINGS

The old standbys for clothing, Anthropologie and Target, offer hot home goods too. Anthropologie particularly keeps tricks turning with totally fun, well-priced objects. This is *the* place to buy on sale, so just keep watching. By scoping the merch and waiting for sales, we've collected some cool shit. An entire set of fine, very delicate, and oddly decorated glasses; they almost look like instruments of medieval torture with odd prongs sticking out—we love them, naturally. A cake stand with red, white, and blue leather stitching that we're dying to use on the Fourth of July. And a stunning mercury glass vase that often keeps our white shell orb company on a black deco side table.

You already know about the Target red orb. Just like they bring in up-to-the-minute hot designers in apparel, they do the same in home goods. We snagged a limited-edition John Derian vase and fab Orla Kiely canisters. Their DwellStudio line of table linens costs a fraction of the Dwell line found in high-end specialty stores. (Maybe not as generously made—but just fine.) We also bought our favorite Riedel Vivant tumblers for pinot noir there. We just love cradling the glass in our hand, and we saved a bundle over the fancy stores.

While we disrespect them for clothing, don't rule out the Home Goods/T.J.'s/Marshalls family of stores for well-priced home goods. Towels, sheets, bath rugs are easy to shop for, and bargains can be bagged. They do a lot of their own sourcing around the world, and you can find stools, wire wall racks (simple, ladies, only simple), and a good assortment of glasses and vases. We bought a set of fancy French steak knives by Langioule for a pittance.

## IKEA: The Mother Ship

Nothing comes close to IKEA for rad accessories and starter furniture. Need a mixing bowl ($3.99)? A red enamel colander ($8.99)? Need to outfit your first pad for under $500? Need nothing at all but want the pleasure of a sleek accent lamp ($14.99), sheepskin rug ($49.99), or set of mod cylindrical glasses ($6.99)? Head to the land o' cheap Swedish meatballs and cheap sweet design (and a workout just walking through their warehouse maze). IKEA kicks ass when it comes to accessories: funky textiles, storage baskets, knockoff lighting, and a thousand other odds and ends. Particularly awesome for kids' stuff—furniture, toys, decorative art—that won't set off a gag reflex. While IKEA has rock 'n' roll design credentials— don't get too excited. A lot of the furniture is assemble-yourself and does not fit in the investment-grade keeper category. (Think disposable and definitely not green.) Be careful: Since everything's so freaking cheap, it's way easy to toss, toss, toss into your cart and wind up with an inadvertently huge bill. Before you step into the checkout, edit your cart like the ruthless bitch you are. Save your wallet and protect mother earth.

# CHEAP (NOT SHABBY) CHIC

......................

## SECONDHAND ROSE

Great things can be found in unexpected places. Consignment stores, charity thrift stores, yard sales, and flea markets are the obvious low-price, down-low entertainment destinations for knickknacks and recyclables. Even a prissy bitch can shop for gently used bargains. Unlike clothing, you aren't going to be wearing that mustard-colored, oversized McCobb platter or that fab red watering can, so ditch the snobbery.

These are the places to go to fill in if you need a random end table, bench, or bookcase. Take 'em home. Sand 'em down. Paint 'em up.

Our focus is vintage wine stems and vases of any kind. Yours now might be old cloth tape measures. The way we sift through the overwhelming array of junk is by putting on blinders. We are *not* distracted by that set of faux botanical prints (although we may be interested in the frames for other things!) or blue-and-white shaker rug. We go straight to the glassware and vases. Period.

Discipline is required. After all your hard work clearing out your own shit, do you want to end up with some other bitch's junk? Pick your fetish and stick to it!

## GET DOWN AT THE DUMP

Recycling stations, in these dire times, should be a frugal bitch's first destination for fabulous finds. That's right, start at the dump. Just like you should shop at the Target or Walmart in the priciest zip in town, if you can enter without a permit, check out the priciest garbage facility that has a take-it-or-leave-it near you. Be crafty as you wait by the entrance for all those too-rich people, or the once-rich people forced to move and now cleaning out on their way down the ladder, to deliver their goodies. Even though it's free, you do not have permission to go crazy. Dignity, ladies. If you are picking through the garbage, at least be picky.

......................

# Chapter 5

# It's Not an Endurance Test, So Get the Hell Out of Town

*L*ET'S GET THIS straight at the outset.

You're prone to seasickness, you've got Raynaud's, and you're ambivalent about birds. Do you *really* want to take a boat to Antarctica to see half a million stinky penguins because no one you know's done it? So you'll feel like shit, vomit along the way, and tire of the birds. (Or—wait—are penguins birds or mammals?) What's a little suffering when you can be oh-so-cool?

Get over yourself, bitch.

How is it that trekking in Nepal is an urgent opportunity to bone up on all the different sects of Buddhism, when you hate religion of any sort, don't hike, and the one time you went above two thousand feet you thought your head would explode?

What is it about sitting on the beach in Fiji that's so appealing when it'll require three flight changes, several nasty inoculations, and there are no great restaurants? Hello, you have a fear of fly-ing, major needle phobia, and live to eat.

What are you thinking?

This is not then. This is now. No more gratuitous traipsing around just because you can. Even if you could, you shouldn't; and if you can't—you're better off for it.

It's time to laugh at all those wannabes taking packaged and exhausting come-home-with-extreme-jetlag-and-parasite trips.

If, in fact, you're a bird lover (yes, bitch, penguins are birds), you can take amazing trips in your own backyard without ven-turing into the freezer. If, in fact, you're interested in world reli-gion and exotic travel, there are fabulous places to explore that won't blow your mind—or your wallet. And there are plenty of beaches to plant your ass on within a single plane flight from anywhere in the U.S.

## LEAVE WRETCHED EXCESS BEHIND:
### Time to Get Going
......................

**TRAVEL IS A** big fat wake-up call, more illuminating than a Sunday-school lesson.

It's time to get on the road again, if only to remind yourself that you're still one lucky bitch.

Despite your depleted bank account and the overhanging malaise of job insecurity, you'll find that compared to people living in the slums of Mumbai, your life is that of a princess in the Taj Mahal.

Besides, who hasn't needed to run away? The seven-year-old who had a fight about cleaning her room; the student at finals who skipped French class all semester; the stock trader who watched the Dow drop by half; the heartbroken girl dumped

145

by her boyfriend on her birthday; the working mom with screaming kids, a workaholic husband, and ailing parents.

Escape the crisis that's hounding your present! Look forward again. Indulge your passions, whatever they are—art, exercise, racing, the Kama Sutra. Head to new destinations to enhance skills or learn new ones. Bring real texture and interest into your life. Not to sound like your mother or anything, but this is the road to truly being rich.

Yes, bitch, it's time to carefully emerge from hibernation. Time for a little smart-spending self-indulgence. Hell, the Obamas go out partying! Everyone needs a break from the routine, an experience to get grounded or get off the ground, a moment to be someone else. Have fun. Escape by joining someone else's world or plunging into tropical oblivion.

No more debating whether to go! You're going. It's decided. Now it's time to figure out where, when, and how to do it.

## TRAVEL INTELLIGENCE

**THE INTERNET IS** your oracle. Whether you're going to Delphi, Dubai, or Denver, what could be more fitting than using the medium that crosses time and space to explore the journey? Rather than bemoaning your confinement, get your hands busy (stay focused—you aren't a boy) and start cruising the Web!

Begin building your trip by thinking of it as a fun jigsaw puzzle. Control (you just love being the bitch on top, don't you?) the entire travel experience by using the Net to piece your trip together. The best bargains are found by being flexible (we know this is hard) about where you go, when you go, how you get there, and where you stay. And the best places to find these bargains are online.

## think sideways

$\mathcal{E}$XPLORE BEYOND the usual. . . . Let one link lead you to another. Unless you're into really weird stuff, cyberspace is the practical first stop in your travel exploration. Challenged on how to begin? Try Googling "Top 25 Travel Sites." Interested in sustainable farming? Google it. Dude ranches? Google it. Spas in Iowa? You get the drill.

The first go-to Internet site for overall drool value is condenet.com. Condé Nast is the publisher of every upscale lifestyle magazine in the world (hyperbole? yes, but mostly true), and this is their corporate site. You'll find no better starting point for chic travel, dining, and style—all on one page. Start by clicking on the link to concierge.com. Check out the ten sexiest summer vacations, then give it up and move on to the ten biggest summer vacation bargains. Skip through the obvious destinations and big hotels or restaurants. Any schmo can zero in on the Plaza Athénée in Paris, Claridge's in London, the Four Seasons in New York. Continue clicking. Move on to Gourmet.com. Maybe a road trip searching out the best fried green tomatoes or a steamboat tracing Kentucky bourbon's route down the Mississippi to New Orleans appeals to some raw part of you.

Once you've got even the vaguest direction (California beach, Chilean wine, affordable spa, historic preservation), think outside the Condé. Now go to the online sites of *Travel + Leisure*, *National Geographic Traveler*, the *New York Times*, the *Atlantic Monthly*, and peruse articles going back a few years. Links in these articles will lead you further, helping you decide where

147

to go and where to stay once you get there. And, if some are subscriber-only, get off your lazy homebound bottom for the first part of your journey—go to the public library (see pages 209–213) and use their resources!

The immediate aftermath of a good write-up will mean the hotel, island, couples massage spa, or cooking school will be overrun by zealous readers. A year or two out they'll be every bit as praiseworthy and more business hungry. For instance, check out the March '09 issue of *Travel + Leisure*'s "Best Affordable Beach Resorts." In the same spirit, since you're a clever bitch and already careful about sources (no Google sidebar ads to distract or odd Web sites to lure you in), be mindful of when articles and recommendations were written—anything before 2005, find current corroborating evidence.

## GO LIVE LOCAL

Next go to local sources. Say you're considering San Francisco for your September vacation. Find local media. Go online to San Francisco–based magazines, newspapers, events calendars. You might find it's an awesome time to be in the city, that in addition to three hotel openings (under construction precrash), a long-awaited restaurant by the city's best chef is premiering. You might read that it's crush time for the grape harvest in Napa and Sonoma and stumble onto a concert featuring your favorite jazz musician.

San Francisco or São Paolo, the same strategy works for visits abroad. Didn't your college roommate spend her junior year in Brazil? Doesn't your next-door neighbor's family live near the Golden Gate bridge? Use your Facebook page to broadcast your lodging desires. A little networking connects you to invaluable inside sources. Plus, expat communities all over the world maintain Web sites of interest. And don't underestimate the value of a good old-fashioned newspaper: read China's *People's Daily* and France's *Le Monde*'s English editions—or have Google Translator amusingly work up a version of a foreign city daily.

*At Your Fingertips*

**get the full scoop**

$\mathcal{T}$RIPADVISOR.COM IS a reliable source for candid reviews of all sorts of destinations. Hear it from the mouths of other travelers.

## HOT TO TROT

We love to cruise through the exotic and expensive tour packages of agencies like Abercrombie & Kent, Butterfield & Robinson, and Smithsonian Journeys. Another favorite teaser comes in the form of college alumni tour travel itineraries. Strictly eye candy. They're selling to the very rich, not anyone as righteous, cool, and intrepid as you. But they *will* have scoped out educational, sexy, and drop-dead-gorgeous places. Exploit their research. Sort of like shopping the major department stores before you buy, use these as your guide to see where the glitterati (or what's left of them) are going.

Thank God the hotels they pick are usually too big and too pricey for our tastes (we like little—in hotels). But destination-wise, their brochures rock. For example, Abercrombie & Kent recently listed a seven-day trip through Croatia for over $7,000 (not including air), which was way out of our league, but they'd figured out the perfect destinations in a country we were dying to see: Split, Hvar, Dubrovnik. . . . And, for those of you with

*149*

ADHD who can't stand reading an entire tour book, we found key sites to visit on their itineraries: botanical garden, castles, wineries, old forts. That's right, find an editor to set the stage.

## THE CONTROLLING FLEXIBLE BITCH

Once you've got the *where* more or less nailed down, it's time to get yourself organized. We're self-proclaimed control freaks and *do not* use travel agents. The few times we've relied on agents, it only confirmed the obvious: We know what we like and how we like it better than any stranger. Once you figure out the tricks, you'll be in control of your destiny. A smart bitch wants to be on top.

## FLYING HELL

You know what we're talking about: air travel. The idea of flying sends shivers down your spine. Long check-in lines. Humiliating security checks. Ever-changing carry-on rules, acceptable bag sizes, weight limits. You arrive hours early to find no lines, or show up in the nick of time only to get stuck in a stalled crowd, blood pressure rising, sure you'll miss your flight. Then you strip and juggle while trying (and failing) to keep a sideward eye on your handbag as it slides its way down the conveyor belt. Later, you're halfway to your gate before you realize your bag is still at the security checkpoint.

Once on the plane, you enter another draconian universe. If they aren't trying to starve you, they're trying to poison you. They're certainly trying to break you, and it makes you wonder if they've conspired with the chiropractors of America and are getting some sort of kickback. And how many flights have you been on where the attendant's flirting with some creepy guy and ignoring a poor old woman trying to get her bag into the overhead, or a mother overwhelmed by two toddlers and a nursing baby? On how many flights has that mother with the gaggle of kids sat next to you? Worse yet, *been* you? Or else you're camped next to the lovely elderly lady by the window who has to keep using the restroom? Survive it by getting into every traveler's best head zone. Dissociate.

*Bitchin' Tip*

## be prepared!

1. Check on the latest silliness at www.tsa.gov.
2. Work to get preferred status on airlines (see "XXX Mature Women Only," below).
3. Print your boarding pass before you leave home.
4. Once at the airport, request a seat change to the exit row, the roomiest place in coach.
5. Bring earplugs to drown out everything.
6. Wear slip-on shoes. Bring warm socks for the flight.
7. Board as early as possible. Don't wait.
8. Stay hydrated. No alcohol. Drink plenty of water—bottled only.
9. Bring your own food, especially energy boosters like fruits and nuts. Just like you're on a wilderness survival trip.
10. Never touch *anything* in the restroom. Use paper towels to handle everything.

To scope out the best flying bargains out there, get your fingers moving overtime.

Lots of terrific sites help you manage air travel. In addition to the big guns (Expedia, Travelocity, TripAdvisor), our current favorites are Yapta and Kayak. Whether it's the buzz feature on Kayak (see below) or the search engine on Yapta that helps you use your frequent-flier miles and notifies you when your preferred destination ticket prices drop—why would you ever use a travel agent? Before you book, go to seatguru.com to find the best spot on any type of plane to plant your pretty little fanny.

In addition to using the big search engines to find cheap prices, we have frequent-flier accounts on every airline we use. Individual carriers will often inform us by e-mail of price promotions before the price changes are picked up by the big travel sites.

## XXX MATURE AUDIENCES ONLY

We have a dirty little secret, but only for mature women; just for women who are in control of their emotions and their finances; women who live within their means and their budgets. Women who pay their bills to the penny every month, no financing charges.

We put everything—yes, we mean everything—on one single airline-linked credit card. Food shopping, gasoline, meals, flying, bus and train tickets, clothing purchases, condoms. Hell, we even bought a car once and put it on the card.

Of course, we collect miles the old-fashioned way, too—we fly. But we picked the credit card airline partner that linked directly to an airline with a major hub in our city. So whenever we fly, if we can (even if it does mean a little inconvenience, time- or route-wise), we fly on that carrier. In addition to earning miles, when you build your status on an airline you get perks like early boarding and exit rows.

We hoard miles. And then we use them for *huge, big, expensive*, unaffordable business-class tickets to faraway, exotic destinations. Places like New Zealand, China, and South Africa. Stop in Calgary and Hong Kong on the way to Auckland. Return from Beijing via Honolulu and L.A. on your way back to Akron. Oh, such a thrifty bitch!

With many frequent-flier programs you can redeem your miles for a ticket that will allow multiple stops. We're not talking endless plane changes on the way to your destination and seeing only the inside of the airport; we're talking getting to visit and stay in different cities all on one ticket. Visit Istanbul via Milan, return home via Moscow. Patience and perseverance pay off when booking these flights. Make sure you talk with an airline agent (this kind of multi-leg, layover travel is tricky to do online) and keep asking questions about what routing options are available. If at first you can't get a seat on the flight(s) you want, keep checking back—availability is constantly changing.

You've worked hard for those miles, so carefully consider how you use them. It may pay to spend cash on trips shorter than six hours; you can manage in the cattle part of the plane for that long. Programs are different and changing, but here's an example. On American Airlines recently, it cost 40K frequent-flier miles to fly coach to Europe, and just 70K coach, 100K business class to China. The cheapest coach ticket from NYC to London was $377, while Beijing was $733 coach and $6,500 business class. Wow, a business-class ticket to Beijing would cost over seventeen times as much in dollars, but only two and a half times the miles. Save those frequent-flier miles for Beijing!

Any trip at least twelve hours is worth your frequent-flier miles (or at least use them to upgrade). Remember, as a bonus on those long hauls, you'll have the flexibility to make stops along the way. Save those miles and splurge.

## PLAY THE SLOTS/PICK A DESTINATION

Kayak.com/buzz. Really, this site should be Kayak/screamforjoy. com. Just like your mom telling you it was just as easy to fall in love with a rich boy as a poor boy (by the way, why didn't you take her advice?), there are so many places in the world you'll be happy visiting. Type in your home city and hit the button—the site aggregates the cheapest fares to twenty-five destinations. You can sort by month, by continent, or by city destination. This is flat-out awesome. It even has a visual for those conceptually challenged—a daily calendar of different airfare prices to a selected destination.

How to make this work for you? Let's say you haven't been out of your cramped apartment in a year, except of course for visits home on the holidays (not exactly vacation, as your mom indiscreetly keeps inquiring about your love life). If you don't go somewhere soon you'll end up homicidal or suicidal. It's been so long since you've had a travel fix, and you've been pretty religious in your savings, squirreling away a secret fantasy fund to ride bareback across a dramatic landscape. Meaning you're flexible, yes, but it has to be movie-sequence quality. You've read about the Camargue in southern France. The more you think about it, the more research you do, the hotter you get. Your fantasies are expanding beyond riding just the horse bareback. You're getting excited typing in Europe. Shit. Too expensive. Complete frustration.

Now you're all worked up.

Smart, educable bitch that you are, you head to the currency-exchange calculator and see what great values are to be found in South America. Could be hot; could work both ways. Bingo. Low-priced fares and, yes, gauchos. Okay, you need to adjust the month of the trip, but you can do this.

If you need to get the hell out of Dodge, be open-minded and flexible about when you leave—this is the first stop in planning your own trip. It's part of the adventure! Let the dice roll, see what's available, build around it. What a wonderful way to surprise yourself and explore something unknown for cheap, cheap, cheap.

## Thrifty Bitch

### 1+1 doesn't always equal 2

USE THE Web to keep current on exchange rates. Find out which currencies give you the most value. For example, take the Chinese yuan. While it's strengthened from a steady 8.2 yuan to the dollar in 2005–2007 to 6.8 yuan to the dollar in 2009, it hasn't wildly fluctuated. So China remains a great value destination. Or track the dollar to the euro as a way to decide when it's safe to go back to Paris. . . . Remember, though, this is not the only determinant! Business is bad the world over, and while currencies may be stronger or weaker, there are other things to consider. Go to oanda.com and learn where travel is dangerous to your pocketbook.

## WHERE TO STAY:
### Hotels, Motels, Inns, Villas, Etc.

DEPENDING ON THE state of your life, you can be all chill, hey-man-cool relaxed about your lodgings or high-strung, snitty, and perfectionistic. For most discerning bitches, the chill, relaxed state is a blue-moon happening. May as well

155

embrace this fact and take advantage of the meltdown. Times are tough for everyone—once high-and-mighty $1,000/night rooms are trading at a fraction of the go-go days' rates. Do your research, triangulate, call in all the resource helpers at your disposal for advice, and you're halfway to finding a great place to stay.

Once you're destination-focused, the mainstay travel sites will offer a host of hotel options. We also like the old-fashioned guidebook—you know, those relics of another era you actually hold in your hand—as a foundation tool in a traveling bitch's arsenal. For instance, we learned in a Fodor's guide that the Hotel Beacon in NYC is a top pick. Who knew? Its location rocks: We're talking upper Seventies, West Side, across the street from the best food stores ever, blocks from Lincoln Center, the Museum of Natural History, the Time Warner Center, and right at a subway stop. The rooms are enormous. Get a suite with a big living room, huge bedroom, kitchenette, and spectacular views of Central Park for as little as $255/night. Make breakfast in, keep sandwiches in the fridge, even host a cocktail party.

## ⚷ Splurgeworthy

### every bitch just *needs* a little paris

MAMA SHELTER
Paris, 20th Arrondissement
Paris should be dead to you. But scoring a room at this reasonably priced Philippe Starck ultrahip hotel makes it affordable—without sacrificing your chicster dignity. Rooms as low as 99 euros. Book early and often.

Don't neglect to sign up for every chain and hotel consortium frequent-stay club: Hyatt, Westin, Rosewood, Four Seasons, Preferred Hotels & Resorts, Relais & Châteaux. . . . Build points, redeem points for stays, hear in advance of new hotel openings, renovations, promotions. Best of all, members receive upgrades and perks like breakfast on the house.

Wherever you find your hotel, do these simple checks:

**Before booking any hotel go directly to the hotel Web site.**

1. Look at the pictures.
   - Just like "blind" dates are a thing of the past, blind stays should be too.
   - Inspect the lobby, rooms, and exterior. If all they show is the front desk and a bed, be worried.
2. How old is the hotel?
   - New is a good sign—you won't find years of hair ground into the grout around the shower.
   - Older is not always a bad thing. It may have more charm. Usually the rooms are bigger, but find out if it's been recently updated.
3. Where is the hotel?
   - Make certain you are close to where you want to be: Look at maps.
   - Check to see if it's near public transportation to the things you want to see.
4. Pricing.
   - Web prices are not necessarily the lowest. Close your computer. Pick up the telephone and talk to a live person. There are often discounts for AAA members, seniors, and other categories.

- Keep checking back. Even after you book. Prices change daily—often dropping. Save big by being vigilant.

5. Get a better room.
   - Check to see about upgrades. Everyone has some kind of promotion.
   - Talk to the reservations manager. Tell her it's a special occasion. Explain your claustrophobia and need for a high floor with a view, or a larger-than-normal room. Tell her about how happy you were visiting the last time (under your ex-boyfriend's reservation name) and how you can't wait to get back and hope they can give you the same upgraded room—of course at the low price she's quoting you—because you are such a loyal returning customer.

6. See if you can negotiate an extra day, breakfast for two, complimentary drinks.
   - Don't be shy! All they can say is no.
   - Work it like you're negotiating in a third-world economy. Sticker prices are just a starting point.

Once you've arrived, check in with confidence and style. Smile. Tell them how you've just gotten off the late flight from Delhi. You're exhausted and, oh, they did get your request, didn't they? You would be *so* appreciative of that really special room. See, you've got an important week of agent interviews coming up. They'll have no idea what you are talking about, neither do you, but it sounds cool. Then, if they still give you a crappy room, complain. One of our sources tells us they save the best rooms for late-in-the-day check-ins, just in case they get snarly customers unsatisfied by small, vanilla basic. Don't be satisfied. Vanilla is boring. Wring every little ounce out of them! Better you in that posh room than the next bitch who happens to walk in (and just finished reading this book).

## GAMBLING GAL

A word about Priceline and other blind, final-sale auction sites where you set your own price and see what comes up. Unless you're totally indifferent to your crib, *just don't*. It's like being a mail-order bride . . . you're stuck with whatever groping loser you happen to get. There are so many incredible deals out there, so many ways to stay in control of your destiny. Think hard. Once you give them your credit card, you're in—and there's no way out.

## FINDING THE BEST FOR NOTHING (WELL, ALMOST)

We use all our tools to stay on top of brand-new hotel, inn, and country retreat openings. In addition to reading PR puff in the local press we put the net out and drag through www.hotelnewsresource.com. During their first months in operation, places are still trying to work out the kinks, to generate attention, and, as a result, they offer way soft prices. If you can live without the in-hotel restaurant or fully operational bar, if you can live with polite but confused desk clerks and the occasional malfunctioning cable connection or hot-water pipes, then these are the roosts for you. Score brand-new rooms in fabulous places for a fraction of what they'll cost when everything comes online.

*159*

## THE INVERSE ROOM RELATIONSHIP RULE

Maybe you're traveling and out all day—walking the city, taking in museums, art openings, opera. In this case, you're using your room only to crash, so it doesn't need to be all hipster-cool or Southern-comfort plush. It can be a big-box mass hotel, clean and safe. Convenience is your main requirement: You want someplace central so you can run around and regroup for all your excursions.

On the other hand, if you're in a remote destination where you actually *see* the air you're breathing and it smells like rotten garlic boiled in urine; if you pull your pants down to use the johns and are attacked by swarms of disease-carrying, horny flies; if the local bottled water comes from the stream you saw industrial effluence being dumped into . . . well, you owe it to yourself to find the best oasis. A hotel to soothe the soul, to replenish you with clean towels and soft sheets as you pray to the health gods you don't get sick.

ROSALYN HOFFMAN

# PERFECT ACCOMMODATION:
## Rent-a-Crib

.....................

**NO ACCIDENTAL TOURISM ALLOWED**

The single best way to stay? Rent a house, villa, or apartment. You not only experience a new place like a local—shopping in the markets, navigating residential streets—but you get more room and usually a more comfortable place. The thrifty bitch in you will light up over the big-dollar savings.

Since most houses, villas, even apartments have several bedrooms, this is ideal for a family or group of friends. You can eat all your meals in, just breakfast in, or mix the week up however suits your fancy. If you love to cook, nothing gets the juices flowing like shopping in local markets. Buy beautiful flowers, decorate the house, and pretend you actually live in Barcelona, St. Maarten, or Jackson Hole.

Check first with local Realtors—they're an excellent source for rental houses.

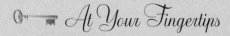 *At Your Fingertips*

**feel like you own the place**

USE THESE sites to explore local rentals:

- vrbo.com
- pap.fr (pull down the English menu on the site's navigation bar)
- homeaway.com
- cobblestay.com
- parisperfect.com

*161*

Once you locate something you're interested in, be curious and persistent. Talk to the owner, get pictures, use Google maps street view to locate the property and view the neighborhood. Confirm that you aren't staying next to a glass-recycling factory, the town dump, or a major building project. Make sure you aren't on the first floor in a sketchy neighborhood. Ask for references from people who've stayed there. Listen, business sucks—if someone isn't helpful, dump him.

*Thrifty Bitch*

### do the unexpected

You're a contrary bitch by your very nature. Put it to work to save you big bucks. The absolute best travel deals can be had by rejecting the conventional. Think South Beach in July. You'll be swimming by day and partying by night in air-conditioned splendor. Think Prague in January—then bundle up. It may be chilly, but nothing is lost: Concerts still happen in the churches at five p.m., museums remain enclosed and, in the winter, gross tourists aren't overrunning the city in their fanny packs.

## SWAPPING IS HOT

Since when have you *not* been that kind of girl?

It's bad out there, and a bitch needs to use all her wiles to get what she wants. Swapping your house or apartment for someone else's palace may be the savviest solution. Remember the chick flick *The Holiday*? Kate Winslet and Cameron Diaz, both equally man-plagued, switch houses—cute English country cottage for slick L.A. modern domicile—and live happily ever after. Yes, if only you could make that kind of swap, and with such good results. Get real. That was fantasy, but it *is* worth checking into this option as a huge money-saving alternative. The biggest site is homeexchange. com. Also, check the back pages of college alumni magazines.

Pictures, testimonials, etc., are, of course, required—you know the drill. Plus, look into insurance in case of damage (to your place).

This is a nearly "free" way to take a vacation and most definitely worth a look, although it works best if you live in a vacation destination or a major city. It's ideal if you're lucky enough to have a second home in a vacation zone—then it's no skin off your back.

## HAVE YOU CONSIDERED CAMPING?

If you're such a complete princess that you must have a hair dryer, hot running water, and a toilet in your room to be complete, then skip this part where we sagely tell you about opportunities to visit some of the most beautiful places in the world on a shoestring so you get to spend the day in just your G-string.

*Green Style at Your Fingertips*

**commune with nature—see the world for cheap**

CAMPING OPPORTUNITIES come in all shapes and sizes. Some are way rough and not every bitch's idea of a vacation, but others have more amenities. Before you dismiss it, browse these sites:

- www.eurocamp.co.uk

*(continued)*

*163*

Some of the most magnificent, unspoiled parts of the world are the least developed, and camping is *the* way to experience them. We know people who know people who go to Cinnamon Bay in St. John every year (now they refuse to talk to us because we let the secret out), a low-key affair right on one of the most sensational beaches in the Caribbean; you can't go wrong. Experience the most sublime warm aqua water, stay practically for free, and commune with nature on an island not nearly as touristy as the other Virgin Islands. Easy to get to: Simply fly to St. Thomas and take a ferry.

*Thrifty Bitch*

### wait to climax

YOU'VE DONE your homework—you're in love. You know what you want and how you are going to get it. Now make it last a long, long time. Long, slow foreplay will build you up, get you excited. Before your trip, save money and spend evenings in. Indulge in decadent, detailed fantasies about your upcoming visit, say to New Orleans.

Start with the movies: *The Big Easy, Belle of the Nineties, The Cincinnati Kid, Flesh and Fantasy* (no, it's not X-rated), *Pretty Baby, Streetcar Named Desire, Suddenly Last Summer.* Read books: *A Confederacy of Dunces, The Moviegoer,* Huey

*(continued)*

164

Long's biography, *The Great Deluge*. Listen to jazz greats Wynton Marsalis and Harry Connick Jr. Watch *Emeril Live* reruns. Cook Creole.

Foreplay like this will keep you hot and bothered until that blissful touchdown.

## TRAVEL PROPHYLACTICS:
### Tips to Keep You Covered

**YOU ARE NOT** invincible. Approach travel with extreme caution. Even reluctant-to-leave travelers, once launched, develop superwomen complexes. Not to get all metaphysical, but something about suspending who they are in normal time and space seems to translate into sublimely stupid decision making. Whether it's buying jewelry you'd never buy at home, looking the wrong way when crossing the street in London, or obliviously wandering into bad neighborhoods, a bitch needs to keep her wits about her.

Just because you're on vacation, most people living and working where you're visiting (unless you are at an all-inclusive, secluded resort) are *not on* vacation. They're leading their normal lives. One great reason to travel is to learn that the world over, people are people. They may wear different clothes, eat different food, speak different languages, and look different from you, but they run the gamut from good to bad, kind to mean, honest to thieving.

**stranger in a strange land**

*D*ON'T BE a *bitch*, bitch. Never argue with a native anyplace you travel. You will always lose. Be polite. Part of traveling is sometimes having the cabdriver take you the circuitous route because you don't know better, or getting over-charged by the unscrupulous vendor just because he can. Chalk it up to the cost of travel.

## THE BITCH'S TRAVEL SURVIVAL GUIDE

**Traveler beware: You are a target.** The out-of-state license plate parked in Austin, the fanny pack, the look of dumbstruck awe on your face at Notre Dame . . . Be smart. No wandering behind giant maps. No slack jaws. Put your bags in the trunk and assume the urban bitch's "I live here" look.

**Get travel insurance.** You'll find two varieties: the got-the-flu-can't-go-want-my-money-back variety; and the need-to-be-airlifted-off-Mount-McKinley-but-don't-want-to-end-up-either-dead-or-bankrupt variety. Get both. Check out www.square-mouth.com.

**Familiarize yourself with the State Department's travel advisories.** To learn where there's a high terror threat, what inoculations you need, and where dengue fever and Ebola have been active, go to www.travel.state.gov/travel, www.who.int/en, and wwwn.cdc.gov/travel.

*166*

**Call your cell phone provider** and set up a plan that makes sense for the region you'll be traveling in. *Do not* use your phone, e-mail, or text messaging if you haven't done this. Your phone charges will be greater than the cost of your trip!

**Inform your credit card company where you're going.** Otherwise, SOBs that they are, they'll end up cutting you off. Beyond a nominal amount, they're responsible for all charges and don't like to see big bucks banged up in an odd pattern of use in Morocco. You could end up seriously challenged when you attempt to charge purchases, and that won't be fun.

**Make copies of all your documents.** Leave one set at home with a reachable, responsible adult. Keep copies of documents with you in a separate place from your wallet.

**Travel lean.** Take one credit card and ATM card (as a means to get cash and as a backup credit card), your driver's license, insurance card, and passport. Remove everything else from your wallet.

**Keep a reasonable sum of local cash money** stuffed into the front pocket of your jeans at all times.

In the event of disaster and you lose everything, have no funds, no means of getting to funds, and can't find the American embassy because you don't speak the language and are too disheveled to use your feminine charm to garner help from a gallant stranger (which you should never do anyway), here's your plan: Find the biggest and most expensive hotel in the center of the town or area where you are staying. Even though you're not a guest, chances are the manager will get in touch with the embassy and even help you contact your credit card company.

## travel essentials: hand sanitizer and pepto

WE ARE not doctors and do not play them on TV. We *are* veteran world travelers. Our two key, over-the-counter, don't-leave-home-without-them travel products are hand sanitizers and Pepto-Bismol. Be compulsive and *bathe* in hand sanitizer. Don't touch anything (unlike our shopping tour, this is not about saving money; this is survival). Keep your hands to yourself. This isn't the time to find every child under five so fucking adorable that you rough up their hair and shake their little hands. They are germ machines—germs you probably have no immunities to. Keep washing up. Touch money—wash up. Grab a handrail—wash up. After any exchange—wash up. Use Pepto at the first sign of tummy distress—nip it in the bud. Pink is good. Don't be alarmed if the inside of your mouth turns black and what comes out the other end matches.

## WHAT'S A GIRL TO WEAR?

**TRAVEL TIME IS** not fashion time. Yes, the movies show beautiful, impeccably dressed people on airplanes where impeccable stewardesses solicitously pour scotch and offer hors d'oeuvres. Yes, all these beautiful people have Louis Vuitton trunks stacked on carts by impeccable porters. It's the movies, you idiot.

## WHAT TO PACK: The Dialectics of Packing

Packing sucks. Everyone hates to pack. It's the ultimate executive task function—requires forethought, planning, and editing. You know, like a big term paper due tomorrow, and you have thousands of library books stacked in your room. It is all there, but you have no idea what you are going to say, let alone in which format. There's no easy solution. One trip you overpack and come home with clean clothes and wonder why you schlepped everything around and had to fold and refold so many things; the next trip you vow not to make the same mistake and find yourself woefully undergarmented.

If it makes you any calmer, unless you are going outside of civilization, you can buy almost everything anywhere.

### The Bitch's Basic Travel Bag Rules

1. Carry-on only. Bags get lost all the time.
2. Keep all meds, your passport, and your wallet in your handbag. The Prozac and Ativan aren't easily replaced.
3. No fancy jewelry.
4. Stay with one color for shoes and bags: black. One pair of comfy shoes, one pair of dressier shoes. A black everyday handbag that slings across your body that you can keep close. A clutch for dinners if you are prissy.
5. Blue jeans rule the world over. A single black skirt or dress and two nice sweaters for evening can be worn everywhere.
6. Assorted knit tops and tee-shirts to dress up or down.
7. A raincoat/overcoat, depending on weather.
8. Pj's (optional), underwear to last the journey (we hate

169

washing them by hand and won't spend the money on the hotel laundry), unless it's a really long trip. Socks and bras, ditto. Pack sexy things in plastic bags—the thought of some gross airport security guy getting his rocks off touching them is nauseating.

9. Backpack. Max out your carry-on space by stuffing your everyday handbag inside. Tuck in books, snacks, laptop (if appropriate), writing materials.

## THE YIN AND YANG OF TOURING:
### Two-faced Bitch

**WE'RE SNARLY AND** not very compromising bitches, and as a general rule don't play well in a big tour group. Unless they're featuring a locale accessible only by tour, we're not in. That said, occasionally tours are worth it.

### BUY ONE, GET ONE

We'll use a guide if we can score a trip for free. If you're a clever bitch (with friends who've managed to keep their jobs), this just may work. The plan? Organize a group of friends to go on one of the fancy, gold-plated tours. Whether it's a bike tour through Vermont, a ski trip in Switzerland, or a trek in the English countryside, many operators will comp your portion if you bring eight or ten friends with you. Sort of like a gift with purchase—their purchase, your gift. (No, you're not screwing your pals—you're the logistics pimp, and for that they owe you.) You owe only the airfare piece.

## NOTHING BONDS LIKE SCORN

When traveling with your family, try hiring a local guide, even if you speak the language. Yes, this means extra *dinero*, but it may be the best investment against typical family tour dysfunction. You know all too well the dreaded "what are we going to do today?" trap. Everyone has a different idea, meaning when one person wins someone else loses. Spare the expense of years of therapy for the kids. You need no more psychodrama! Remember the time you all went on the long college tour that finished with a free afternoon? You spent forever debating where to go, and by the time you rented the car to drive to Louisa May Alcott's house (you always wanted to be Jo), got lost trying to navigate out of the city, and arrived, it was two forty-five. The place closed at three (someone did not do their homework).

Little Timmy had longed to go to Fenway Park; Annie demanded Filene's Basement (despite your true and sage advice that it was not what it used to be); your husband wanted to find Sam Adams's home (the beer guy, not the revolutionary firebrand). By the end of the day everyone was mad—at *you*.

If you'd hired a tour guide, he could have brought you to the U.S.S. *Constitution*, Paul Revere's house, and the Freedom Trail. Then on to his friend's struggling pizza parlor in East Boston—under the false pretense that he was taking you to the place all the locals favored. Someone else would have worried about logistics, you'd have gotten a full-flavored feel for the city, and, most important of all, the tour guide would own your family's scorn. Better to have endured trudging around, and later laughed together about his ridiculous accent and how bad the pizza was—nothing bonds a country tighter than a common enemy.

## PLAY THE CONCIERGE KEY: Get the Lay of the Land

On arrival, go into the best hotel in the city—of course you're not staying there. Loiter in the lobby a moment. Breathe in the aroma from the fabulous flower arrangements. Ride the glass elevator to the top, take in the view, or check out the cedar-scented spa and posh restaurant. Linger awhile. Come back down again and exit the elevator as though you've just gotten up from sleeping in late. Confidently march over to the concierge desk. Light up with a glowing "I belong in pictures" smile—you know, somewhere between cool bitch and warm, down-to-earth gal—as you introduce yourself. Pretend you're a world-traveling French-style sophisticate. Extend your hand.

"I am Jewel Astor and we're here for the next week. My husband I are complete foodies and *live* to explore small, interesting places wherever we go. What do you recommend?" Then in a conspiratorial tone, add, "Aren't we all so sick of pretentious restaurants that don't deserve the hype?"

You haven't lied. You never said you were staying in the hotel, did you? Besides, these folks are *bored* . . . who can afford their establishments these days? You're doing them a favor by making it look like their services are needed. Hell, you're helping them keep their jobs. Nine times out of ten, they'll happily sit and schmooze, and you can slyly extract information about the best restaurants, off-the-beaten-path walking areas, new museum openings, and free concerts. Sometimes hotels offer passes to cultural events, which not only save you the entrance fees but also time waiting in lines. (Ask about these passes at the hotel where you're actually a paying guest.) Unless you found a snotty, unhelpful asshole, be a mensch and always give them a tip. They saved you buying a tour book.

**feel like 007**

*C*HECK OUT the latest dining trend around the world: underground dining. Do a little Web research. Scout the blogs. Find out if there are any off-the-record "supper clubs" in the city you'll be visiting. Okay, no health inspectors have been there . . . but you just may be served an incredible meal by a cutting-edge chef. This is a way talented chefs debut their style before they've got the overhead to open their own places.

## STOP LUSTING:
### Just Do It

**GET OFF YOUR** ass and go.

It's been so long, you're starting to think you don't need it anymore. You think you're satisfied with the tools you've got hanging around. You're starting to believe the thrill is the same, even if you're just at home alone sprawled on your bed with a few magazines, a movie, or some odd cyberspaces to explore. Trust us: While there's virtue in virtual, once you get back in the action you'll remember why *nothing compares* to the real thing.

Now you know what sites to cruise, what tricks to use, and how to take a thrifty vacation guaranteed to get your rocks off. The question remains: Where to go? The following are some suggestions. But be your own bitch! Use these ideas as inspiration—then chart your own path.

## ROAD TRIP—HELL, YES!!

You think you need to go to Europe to be a tourist? No, not really. Check out your own backyard. Take a road trip. What better way to regain control of your destiny? Jobs be damned. Stock market be damned. Housing woes be damned. Screw the lines at the airport and the groping security people. Get behind the wheel and just *go*. With your BlackBerry or iPhone in hand, map your trip, find your lodging, discover places to eat on the fly. Everyone speaks English, and, if you don't like the scene, pick up and leave. It'll amaze you, excite you, add years to your life. Write a journal, blog it. Hell, maybe you'll sell the movie rights.

Why do all the classic road movies belong to the boys? Sure, we've got *Thelma and Louise*, but it doesn't end so well, now, does it? Reimagine the wonder of the open road. Explore your own backyard—but make your own cheesy happy ending!

## DRIVE—AMERICAN

Have you ever camped in the desert? Hiked the Grand Canyon? The Grand Tetons? Dropped your jaw at Montezuma's Castle or Taliesin in Arizona? Driven across Death Valley? Visited the Art Institute and taken a grand architectural tour of Chicago? Won a blue ribbon at the Iowa State Fair in August? Backpacked the length of the Appalachian Trail? Gone lobstering off the coast of Belfast, Maine? Explored the Alamo? Spent a night partying in South Beach? Attended a play at the Guthrie in Minneapolis? Run the Nike Women's Marathon in San Francisco? Mushed the Iditarod in Alaska? Picnicked while the Boston Pops play the 1812 Overture as fireworks go off on the Charles River in Boston on the Fourth of July? Cycled through the Big Apple after midnight? Viewed Art Basel in Miami? Reenacted the Battle of Gettysburg? Painted, wrote, played music at Interlochen Summer Arts Camps for Adults? Sliced your finger at cooking class at the Culinary Institute of America in Hyde Park? Made cheese in Wisconsin? Watched orcas breach in the San Juan Islands? Drunk Oregon pinots at the vineyards? Golfed Pebble Beach?

The point is, bitch, the US of A is teeming with things you've never seen or done. And so much is for *free*. Places you can go to veg out (amazing beaches), or learn (astonishing historic sites), or get fit (mountains to climb, caves to explore).

Put down the top, wrap your scarf around your head, crank up the radio—and drive.


## PASSIONS PLAY

Pick your passion as a starting point for a road trip. Movie buff? Look for film festivals around the world. Discover that the Nantucket Film Festival is in June. Once you begin to cruise you'll realize this is preseason Nantucket, well before the island hits August peak craziness. No, it's not the biggest or most prestigious of the festivals, but it's lots of fun. Check weather.com and you'll see the weather is delightful in June. Go to the local chamber of commerce for lodging options. To your surprise, you'll learn this is a budget opportunity. Consider renting a house for a week with friends—cheaper and more fun than an inn or hotel—and morphing this into your early summer beach vacation. You'll discover some of the most beautiful beaches and best restaurants in the world on this little gem of an island thirty-five miles off the coast of Massachusetts. Skip Cannes, save a bundle on air travel, escape to an island, but stay American. All because you love movies!

Friend of flora? How about a tour of botanical gardens? Your government (in wiser days) nurtured one of the most gorgeous gardens in the world right on the Mall (no, not the shopping mall), smack-dab in the middle of D.C. Recently renovated, it's the oldest continuously operating botanic garden in the States, and stunning any time of year.

For just a moment you stopped being a shallow, materialistic bitch and followed your love of orchids to the capitol—little did you know you'd find so much hidden culture in plain sight. These days D.C. is hot, hot, hot. The shame of unregulated greed has (at least temporarily) knocked the Big Apple from its perch at the top of the power tree. D.C. has displaced NYC, as only a trillion-dollar sugar daddy and second-coming Camelot could do. There's nothing sexier than power, and the new locus of power is Capitol City.

For starters, the entire Smithsonian Museum complex will knock your socks off. Trust us, you'll feel like a dope if you haven't been since your sixth-grade field trip. The list of wonders is long: The National Portrait Gallery, the National Air and Space Museum, the Hirshhorn, and on and on. The city itself is one of the most beautiful in the world, laid out by the French architect Pierre Charles L'Enfant in 1791. (See www.nps.gov/history/Nr/travel/wash/lenfant.htm to find out more and discover the National Register of Historic Places.) Walk until your feet fall off. And since this is a city of transients—diplomats, immigrants, politicians—the restaurant scene is hyperinternational: Ethiopian, Moroccan, Malaysian, Vietnamese. . . . Make Seventh, Eighth, Ninth at E, F, G your destination.

At night, pool your funds, hire a limo, uncork the champagne, kick off your shoes, and drive from illuminated monument to illuminated monument. You'll get goose bumps—and not from your state of undress.

## ALL-NATURAL BITCH: For the Birds

If you're a closeted bird fetishist, come on out! No need to
be ashamed, even if you do have that habit of making bizarre
sounds to draw birds to you. We admire you for your love of
nature, your thriftiness, your incredible powers of observation
(though not so much for your fashion sense).

And you who sit in judgment of those feathery fetishists—get
over yourselves! Bird people know the *absolute best places*. You
can learn a thing or two about gorgeous (and free) spots to visit,
about slowing down, about listening, from those binoculared
bitches. Think you need the rainforest for otherworldly scenery? Think you need a Japanese monastery to get all chilled out
and Zen? Think again. Go to Audubon.org to find the sanctuary
nearest you.

Nature and New Jersey you thought an oxymoron? Get over
your prejudices. Head over to Cape May, famous for seabirds in
summer and birds of prey in fall. Plus you're just three hours
from New York City, two hours from Philadelphia. Get your
nature fix, then head to the urban areas and hit some of the best
art museums in the world.

## from sea to shining sea

TAKE A road trip to stunning beaches every red-white-and-blue-blooded American gal must strut her goods on before her bikini-wearing days are done. We suggest Ocracoke Island off the Outer Banks, reached by ferry—Blackbeard, that discerning rake of a pirate, was there before the crowds. Key West, at the very tip of the Florida Keys, is cool, gorgeous, and, when you're sorely in need of a Caribbean fix, proudly represents the southernmost point in the Continental U.S. Or crank up the Beach Boys and head over to Surf City, a.k.a. Huntington Beach, OC, CA, USA—need we say more? When you're finished being all hip and chill Southern Cal girl, head north and gasp at Big Sur. Then spend the night looking for Clint in Carmel—he's old but iconic, and the perfect road trip sighting trophy.

## GET ROUGH AND CHIC: Just the Way We Like It!
## Shanghai, Beijing, and Beyond . . .

You just gotta go.

Now that you know the lay of the land, now that you're feeling confident and thrifty, start planning the trip of a lifetime—to China.

Go because you're an adventurer at heart. Go because it feels like you've been in jail. Go because you travel to grow, to experience other ways of living, to see beyond your four walls. Go before the world becomes one big boring mass of global commercialism. Most of all, go because you have a small budget and a big travel appetite. And there is simply *nowhere else on earth* you get more of everything (except relaxation) for your travel buck.

Five thousand years of unrivaled discovery and sophistication are roaring back after a measly few-hundred-year stall. Hell, we're a little hiccup in history by comparison. Get over there and see it happening. See the contrasts between old and new, East and West. The world is your oyster—go get covered in the wet, briny slime, slurping for the pearls of Asia.

*Thrifty Bitch*

## the pearls of asia

YOU'LL FEEL like the empress who lived at the Summer Palace when you bring home a chest full of pearls from the Hongqiao Pearl Market in Beijing. These prices are so low you'll be actively hostile toward all those jewelry hawkers back in the States—you know, those hipster designers selling really expensive pieces using mere moonstone, seed pearls, and oversized freshwater pearls. You could finance your trip reselling the necklaces, bracelets, and rings you'll be coming home with! Allocate a morning—and then end up going back for more. Find a vendor you like, go from stall to stall, negotiate prices, and design your own necklaces. Take pictures as they string them before your eyes. This is the bitch's perfect souvenir.

......................

# Chapter 6

# A Bitch on Wheels Knows Her Limits

*M*OVE OVER, BEVERLY Hills bitch, with your fake boobs and big honking Mercedes XL. Step aside, little miss sporty-and-outdoorsy, with your Lincoln Navigator transporting ski equipment and kayaks, well . . . *maybe* once a year. And *you* . . . suburban goddess with your juice-box-clutching kids nestled in the Dodge Caravan: We get your dilemma, but sorry; it's time to hit the road. Your fancy overused cars are an embarrassment, not a status symbol. Do you really need to pull out the big guns just to pick up your meds, when you could simply hop on your mint green retro cruiser bike or jump the local number two bus?

It's time for a tune-up. You've got different accessories for different occasions, right? So use different modes of transport for different tasks. Your new assignment: to get acquainted with a whole new class of cars. To learn how—and when—to buy them. To take a long, sexy ride on the hottest two-wheelers on the market. And, most of all, to expand your consciousness. It's time to think of wheels as a communal resource rather than a new toy that's just for me, me, me. By ending your dependency on one filthy, money-guzzling beast you'll reduce your monthly expenses big-time, and do your part to help the environment. The chicest people the world over have known this for years . . . a modern bitch rolls on all wheels.

## A BITCH ON FOUR WHEELS

**IF YOU'VE JUST** tanked up for the third time this week (gas, not booze!), and charged another hundred bucks to your credit card . . . If you're waking up at three a.m. to call your bank's ATM hotline to make sure they're still in business, then turning to that jumbo tub of cookie-dough ice cream to soothe the heartburn . . . If you have to restrain yourself from calling the "get rich quick" 1-800 number pulsing across the infomercial . . . then we have news for you. Ending your unhealthy relationship with your car can provide the single biggest savings outside of a massive rent or mortgage downsize.

No, we're not suggesting that you do something rash like file for a car divorce; quite the contrary. We're telling you to stop craving a flashy new model every few years, and renew your vows to your baby despite its limitations.

And, for the virgins among us, lusting for the first ride they can call their own: We'll share the modern new rules for finding Mr. Goodcar. Park your ass and we'll tell you when it's time to buy a car; whether it should be shiny and new or gently used; how to avoid lease seduction; which new cars are right for the new green and thrifty you; and what car keeps you looking your chicest.

## NO CAR PURCHASE FOR BABY

When do you need to buy a car? Rarely, if ever.

Cars are *not* a fashion accessory. Get a grip and resist the auto industry's new-model cycle. Beware that new-car smell luring you into "premature purchase." Most cars should last at least eight to ten years before very costly repairs are necessary, and experts agree that timely maintenance and minor tweaking will always cost you less than a newly purchased car's coupon payment book. Remember, the economy sucks. So those nascent rust spots? They're now *très* cool. There are less expensive ways to announce to the world just how hot and sexy you are—like a new pair of Manolo stilettos—a bona fide bargain compared to the cost of a new car!

## THE ONLY TIMES TO BUY

*Do not* consider an automobile purchase unless:

- You don't have a car and need one.
- Your car has been stolen.
- Your lease is up.
- Your gas expense is now more than your mortgage expense (see edmunds.com/calculators/gas-guzzler.html for a calculator to see if it really pays to turn that gas-guzzler in).
- Your family circumstances have changed. For example: Your real estate company folded and you've moved from Florida to Alaska and the BMW Z4 really needs to be a Toyota RAV4.
- Despite your best efforts your car no longer starts.

## IF YOU DO QUALIFY

The first rule of car buying is to remember that *you are a woman*. Your car is not an anatomical extension of your body. *You do not have a penis* and therefore have no need to proclaim to the world that yours is the biggest! Don't even think about a Navigator or Mercedes S 550. And sadly, those seductive European sports cars are way too expensive to buy and to service, especially since they cannot deliver on their implied promise of "returning the favor" by lavishing you with "multiple Os." Scratch them off your list: sorry, no Porsche Boxster this year.

The second rule of car buying is to beat the assholes at their own game. You know the ones we're talking about—the guys using more hair product than you, who talk directly to your breasts as they ask when your husband or father will be joining you. Don't they know that women pay the bills and influence the majority of car-buying decisions? Knowledge is power, so before you begin shopping, do your homework.

*At Your Fingertips*

### queen of the road

- ◆ For general car-consuming advice turn to www. consumerreports.com, the bible of the good, the bad, and the ugly when it comes to auto reliability and safety. If you don't have a subscription, wheel yourself down to your local library.

- ◆ To find out what dealers paid for their inventories, for up-to-date manufacturers' incentives, blue book

*(continued)*

values, used-car buying guides, as well as more
detailed specifications, consult www.edmunds.com
and www.kbb.com.

◆ To obtain valuable fuel savings information go to www.
fueleconomy.gov.

◆ Every woman should read edmunds.com's "The Gender
Gap." It will rile you up so you don't take their crap
when they try to screw you out of a fair deal (www.
edmunds.com/advice/womenfamilies/articles/45991/
article.html).

## NEW OR USED?

In the good old days this might have actually been a valid question. Now it all comes down to living within your means, so you
can sleep through the night. We'll pretend for a moment that
this is still a valid question. Bitch, "cutting back" is the new conspicuous consumption, and there's no better way to flaunt how
au courant you are than by buying a gently used beauty.

## USED CARS: A Girl's Best Friend

When you buy a new car, you're getting screwed from the
moment you drive that shiny new trophy off the lot, since most
cars depreciate by 45 percent during the first three years of ownership. Used cars, on the other hand, are both significantly less
expensive and the best example of über-recycling (particularly
if you can score a hybrid). They also come with "a gift with purchase": lower sales and excise taxes and lower insurance rates.

## kick the tires

- Buy only from a local source. Whether it's your neighborhood dealer, Craigslist, a friend of a friend, or your local newspaper classified, you *must* check out a used car in person.

- In the same way you'd ask your best friends to give your latest boyfriend the once-over, you *must* bring a used car to a trusted mechanic for a thorough physical before signing on the dotted line.

- Beware of unscrupulous salespeople: *Never* sign an agreement with an "as is" clause; this will void your ability to return a defective car under most states' lemon laws.

- Check carfax.com to research the car's lineage before you buy.

## WHEN ONLY NEW WILL DO

**MAYBE YOU'RE ONE** of those women who never took to the vintage-clothing craze; it all felt a little too up close and personal. Buying a used car feels like wearing someone else's underwear. Or maybe your parents thought they were bestowing words of wisdom with their "Don't buy used; you're just buying someone else's problem!" which still rings in your ear. Or maybe you're just one of those chicks with too much testosterone who needs a big new thingy to feel complete. If you're one of these poor

185

unfortunates (yes, the tables have turned—we now feel compassion for those so unsavvy, they *must* buy a brand-new car), remember this:

Your car should cost you no more than 15 percent of your monthly budget.

It absolutely must be a car with excellent resale value; this is the one hedge against depreciation.

⌐━ *Bitchin' Tip*

## make sure it's a keeper!

*So*, YOU passed all the hurdles and qualify for a used car—or you're a spoiled princess and need one that's brand-spanking-new. Either way, make sure it's equipped with antilock brakes, electronic stability control, and, depending on your driving conditions, traction control. If you're buying new, choose one of the Kelley Blue Book top ten cars for resale after five years of ownership.

## FINDING THE MODERN CLASSIC THAT WORKS FOR YOU

Are you a single person living in a big city? Check out the adorable and affordable Honda Fit ... *and buy it in red.* Do you have snowy winters, kids with skis, and family pets? The sanely sized, competitively priced Subaru Forester rocks. Need a stylish family sedan? GM is still in business and the Chevy Malibu gets high marks for looks, drive and value. Are you a traveling sales rep racking up mile after highway mile? A hybrid is a must, so choose between the Honda Civic Hybrid, Ford Escape Hybrid, or the gold standard, Prius. Every one of these cars is chic, reliable, and costs less than a year of rent in Manhattan.

## a hybrid is . . . ?

IN CASE you've been living in a cave, here's the deal with hybrid cars. A hybrid is not a new crossbreed Chihuahua and Great Dane designer pooch. (Ouch! Poor Chihuahua!) Simply put, it's the "it" car, fueled by both a regular internal combustion engine and an electric engine assisted by a battery pack (recharged by the kinetic energy of the car itself!). Their emissions are significantly less than those of a conventional car, and their slightly higher price point can be justified by the big bucks you save on gas.

## AVOIDING LEASE SEDUCTION

Never lease a car.

Car makers suck you into lease programs with no or low down payments by promising lower sales taxes and the allure of easily rolling into bed with a younger, slimmer, better-endowed ride as soon as the lease is up. (Who wouldn't want a three-way massaging, air-conditioned seat?) Hold your ground, baby.

While the expenses of a loan and a lease on a monthly basis may *appear* to be even, once your lease is up—after all those months of payment coupons—you have nada, zip, absolutely *nothing*. And to add insult to injury, you need to go buy or lease another car!

Leases usually come with nasty fine print that will bite you in the ass. You rack up huge penalties for driving over the terms of the mileage contract or returning the car in less than pristine condition. If you need to break the lease, brace yourself for the ultimate punishment of all: You still owe the payments! GMAC

187

doesn't give a shit that you're going through a tough time. (They have their own problems.) Besides . . . didn't you say you were through with masochistic relationships?

## THE ONLY TIMES TO LEASE

Never consider leasing unless:

- Your accountant says you can benefit from the deductions.
- It's a very short-term solution: perhaps relocating to an urban "no-car zone" is on the horizon; or you're planning to start a family but want one last "quickie" before your "suburban chunky" days.

## THE CHICEST OF THEM ALL

OH, TO BE cute, chic, and green (almost): Our to-die-for brand-new car is the Mazda MX-5 Miata. It's a blast to drive, easy on the gas budget, high on the resale meter, a great urban size, and a rocking cool convertible. Perfect for your road trip (see page 174). The chicest and only choice: true red (okay, we have a thing for red). Period. Control yourself and go for the baseline with a $22,700 sticker price. Yes, you now need to learn how to drive a manual, which is far more fuel-efficient than an automatic. How else are you going to get exercise when you're driving?

## the right hands for the job

*T*HE MOST important car accessory is a good mechanic. Canvass your friends and neighbors to find the best repair guy in your area. Nothing makes for a smoother ride than a hottie with good hands who can assess the body, then keep servicing you under the hood and inside. According to the U.S. Department of Energy, a properly tuned and maintained car can save up to as much as 19 percent per mile in gas costs.

## A BITCH ON TWO WHEELS

**WAKE UP. LOOK** around. They're swishing past you on the road in a cloud of pink or cream or classic black, and claiming your secret parking spots as their own. And the women motoring these vehicles . . . why do they all look so damn happy? The answer is simple: If the most evolved creatures on earth move on two limbs rather than four, it's only fitting that the most sophisticated among us are two-wheel bitches.

Two-wheelers are cheaper than four wheels, easier on the environment, and sexy as hell. Whether you dump your car in the nearest junkyard or incorporate two-wheelers into your transportation repertoire, you'll save major money on gas and taxes, and may even be able to cut back on your antidepressants. So, grab a helmet (stylishly black) and spice up your wheel mix with hip Vespas and hogs, your vintage bicycle or a speedy new one, or the funky two-wheeler that's just rolled onto the market.

189

## VESPAS: Cheap Chic

The hottest bitch on two wheels . . . drives a Vespa! Screw four-wheeled machines. It feels oh-so-good to have the handsomest two-wheeled vibrator in town running between your legs as you scamper to work or run errands. Not only can you scoot in and out of traffic at will, get up to seventy miles per gallon of gas, park willy-nilly at odd angles (in some places even on the sidewalk!), but you also tool around town astride a little machine that comes in the most delicious color combinations.

## THE PRICE IS RIGHT

The opening price point on a brand-new Vespa is $3,200, and used ones can be found for as little as $1,000—a massive bargain compared to their primitive four-wheeled cousins! Vespas also have excellent resale value, news that should get a thrifty bitch's pulse racing. With prices like these, you owe it to yourself to pull out that old Hermès scarf (ah, the good old days), wrap it around your head and tie it under your chin, don your thick-framed black sunglasses, and apply a beguiling stroke of Charles Revson Red. Now, morphed into Sophia Loren, march yourself out your door to test-ride one: Right now!

## YOU'VE HEARD IT BEFORE . . . SIZE MATTERS

Vespas come in many models. Most states allow you to drive the smallest engine job, the Vespa LX 50cc (maximum speed thirty-nine mph), on your regular car operator's license. These are fabulous for short, simple commutes. The smaller the ccs, the less power you have, so depending on your driving conditions, you may want to check out larger-engine models. They'll give you that extra burst of power for more agile and safer scooting.

## HOG RIDERS WEAR LIPSTICK, TOO

If you have more hard-grinding fantasies—say, black leather jackets, studded neckwear, and big black boots—you're not alone. Women riders are the fastest-growing sector in the motorcycle business. Tired of taking a backseat? Try straddling this two-wheel classic for its manageable price and excellent fuel efficiency. If you want to try some low-altitude flying, go hog-wild with a Harley.

The Harley-Davidson Sportster 1200 is made for a woman, since it's built smaller and lower to the ground than most other models. Big hogs are a different animal from and pricier than Vespas, but they're still far cheaper than any car out there. The Sportster starts at $10,000 new, and can be found used for nearly half that price. If you do choose the biker-chick route, then keep the faith, baby. After all, you're buying a mean machine, so only buy black.

O⊷━ *At Your Fingertips*

### safety, baby!

WHETHER YOU'RE Sophia Loren on your Vespa or Jane Fonda on your hog, you *must* take a safe driving course. They're only $25 and the best investment you'll ever make. Check them out www.msf-usa.org. According to the Federal Highway Administration, motorcyclists are thirty-four more times likely to die in a crash than car drivers (duh), so be supercautious . . . and don't tell Mom!

# LIBERATE YOURSELF ON A BICYCLE!

**WE KNOW: VESPAS** and motorcycles can be dangerous and are definitely not for everyone, but everyone can—and should—ride a bike. They're the new status symbol for all things hip, lean, and green, and the single most cost-effective way to get around; you save big-time on parking fees, taxes, insurance, and gas. They're also the healthiest form of transportation you can find. Pumping your legs on a bike burns six hundred calories per hour (going fourteen to sixteen mph), while pumping your legs during . . . well, you know *what* burns only a couple of hundred calories per hour.

So give the car a rest and join the cool new bike culture before it whizzes past you, potential savings and all. Hop on, and we'll show you how to buy a bike with our handy-dandy bike-buying bible, and which bikes and accessories make the most sense for the modern bitch.

## THE BIKE BIBLE

By following these simple bike-buying commandments, you'll end up with a bike that goes the distance, rather than a constant reminder of how much money you just flushed down the toilet.

- If you have a bike that you like and it works, hold your hand. The economy sucks and you know what they say: If the wheels roll, use them.
- You are a woman. Unless you're extra tall, with a long torso and long arms, buy a bicycle engineered for your body.
- Buy the best bike you can afford. A big aftermarket means great bikes hold their resale value.

- *Do not* go to Walmart or Target. Visit a reputable local bicycle store and have the sinewy stud help find the right size and styling for you. Take different bikes out for test-drives. Compare and contrast models. Ride up and down hills. Zip around on a busy street. Try stopping short on a stretch of sand or gravel.
- Get out and ride the bike you've invested in.

## MODERN BIKES FOR THE MODERN BITCH

Walking into the bike shop can be intimidating. Hanging from the ceiling are hundreds of bikes made by dozens of different manufacturers. Clip-clopping past you with purpose are packs of riders, clad in Spandex, wrap-around sunglasses, and bike shoes. Calling out to you are rows and rows of cute little bike accessories. Yes, it's overwhelming. Wait! Don't leave. Here's a quick tutorial so you can sidle up to that bike shop guy with confidence:

- Road bikes are built for speed and are made to ride on relatively smooth pavement on narrow tires with aerodynamic dropped front handlebars: Think Lance Armstrong.
- Mountain bikes are built for off-roading, have fat, knobby tires, flat front handlebars and suspensions built for abuse: Think teenage skater boys blasting indie music.
- Recumbent bikes are the most ergonomic but scare the shit out of us because their low profile makes them nearly invisible to car drivers: Think MIT professor with full beard, potbelly, and legs better than yours.

193

All of which means, unless you're viewing your bike as a fashion accessory to complement your image (think Racer Barbie, Dirt Devil Barbie, Recumbent Geek Barbie), the best all-purpose choice for a hip, budget-conscious bitch is either a hybrid or comfort bike, or the new retro-chic cruiser.

## HYBRID AND COMFORT BIKES

They're plush, they're fun, and they're all-purpose. Hybrid and comfort bikes are just as perfect for commuting as they are for cruising aimlessly around town while you give your car's filthy footprint a break. A hybrid bike is a cross between a road bike and a mountain bike, with treaded tires and flat front handlebars. A comfort bike is a specialized version of a mountain or hybrid, with more of an upright riding stance, softer seats, and easier gearing.

Once you've taken the hybrid and comfort for a spin and determined which style feels best, tailor it to fit your personal comfort level; seats, handles, even pedals can be customized. Buy the most comfortable seat you can find: Remember, you *do not* have a hanging appendage but lots and lots of very delicate tissue. It should be soft and breathe (the seat, that is). After all, there are more exciting ways to get a yeast infection!

○━━━ *Splurgeworthy*

### a bike with benefits

*N*EW HYBRID electric bikes have batteries parked above the back wheel and a control switch, so you can decide when you need that occasional nudge to help you pedal uphill. If you're committed to commuting by bike, but coming home

*(continued)*

too exhausted to even crack open that wine bottle, then this may be the pick for you. Check out the Twist Freedom line at www.giantbicycle.com.

## CRUISERS

For all you pussies who don't want to sit astride that Vespa, wrap your legs around the next best thing: a cruiser bike. Cruisers are one-speed or multispeed old-fashioned bicycles for flat town driving. Not only are they affordable, but they're gorgeously retro, with fat tires, high handlebars, real kickstands, and whimsical, girlie colors. (Think of an updated version of that Schwinn or Huffy you used to pedal around the cul-de-sac). Our all-time favorite is the Trek Women's Cruiser Classic with a white-and-soft-yellow aluminum frame, saddle-colored seat, and a turquoise-banded tire.

*Splurgeworthy*

### it's a girl thing

WE LOVE Terry bicycles, made by a woman for women, which means designed for wider hips (like we need to remind you), shorter arms and torsos, and a different center of gravity from most men. Check out www.terrybicycles.com and watch the YouTube video series about how to design and build a bicycle.

195

## SECONDHAND SPINS

Shiny new bicycles depreciate (just like cars) the minute they roll out of the bike store. The used-bike market is another good way to find a killer deal, but when you test-ride a new set of wheels (and you wouldn't buy a bike you didn't test-ride first, right?), bring along a biker friend who knows about them. One note of caution: The biggest rage among hipsters is fixed-gear bikes without brakes; stopping and starting requires a skidding-and-reverse-pedal technique suited to eighteen-year-old boys (the ones listening to indie music). Do not delude yourself into thinking you are such a cool bitch that of course you'll be able to get the hang of them. They are up for sale for a reason. Buy a bike with brakes. Being able to stop is a good thing.

## ONLY THE NECESSARY ACCESSORIES

Your top accessory is a bike helmet. No, you don't get to feel the wind blowing through your hair as you pedal alongside traffic, but you do get to strut into the bike shop and say to the hot, cycle-obsessed guy behind the counter, "Show me the best helmet you've got!" This is one place to treat yourself, no shortcuts allowed.

And just because you've been feeling accessory-deprived lately doesn't mean you should make up for it by dropping hard-earned cash on every gleaming accoutrement on the display rack. Buy only bike accessories that make your riding safer and easier: gloves, a rearview mirror, a bell, a great lock, and a kickstand and saddlebags if you'll be cruising around town running errands.

**pave the way**

*So* YOU'RE going to live better, spend less, and be good to Mother Earth by rolling on two wheels, but, darling . . . where does all that rolling actually happen? Lobby your local pols for dedicated nonautomobile travel lanes suitable for bicycles, Segways, Rollerblades and Razor scooters!

## THE SEGWAY COMMUTER:
### Be Jane Jetson

**YOU MAY NOT** think of yourself as the sci-fi, futuristic type, but keep an open mind and scope out this unconventional, totally juiced two-wheeler that's sped onto the scene. It's innovative, hip, green, and, if you travel only short distances, could be a cool alternative to the more classic two-wheelers. In terms of price . . . we'll help you rationalize the cost.

### GEEK CHIC

Think of a two-wheeled electric "people mover" that looks a little like a dolly . . . except it isn't. You ride it by stepping aboard, standing straight up, placing your hands on a crossbar, leaning forward to go, go, go, and leaning back to stop. Meet the Segway, the coolest, most intuitive two-wheeled machine on the market. The downsides? It can go only twelve and a half miles an hour, needs a charge after twenty-five miles, can't accommodate much cargo, and oh, yeah . . . retails for $5,000 new, $2,500 to $3,500 used.

197

If a Segway will actually replace your car for work and light travel, then it should pay for itself after three years in what you'll save in gas costs . . . in which case, check out your local bylaws to find out if it's permitted on a sidewalk near you!

O⸺ *Green Style*

### chic schlepping

OF COURSE you would walk to the market, but how do you get your environmentally correct recycled bags full of groceries back home? In your incredibly handy, incredibly hip shopping cart trolley. These rolling carts, once restricted to granny types, are shopping companion and fashion item rolled into one, and used all over the world on market days. Basic metal grid types are available at every corner hardware store, but we're in love with the cart made by Rolser with the Marilyn Monroe graphics. If you're lucky enough to find one, snap it up.

## A BITCH ON BORROWED WHEELS

C'MON, LADIES. IT'S high time to reach out to all those community transit programs you've dissed and dismissed for years. Stop complaining about the forced intimacy, the lack of control, or the occasional inconvenience. Unless you want to be broke and outdated, extend your wheels beyond the glorified bauble parked in your driveway. Shift gears and bring some hot borrowed wheels into your life. Not only will they get the job done; they'll leave you blessedly free of endless demands for attention.

That's right, baby. Car sharing, carpooling, and public transportation. These options have a hip, new cachet. The benefits? More cash to play with, status for being the most forward-thinking bitch in town, and the joy of getting to lay a guilt trip on your auto-owning friends for being so much less environmentally conscious than you!

## CAR SHARING:
### Free at Last, Free at Last!
......................

CAR SHARING IS like dating a hot guy who wines and dines you, is great in bed, but leaves before you have to share the bathroom in the morning. With car sharing, you get all the benefits: an ultrachic car, a full tank of gas, reserved parking. And none of the aggravation. Forget about overnight parking fees, expensive auto insurance, rising gas prices, oil changes, washing the MF, messy contracts, and the occasional, "Oh, my God, do you hear that rattle?"

This is your gigolo, baby. Rent him by the hour.

### How It Works

- Reserve a chic and sporty car that lives nearby (will you be Audrey Hepburn in *Two for the Road* or Charlize Theron in *The Italian Job*?).
- Go get your car (hopefully it's just a walk down the block, but depending on your circumstances you may have to hop on the bus or subway, or suck up to someone for a ride).
- Unlock the car. This is done by waving the proximity card you've just downloaded across the windshield (feel that minirush as the car unlocks).

*199*

- Check above the visor for the gas card you use for fueling up, *on them*! This is the closest you may ever come to having a real sugar daddy!
- Drive away in a snazzy little MINI or Prius, Jetta, or BMW 3 for as low as $6 per hour or $55 to $62 for the day.

○━━ *Thriftiest Bitch*

## horning in on the market

ZIPCAR MAY be the biggest and most well-known option, but it's not alone. You'll find City CarShare in the Bay Area, HOURCAR in Minneapolis/St. Paul, iGo in Chicago. Even rental companies like Hertz and Enterprise plan to make moves into this market. More competition means lower rates. As always, ask for special introductory pricing.

**HOW IT PAYS: Comparing Car Sharing to Car Ownership**

Should you take the plunge? If you live in a city and drive less than sixty hours a month, take a long, hard look at car sharing as the best way to save some big bucks, not to mention rattle-and-roll headaches.

Do the math. No complaints. You have time on your hands. Go to AAA (www.aaanewsroom.net/Assets/Files/200844921220.DrivingCosts2008.pdf) to figure out how much it's costing you to own and run your automobile. You may find that it pays to think about dumping that high-maintenance car and hopping into a peppy little for-hire Mustang. Then motor that lean, mean, *borrowed* machine right over to the savings bank.

200

**the downshift**

*M*ANY CAR-SHARE vehicles could often benefit from a day at the spa. Before you get too comfortable in that borrowed baby, check the seats for dog hair and other disturbing, sticky substances, or all your savings will be sucked up at the dry cleaner.

## CARPOOLING:
## Avoiding the Creep Factor

**IF YOUR PROFESSIONAL** image isn't exactly folding yourself origami style into the backseat of a two-door 1997 Toyota Corolla, then think again. Carpooling is one of the most efficient forms of motorized transportation. Not only does it make you feel like a good green queen, but joining another person in their car cuts your commuting costs. Oh, we can already hear you whining: "You expect me to ride to work pressed between two sweaty, sleazy strangers?" Absolutely not! We'll show you how most cost-saving, online-carpooling communities work, and why a high-maintenance, discerning bitch who's entitled to a carpool that's safe . . . should be creating her own!

**the bff carpool**

*C*OORDINATE DULL errands with friends. Turn the trip to Costco into a social event. Bitch about work, brag about kids, fill your larder (keep each other on budget), save on gas, and conclude with a latte or glass of pinot. Find fun in the simple stuff—life is sweeter (and cheaper) this way.

## THE ADVENT OF THE ONLINE CARPOOL

Joining an online carpool can be sketchy, sort of similar to online dating: without the photo, the video, the profile, the coffee, lunch, or requisite glass of wine. You log on to one of the several national online programs and voila! *40-ish SWM with Ford Escape* is matched with *30-something Professional Woman Seeking Ride to City Three Mornings per Week.* There's no paperwork, no paper calendars, no messy ride-share boards, just an e-mail exchange between driver and passenger regarding where, when, and how much.

But then what? Do you blithely hop into the car of Big Jimbo with the visible ass crack and pay him $3.50 for your forty-minute commute? Uh, we don't think so. Without a reference check from a third party, never put your pretty ass in a car with a stranger. You may have become a community player extraordinaire and the savings may sound yummy, but, baby, you still have your standards.

## CONTROL THE ELEMENTS: Create Your Own Carpool

The Web is great at matching strangers, but to find potential carpoolers you either know or almost know is a very old-fashioned process. Start by checking in with the administrator at your kids' school or camp, your workplace, or any other institution you're commuting to. Chances are there's already a list of people in your area looking to carpool. Ask the administrator or anyone in your network of friends and acquaintances if they can vouch for any of the people on the list, then follow up with a face-to-face. Without a third-party endorsement you might as well stand at the edge of the highway, hike up your skirt, and stick out your thumb.

Once you've arranged your group, set the carpool rules. *Your* rules; no consensus, no democracy. If you don't want to listen to *Cats* at eight a.m. on your way to a board meeting, then shove Andrew Lloyd Webber out the door. If the sound of a dewy young thing cooing to her boyfriend on her cell phone makes you want to vomit, then lay down the law. If your blood pressure rises while you're waiting five minutes for a passenger to breeze out the door after you've rushed your guts out, then hand them their walking papers. Everyone may be saving money by sharing the HOV lane, but, baby, it's your show.

## PUBLIC TRANSPORTATION:
### The Cheapest Way to Go

YOU CITY FOLK who take the subway, T, el, metro, or underground: Pat yourself on the back—this section's not for you. You already know that you can get from work to the therapist and back again without enduring hair-ripping traffic and exorbitant parking fees. Nor are we talking to those country mice living in towns so small public transportation doesn't exist.

This is a message to public-transportation cowards. Those of you who're scared of the big, bad bus. Who complain that hopping the light rail is inconvenient, since it takes a little longer to get to your destination. Who can't be bothered to read a schedule, or to walk a few extra blocks. If you live with a decent (even a semidecent) system at your disposal and choose not to use it, the joke's on you.

## SAVE, SAVE, SAVE!

Public transit for the daily commute is the cheapest way to go! A monthly transit pass costs anywhere between $50 and $90. Remember you are a math genius now, and the cost per mile to get to work by yourself in your greedy little car is on average $.54 (assuming you drive fifteen thousand miles per year). So if you commute twenty miles round-trip, you'll save between $130 and $150 a month by using public transportation! Plus, there's nothing like public transit to make you wave the green flag in the faces of all those bitches so much less hip than you.

## GET EVERYTHING—OR NOTHING—DONE

You may be paying your public transit system for a ride, but what many stressed-out, anxiety-ridden women don't realize is that public transportation pays something precious and meaningful back in return: time. Sitting on the train or the bus gives you a chance to read that novel you've been dying to get your hands on, write in your journal about your "so-called life," listen to your iPod, return calls to bill collectors, or take a mini snooze. If it's standing room only, you can give your mind a little vacay and zone out entirely. The beauty of the bus is that you don't have to stay alert and you don't have to make inane small talk with strangers the way you would in a carpool. Although you may be sharing your ride with the masses, public transit allows you to remain gloriously anonymous.

## learn the line

*So*, IT'S just all too confusing. You would *love* to take the bus or subway but have no idea how to navigate through the public transportation maze. Well, that's one hell of a lame excuse! Go to publictransportation.org and get up to date on all public-transit options in your very own hometown.

...................

# Chapter 7

# Get Out, Get Entertained

## WELCOME TO THE *NEW* GOOD TIMES

INNER AT ONE uptight fancy restaurant after another—nauseating. Symphony tickets every Friday night—soporific. Rock concerts every weekend—deafening. Season tickets to all eighty-one baseball games—boring. Sitting on the couch watching television night after night—mind-numbing.

Over-the-top, unvaried, not stimulating entertainment is deadly. Whether you're paying big bucks going out or just the cable bill staying in, now is the time for a bitch to reevaluate how she gets her pleasure.

First, separate the things that give you comfort from the things that give you pleasure. Haven't thought about this before, have you? Mac and cheese, TV, soft fleece. A clean apartment, room-darkening shades, Valium. Yes, comfort is found in the predictable, the time-saving, the stuff that helps us avoid distress. Bitch, you can buy comfort (who wouldn't want someone else changing her sheets?). But pleasure, ah, that's another story.

Pleasure is silky, rich, simple, delicious, thrilling, joyous. No bank account, stock certificate, high-value real estate assets needed to get (or give) pleasure.

Lose yourself in the library reading *The Sound and the Fury* or *Pride and Prejudice*. Slide your hands up and down a cool, smooth marble obelisk in a sculpture garden. Learn a thing or two at the Museum of Sex. Get excited listening to the next Leontyne Price at the conservatory near you. March to the music under hot blue skies at a summer band concert. Find fabulous, affordable restaurants. Feast for less at the old shrines.

Despite common wisdom, spending money doesn't bring true, long-lasting pleasure. Yes, we know the rush when you snag a table at that hot new restaurant or score tickets to a sold-out concert. But how long does that feeling last? Is the experience itself truly satisfying? Did you really *love* the deconstructed, reconstructed, molecularly reengineered food? Did you truly *adore* the narcissistic spectacle—gyrating hips, fireworks, overpriced tee-shirts—of that stadium concert? (Oops! Did you do it again?) Unless you're a true foodie or raving Britney fan (that's okay—just keep it to yourself), wasn't it really the thrill of that hard-to-get catch you reveled in? Be honest: You were stuck in that old paradigm of more is more, the empty excess of the go-go days.

This is your opportunity to stand up and rethink the activities that you've been spending your time on. Money and things can be re-earned and remade, but time is a nonrenewable resource, and only you have control over how you spend yours. So get back in touch with what you love—break the "more is more" cycle.

Bitch, welcome to the new good times.

207

**WHICH BEST DESCRIBES YOU?**

- **You do an activity because you love it.** You forget everything else around you, time passes, worry dissolves, you feel enriched, energized, engorged. Even though you haven't run a 5K, you have that endorphin high (not that we'd know what that feels like). The perfect, pleasure-principled bitch. **You get a gold star.**

- **You do an activity because it seems like a great thing to do.** The ballet subscription, the share in the pro-basketball seats, the outdoor Pops series. Unfortunately, while you appreciate dance, Wednesday night after a long day of work you fall asleep to Tchaikovsky. Basketball? You like the game but you don't drink beer and are surrounded by middle-aged married men with bad hair and big paunches. And sitting on folding chairs in the grass being eaten by mosquitoes is not your idea of a good time. No, this is not giving you pleasure. Kudos for trying. Start organizing activities you actually *like*. **You get a silver star.**

- **Your "friends" love to eat out.** Every night. Big, bad, uninteresting three-course meals. Whenever you're together you supportively listen to Marley's nanny troubles (even though she's an at-home mom with one eight-year-old), Annie's nightmares with her decorator (whom she refuses to fire even though she hates him—haven't you wondered how it is she is the only person left in America spending big bucks on new furniture?), and the trials of Cherisse's meddling in-laws (their crime is wanting to gift Cherisse and her husband with a summer beach house). It's killing your waistline and your budget. You're a kindhearted bitch, but you need new friends with less money and better taste. **You get a bronze star.**

■ **Weekends are spent with dull Tammy and Sue scouring outlet malls for bargains.** Mostly you're trying to keep up with the other bitches in your neighborhood by hunting for a David Yurman ring or Escada jacket at a deep discount. Your trips are getting farther and farther afield, since you've already raked through the local centers. While you're seeing some of America's finest superhighways (and getting a firsthand glimpse at your stimulus dollars at work repairing America's aging infrastructure), you're just burning two precious, nonrenewable resources: time and fuel. Oh, honey, you can do better than this! **No stars for you.**

Listen, here's what you may have forgotten: *You deserve that gold star. You're worth it.* Life is short—why settle for less? And, contrary to popular opinion, it doesn't cost a lot to ace your grades. We're going to show you how to get high marks in high culture.

## BIG STACKS

**WHENEVER WE WALK** into a library, a sudden surge of excitement followed by an ethereal, soft, warm feeling washes through us, leaving us with a transcendent calm and effervescent glow. (No, bitch, we did not lose our virginity in the stacks.) There's just something about the air, the hush, the warm dust dancing in shafts of light that makes us want to drop to our knees. Reverence and awe sweep through us as we consider the contents.

For us, libraries are the holy of holies, although there's something about people who choose to master the Dewey decimal system we've yet to figure out. Perhaps it's the inscrutability of personalities at the other end of the spectrum on the Myers-Briggs chart . . . or overdue-book-induced trauma—we just don't know.

If you haven't hung around your local public library lately, then join everyone else in America who's suddenly figured out what an amazing resource it is. Besides, you should be getting your money's worth—whether you like it or not, you're supporting it through your tax dollars.

Besides letting you borrow books for free (duh), libraries lend movies, music, even art. When you're bored and broke, you can always get out of the house and sit in a cushy leather club chair in the reading room, thumbing through the latest issues of *Us, People,* and *Entertainment Weekly.*

Oftentimes, the main branch of your city library will have carefully curated art exhibits—sometimes slightly offbeat and interesting—subjects that you might have never considered before, like the Dallas Public Library's exhibit of hobo signs (how timely), or the Cleveland Public Library's celebration of FitzGerald's "Rubaiyat of Omar Khayyam" (such gorgeous illuminated books).

Great lectures on totally random subjects—divine for clever dinner-party conversation—can be heard for free just by showing up and sitting in an uncomfortable folding chair for an hour.

Recently we were in Boston and went to hear Stephen Puleo, author of *Dark Tide,* talk about the great molasses flood in Boston's North End in 1919. Did you know that molasses was used in the manufacture of TNT? We didn't. We'd heard about the flood, knew about the casualties, seen images of horses stuck in the gunk—but we always thought the city just had a really big sweet tooth. In fact, the molasses was stored in a huge container on the waterfront, and the catastrophic events that surrounded the collapse of the tank involved the war, anarchists, bad design, and company mismanagement (sound familiar?). The flood was a catalyst for the strict building codes that exist today. Such drama, such interesting free stuff!

Beyond lending, lectures, book readings, films, and interesting exhibits, libraries are branching into classes, like yoga, digital photography, and Web design. Some offer writers' groups and art classes. Sadly, though, as municipal budgets are being cut, some of these programs are too. Take advantage where you can.

## BOOKS?

If you're like us, you may be gun-shy. You know, you had that huge wave of enthusiasm the last time you borrowed those novels. All the books you got to check out, slip in your bag, and take home—a bitch's shopping rush—didn't cost you a penny. You read one or two and then they were due. And then they were overdue. So overdue you felt shame.

When the notice came that you were going to be arrested for a felony—who knew keeping overdue library books could get you jailed?—you finally took them back. You walked into the big hushed hall, got to the circulation desk, and suddenly felt the need to explain yourself. You offered a phony excuse (the slow, painful death of your nearest relative), but your soul twisted in agony. Had you just visited a death curse upon your relative? For months after you prayed that everyone in your extended family stay healthy.

211

Yes, it's been a long time since you took a book out of the library. Be brave. Go back and try again. You're older and wiser and poorer than before.

## At Your Fingertips

**no more overdue fines**

SIGN UP for e-mail reminders from www.libraryelf.com. These little bookish creatures—between baking cookies and cobbling Christmas gifts—manage to send you notices before your books are due. What multitaskers.

This time, try harnessing your compulsions in a healthy way: Be a binge reader. We're big mystery fans and love to take out a half dozen of one author's books at a time. Create your own P. D. James or Josephine Tey festival. Compare and contrast for style and character Robert Parker's *Spenser* series with the early works of John le Carré, featuring George Smiley. Or if you have time on your hands, lots of time, try Naguib Mahfouz's richly written and gorgeous Cairo Trilogy. Investigate new authors. No money need change hands, so take risks on books outside your comfort zone. Put your name on the waiting list for bestsellers. Those librarians are so, so organized they really will call or e-mail you when your turn comes around.

**in the know**

Updike's dead. Grisham's formulaic. Danielle Steele rots your teeth. If you want to knock the socks off your friends and your book club (see pages 249–250), check out these smart, up-and-coming writers: Sarah Shun-lien Bynum, Ron Currie Jr., Amity Gaige, Salvatore Scibona, Justin Tussing, Malena Watrous. Years from now they'll be the literary bigwigs—get in on the ground floor.

The best section in the library?

The children's reading room. Go for story hour. Borrow a kid if you don't have one, or just quietly slip into the back. Nothing beats the peaceful feeling that washes over you as you sit in the undersize chairs, or on the floor, listening to that nice librarian reading *Goodnight Moon*. Then go home for a nap.

## A IS FOR ART

**ADMIT IT.**

You mean to go to the museum. You read about the block-buster Tintoretto or Chuck Close show that's coming soon and make a mental note to get your ass over there. But what happens? It's raining and surely the museum will be crowded, it'll be hard to park, you don't want to get wet. Or it's gorgeous outside; why go to the museum when you can ride your bike or play Frisbee? But then the day slides by with no Frisbee, and you become increasingly bored and desperate. You end up arranging to meet a friend for lunch and a quick shop.

*213*

But the restaurant's crowded and mediocre. You spend good money for that extra pound you didn't need and see-through blouse you really didn't like. Your "friend" fills you in on your ex-boyfriend, how he's found eternal happiness in the arms of some bimbo. You feel overweight, broke, rejected. And you could have gone to the museum. What were you thinking, bitch?

We love museums for almost everything. While they don't have that moldy, musty, papery smell, there's a crisp, aristocratic quality to that curated air. Like libraries, they're not just for looking anymore. Films, lectures, gallery talks, poetry readings, visiting artists, and art classes all flourish under one roof.

Step up to the ticket window to a Zen-like calm. Hear chamber music playing, reverent whispers echoing. A pulse of happiness surges through you as you promise yourself (just like the last time you came, a year or two ago) that from now on this will be your Saturday destination. Feel a rush of glee when they give you that little pin in exchange for your admission fee. (It's so chic to be seen in public later with a museum lapel tag . . . much better than that tiny cheesy horse.)

Be a sophisticate as you join visitors from all over the world. They'll be quietly walking by in their sensible Mephistos—get a peek at upcoming world fashion trends, or play a game and see if you can guess where they're from by their attire.

Finally, let's be honest: Haven't you always harbored fantasies of a museum fling? You know, running into that sensitive guy somewhere between the Etruscan and early modern galleries. He'll be staring intently at an ancient bronze horse; you'll walk between him and the display case, suddenly stop, turn, say, "I love this period . . . my favorite example is at the Florence Archaeological Museum." (You're allowed to be a pretentious flirt in the halls of a museum.) He'll be wearing perfectly worn-in blue jeans, an open-collared shirt, maybe a blue blazer or

214

simple crewneck sweater. His hair will be slightly longish. He'll have a day's growth of beard. . . .

So what if financial Armageddon has arrived? Is that any reason to give up on your fantasies?

## *Bitchin' Tip*

### shut up and listen

*A*TTEND LECTURES and programming at the cultural institutions in your neck of the woods. Recently the Art Institute in Chicago offered a free lecture titled "Bauhaus to Green Haus," about the Bauhaus movement and its applicability to sustainable architecture and design in today's urban areas. Learn how the past colors the present.

## *Thrifty Bitch*

### culture on the cheap

*M*OST MUSEUMS have a day or night of the week when admission fees are waived. Students and senior citizens often get a free pass or discounted rate, so bring your ID cards. Read the sign: Some museums' admission fees are actually a "suggested donation"—you can pay whatever you want! Also, if you're a member of a different museum or institution, you may qualify for free entry; and oftentimes your local library (the library is the best!) will have passes you can borrow. If you fall in love (we mean with the museum—not the dude you just met), consider a membership; it'll be much cheaper than paying each time you go.

215

## MONA LISA SMILES

Here's a novel idea: How about really looking at the art? No, not just walking through and admiring the pretty colors. Train your eye to really *see* painting and sculpture. Learn about the periods, the techniques, the evolution of styles. Why is it that for centuries all that luminescent artistic talent was so obsessed with the Virgin Mary? Those scrolls from Asia, why do they all seem to look the same? A black line across a white canvas sold for millions—are they kidding? Start by renting a guided headphone set, sign up for gallery tours, progress to attending lectures and taking classes. This is the rich stuff.

Or head into the portrait gallery with just one question in mind: Did the artist like his subject? Or find the landscapes and think about where the sun was in relation to the painter . . . can you find the light? Or find the Picassos and see if you can reconstruct the figures—can you spot the nose, the eye, the breast in a cubist piece?

## THINK OUTSIDE THE BOX—UNLESS "THE BOX" IS ON EXHIBIT

"Oh," you say, "I just went to the Art Institute in Chicago a few months ago," or, "I went to the Philadelphia Museum of Art the last time I visited Aunt Emma." Well, bitch, museums come in all shapes and sizes. Expand your horizons. Don't forget science museums, children's museums, natural history museums. Outdoor sculpture. Modern art; folk art; textiles. There are museums devoted to nineteenth-century mill girls, chocolate, dolls.

It goes without saying, but our all-time fave is in New York City—the Museum of Sex. Next time you're in town (wear your Worth hat with the big, big brim if you're a shy girl) head down

216

to 233 Fifth Avenue and take a gander. Recent exhibits include "The Sex Lives of Animals" (haven't thought much about that since you had little Maxie fixed), "Vamps and Virgins: The Evolution of American Pinup Art 1860–1960" and "Get Off: Exploring the Pleasure Principle." The sex machines in their permanent collection are a *must-do*.

○━━ *Bitchin' Tip*

**a reminder**

LET'S COUNT some of the other things you haven't done since you were a kid.

- The zoo
- A botanical garden/arboretum
- The aquarium
- A famous local author, president, Civil War hero, Underground Railroad homesite
- An amusement park

## BE A MOOCH

Since you're now so arty, cultured, and sophisticated, it's time to visit the galleries. No, you're not buying, unless of course it's your neighborhood artists' association (see page 124). One night a month most cities' art galleries have openings—usually from five to eight p.m.—where they show fresh exhibits of the artists they represent. To lure you in they offer free wine and cheese. Most of the time the artist will be there to meet and greet their public. Sometimes, usually on a different night, the artist will give a lecture and open the floor to questions. If you see something you like, ask if there's an upcoming talk; then go back to learn more.

Don't feel bad about gobbling their cheese and chugging their jug wine. Galleries compute your consumption into the cost of doing business. (Besides, these guys are pimps, raking in 50 percent commission on each work they sell.) They like the buzz of big crowds, which creates energy and convinces insecure buyers with money that the artist is really popular, thus boosting sales. So do your part for art—drink up, sister.

Visiting galleries is an excellent way to train your eye and educate your palette—uh, palate. Who knows, one day you may even be able to afford to buy pricey art again—when you do, you'll have taught yourself about the market, watched what sells and what doesn't, and developed a sophisticated eye.

If you find that looking at art gets you excited, spread your net wider. You may have to work harder to locate them, and travel farther afield, but find young artists in cheap gallery spaces, or haunt art-school shows and watch talent emerge.

*Thrifty (Do-gooder) Bitch*

### auction a day

*B*IDDINGFORGOOD, AN online ticket-auction company, supports charities and nonprofits all over the country. Seeking a good deal on splurgeworthy events? Trying to maintain (or develop) a social conscience? Bid on tickets (as well as other products and services) for events all over the place.

## ENTERTAIN ME!

YOU'RE ON YOUR way to the pinnacle of pleasure. You've already hit the gallery scene; you've scoured the local museum Web sites for free evenings; you've searched the library stacks and come home with awesome new music and that book about the molasses flood. Feeling smarter?

Great.

But what about when you want to be entertained? When you want to sit back and watch?

Just like you're no longer lusting for the Hermès bag, the grandiose vacations, the La Cornue range, it's time to break the bigger-is-better entertainment cycle. Biggest is not always best. *We're* saying that? We are. Believe it.

It's time to consider a separation from the jaded majors in favor of playing the field with the sweet farm teams. After all, why would you want Alex Rodriguez when you can have a fresh, waiting-to-be-broken-in, pliable, up-and-coming prospect? (Yep, that's how we like them: up-and-coming.)

Are you so sophisticated that you notice a qualitative difference between the professionals in the symphony and the students in the conservatory orchestra? Besides the obvious price savings, there's so much pleasure to be derived from witnessing new talent pursuing their passions. Experience the drama as you sit nervously on the edge of your seat, hoping the young opera singer successfully hits that high note, as you watch the emerging basketball prospect dunking on the breakaway, or the regional theater actor sweating through Hamlet's soliloquy. You can even be one of those bitches who says, "I saw her the first time she performed that piece, when she was still just a student, and I just knew how *fabulous* her career was going to be."

This intimacy with the performance—this exposure to fresh, raw talent—is nearly impossible to find in a professional arena. Educate your ear, train your eye, learn the rules. And on the rare occasions when you *do* attend a Lakers game or the American Ballet Theatre, you'll have a new appreciation for the rigors of the sport, the challenge of the art, and what it truly means to have the privilege of witnessing those who are at the peak of their professions.

## SPORTS STORIES

Rooting for a sports team can be as exciting as playing yourself. Rooting for a sports team can be a very cheap form of therapy. Rooting for a sports team is just plain fun.

It's thrilling to see a soaring walk-off homer in the ninth or a goal in sudden death. Nothing's better than cheering on the underdog, watching them win, hugging perfectly cute strangers in the stands. Ah, if only your life could work out with the same fairy-tale win in the end.

Think of the psychological opportunities sports fandom presents: Work out your aggressions screaming obscenities at the television set. Indulge your secret libidinal desires by longing publicly for the hot rookie—it's allowed. Affiliate with others—we mean besides your cat. Be part of something bigger than you are—desperately important in this downsized age. Learn to deal with failure the best way possible: by blaming others—the ref's bad call, frigid weather, bum players. In the end, being a sports fanatic is a cost-cutting measure: It eliminates the need for your therapist. We can think of no more effective vehicle for all your transference needs.

Sure, it's better for your heart (and butt) to get out there and run the bases, swing the racket, cycle the hills. But sometimes a bitch just needs to kick back, pop a beer, and ogle those gorgeous muscled men.

## BIG LEAGUE 0, MINOR LEAGUE 10

Major-league professional sports teams and athletes are big money and marketing machines. These guys seem to be all gooey and community-minded—you know, sponsoring charity bowling, golf, and poker tournaments. (Like you can relate, right?) They talk about how *deeply honored* they are to be playing in your town, the greatest city on earth—and when they get traded, say the same thing in the next locale. You've seen the pictures of them showing up at schools and homeless shelters, smiling broadly into the camera as they dish mashed potatoes or sit with a kid in their lap reading *picture* books. Then next week you see them on the front page of the *Post*, arrested with a gun at a club, slipping into a motel room with a woman who's not their wife, or confessing to Congress about their steroid use.

Good for them.

Do you really want to be giving those club owners and overpaid celebrity athletes your dwindling dollars? Think about the obscenely huge amount of money they're making! Should you be going to the ballpark to watch the grounds crew come and remove—yes, *remove*—the bases after the second inning so they can end up as sports memorabilia? C'mon, bitch, there are lots of better ways to find third—and they're free.

On average, a game at a major-league ballpark will run a typical American family slightly over two hundred bucks (parking, food, souvenirs, tickets).

Wise up.

When the New York Yankees opened their brand-new park, they charged $2,500 *per ticket* in the premium section. A case of bad market timing and remarkably excessive greed—and what happened? The seats went empty.

Smart fans were hopping the ferry to Staten Island to watch the SI Yankees at less than ten bucks a pop.

Bitch, if you get all hot watching the big boys play, then look for the minor version of the major team. Get up close and personal as you watch players on the way up, players on the way down, famous players on rehab assignment, and guys just playing for the love of the game (or guys who have no other marketable skills).

221

Pick your sport and use the Web to find its minor-league cousin. Unless a major celeb is on rehab assignment, most of the time you can just walk on over, buy tickets at the gate, and cruise in. Some parks sell refreshments; other let you bring picnics. Just check before you head out the door, because some parks are BYOLC (lawn chairs).

## Thrifty Bitch

### major withdrawal

IN CASE you couldn't tell, we're baseball addicts. Can't help ourselves. While we used to sit in the bleachers for five bucks, those days (even if we could score tix) are long gone. A smart bitch never gives up. Now, when we're jonesing for the home team, we have two strategies: friends and the clicker. Yup. We still have friends with dough and seats, so we promise good things in exchange for an invite (don't get all dirty; we're fabulous cooks). But since we are such devotees, we actually prefer watching the game on TV—it's way less distracting and you can actually see what's happening. Besides, we get to drink our own beer (microbrewed, of course). Oh, and don't dismiss the radio. There's something awesomely old-school about sunbathing in the backyard, tall glass of lemonade by our side, listening to a Sunday-afternoon game on the radio.

## THE UNUSUAL SUSPECTS

There are a hell of a lot more sports to get excited about than just the usuals.

Start going to reasonably priced, under-the-radar sports like lacrosse and wrestling (think of the moves you can learn). Soccer, the most popular sport in the world, is still like an orphan in this country. Come on, bitch, you already know the rules (remember getting your shins slashed in school?). You know what grace and athletic prowess is required to play at the pro level. While we're big women's soccer fans, we must admit those guys are hot and, unlike football and hockey, you can actually appreciate what they look like.

Think about becoming a college sports booster. If you're a serious football, basketball, or baseball nut and live near one of the powerhouse schools (like Ohio State, UConn, or Arizona), then you're already onto the pleasure of rooting for a college team that's nearly professional.

## LADIES BEAR WATCHING

Get out there and support the professional women's teams. WNBA, WPS, LPGA, to name a few. Check out amateur leagues like roller derby—so athletic, so camp, so much fun! Or go online to the college or university near you to find their athletic schedules. Fall, winter, and spring stay busy with a full lineup of sports. Everything from the prosaic to the unusual and, best of all, thanks to Title IX, equal.

*Bitchin' Rant*

### women deserve equally egregious salaries

*S*UPPORT WOMEN'S teams.

We bitches need to stick together, and there's no better way to show support than by cheering on women athletes.

*(continued)*

223

Corral your daughters, your nieces, your goddaughters to watch other women play at a high level. Team sports can teach a bitch lessons beyond hard work, perseverance, and staying in shape. Finding your personal best while also learning to share and be a good winner, or good loser, are invaluable life lessons. No matter what the season, there's a free or near-free opportunity to become a follower.

Or think Olympic events. Instead of just watching a sport every four years on television, go to where the serious women athletes train. Since you fell over the hurdle in high school gym class and broke your wrist, how close have you been to a track-and-field event? Check out pole vaulting, discus throwing, sprints. Synchronized swimming? Sort of strange, but kind of cool. Ice dancing. Speed skating. Drag out the old houndstooth jacket and hunt down equestrian events.

$0\!\!\!\!\!-\!\!\!=\!\!\!\!\!$ *Bitchin' Tip*

### local little leagues and school teams

WHILE THEY'RE free, these games can't meet your entertainment needs. You may not release pent-up rage on these innocents. Yes, you should go as a positive and supportive parent. Yell encouragement, clap with enthusiastic support

*(continued)*

224

for all the players. But it's ugly and unacceptable to be an uninhibited, nasty, and rabid fan when your kids or your neighbor's kids are involved. If you find yourself screaming with disappointment at children as they *play*, race yourself to the nearest community mental health center.

## FOR A SONG

Just like the majors in sports, you'll find "majors" in dance, music, and theater. The Chicago Symphony, Metropolitan Opera, San Francisco Ballet, the Guthrie: Most are struggling to make ends meet. It's hugely costly to pay companies of gifted performers, to build and maintain sets, to upkeep venues. Unlike the pro sports, the concert halls are not ringed with Gatorade, Budweiser and Gillette advertisements and there are no big television deals. And with charitable and foundation funding down, these companies are often in the red. Under normal circumstances they'd fall within our splurgeworthy category—but, bitch, we share your pocketbook pain, and these tix are way expensive.

Stay loose, be flexible, and you can still go out to listen to great music or watch wonderful dance and theater performances for a song.

Unless there's a hugely famous headliner or a totally overhyped pre-/post-Broadway run, you should be able to snag half-price tickets by going online, heading over to discounted ticket destinations, or swinging by the venue itself on the day of the performance. Check the Web sites of the major dance, symphony, and opera companies near you to see if they offer free or deeply discounted tickets to dress rehearsals. While afternoon performances may not be perfectly convenient or the maestro may interrupt Bartók's Violin Concerto No. 2 to scold the second violinist, a flexible bitch makes out. Or she finds something else to do.

225

**think local**

$\mathcal{G}$ET ACQUAINTED with your local arts section of the newspaper (if it's still printing) or check out its online listings.
You'll be amazed (and embarrassed it's taken you this long
to look) at how many art, music, theater, and dance performances are available for free—or very nominal amounts—
right in your backyard.

## SMALL BALL

Local community arts companies abound.

What do you think happened to all those geeky kids carry-
ing violins and cellos to elementary school? The stars of high
school musicals? College dance majors? Hello! They're your
neighbors! They're still singing opera. They're still acting, ballroom dancing, doing ballet. They're still playing in neighborhood symphonies, chamber groups, bluegrass, and rock bands.
Yep, they're filling their passions and getting their pleasure,
right around the corner.

## TO BELIEVE OR NOT TO BELIEVE

**EVERY COMMUNITY HAS** a local theater, often filled with very
talented thespians. Wander in on a Saturday night. Ticket prices
will be so cheap you'll feel guilty. The fun part of staying local is
that you're bound to know people in the cast.

Look, there's Jill, the teller at the bank—my, does she resemble

226

Natalie Wood; no wonder they cast her as Maria! George, the guy who cuts your hair—who knew he could sing and dance? He's a little short and stout for Tony, although his hair does look damn good. Wait a minute, is that your dentist as Krupke? Sit back, relax, see if you can forget you know them by the end of the performance. Tomorrow they'll be themselves again. You'll see Jill counting out your withdrawal . . . George cutting bangs too short . . . and that dentist—well, he'll never touch your teeth again!

Or head back to that college campus and watch their student dance company or their symphony perform. If you live near a conservatory, it's a no-brainer: Start supporting their orchestras, theater, and dance groups. The caliber of performances will rock your world. Check out the college or conservatory calendar of events for other performances. Often high-profile talent will come into a university town and the tickets will be cheap, cheap, cheap.

While we know you don't believe in much anymore, see if your local church offers free jazz and chamber music concerts. For years we traveled through Europe and would go to free early evening performances in stunning cathedrals and churches (see page 162). It took a long time for us to figure out you can do this in our country, too. Head over after work, listen to the music, stop at your favorite bar for a glass of wine, head home saved and sated. How civilized.

What could be lovelier than going to the nearest town center on a warm summer evening, unpacking a picnic, and sitting on the grass as a local community band plays? Watch all the little kids march around clapping to "Seventy-six Trombones" and "Stars and Stripes Forever." Hell, don't be such an uptight little bitch. Feel that patriotic little tickle surging right below your belly button. Get up and join the kids.

## CLUBBING

Not that kind of clubbing. No $300 bottles of vodka, loud, bad deejayed music, long lines of ho-ish women trying to get it. We're talking about local clubs and bars that book acts. The kinds of places performers go on their way up—or down. The kinds of places with cheap covers, where you drink warmish beer and eat bad burgers with soggy fries. The kinds of places that get crowded on the weekend, where you jam six to a table for two after struggling to find enough chairs. The performers are so close they spit on you as they sing, or the clarinet deafens your right ear as you try to hear the vocalist. Yes, these are the places where you should be doing your clubbing.

Head over on a Wednesday. They're never too crowded. Parking is easy. Mix up your genres. Where do you think Joan Baez, Bob Dylan, John Mayer started out? Country, rock, jazz—you can hear it all better and for less. We love the comedy places; even when they're really bad you end up laughing.

## DINING OUT: Small Bites Are Better than Big Ones

For most of us, eating out has become the number one dollar suck in our entertainment budget. Does this mean you need to give up on dining out? Heaven forbid. Absolutely not. Never.

Bitch, do not let this little economic adjustment drive you further into the depressing paradox of modernity: loneliness and alienation in an ever-connected but isolated world. If there's ever a time to get in touch with the old-fashioned virtues of family and friends gathered around the table, this is it. So get your hands off the keyboard, stop the Facebook stalking, quit that annoying promotional tweeting—no more socializing with giga- and megabytes. This is the time to get out and eat *real* bites—with real peeps.

Sharing *great* food with friends is number two on our list of life's pleasures. We're girls, we're yakkers, we're social, and food is theater, is play, is connection, and, most of all—is so damn delicious. Who doesn't want to get together and drink a glass of wine (or two), catch up on the latest neighborhood gossip, family dramas, love crises, work worries, kid problems, all while eating yummy food?

Do not give this up. Here's what you need to give up: The too big meals. The pretentious meals. The mediocre meals. The overhyped meals. Make changes to where you go, what you eat, and what time you eat it. Become like Marco Polo, an explorer in search of the new and the delicious. What you must sacrifice is frequency. You can't eat out every night, or even every weekend anymore. Sorry. Look, there are all kinds of things we wish we could do every day, but it's time to finally grow up. You just can't have everything you want.

## QUALITY OVER QUANTITY: The New Dining Equation

Yet again, less is more. It's better to have a single delicious course of food in a place you love than three mediocre courses in a marginal restaurant. You will no longer go for mediocre, unhealthy meals just because they're cheap. Red Lobster, Olive Garden, McDonald's—WTF are you thinking?

Or you love that cute neighborhood bistro. They give you the menu, spend ages explaining the appetizer and dinner specials, tell you they need your dessert order before you begin so they can handcraft and custom-bake it just for you. You can still go, but no more three-course meals. Period. If the waiter looks down his nose when you want only the slow-cooked octopus appetizer with the chorizo emulsion, or if you order just the carpaccio topped with parmesan shavings, arugula, and truffle oil—tough noogies.

Eat less. Consider sharing a main course with your partner and split a salad. Leave a big tip. In this economy, if they want to charge you for sharing—actually in *any* economy—walk.

---

## ⚷ Thrifty Bitch

### tank up before hitting the road

*H*AVE AN appetizer and a glass of wine before you head out. Meet up with your friends and take turns serving predinner cocktails and hors d'oeuvres at different houses. . . . You can share the expense and the cleanup. Then go to a restaurant (*designate a driver—a nonnegotiable rule*) and order minimally without fear of going hungry. Or consider going out for a light bite followed by dessert and coffee back at your place.

---

Once at the restaurant, order your libations carefully. Feel free to be festive and order a cocktail, but if you're a lush and want more than one martini you'd better be on a date—where he's paying. Four bucks for a soda? Just say no! Water is better for you and free (you aren't still drinking the stuff in the toxic plastic bottles, are you?). Wine with dinner is often the biggest expense on the bill. If there's a group it'll be cheaper to order a bottle than for everyone to order by the glass. Try not to order the second-cheapest wine on the list. A reliable wine distributor told us common wisdom says patrons won't want to seem like "cheapskates," and therefore won't order the least-expensive wine on the list—instead jumping up to the second-least expensive. Slam. Some restaurants will mark up that bottle to the nth degree and make a killing. Order the least expensive wine. Tough. Remember, it's now chic to be cheap. Bring home the wine that's not finished (yeah, right).

Look for restaurants that are BYOB. We've found that the expense or ability to get a liquor license leaves many new restaurants willing to let you bring in your own. They'll charge you a slight corkage fee (although this seems to be more negotiable than in the past). These owners tend to be true foodies, desperate to cook for the art, for the pleasure, for their passion. You can save huge dollars bringing your own wine and often end up eating wonderful food to boot.

## WHERE TO GO: Explore Yourself

The strategy:

Read everything you can about new restaurants in your town or the places you'll be visiting. (For good recs when you're away, swing by the best hotel in town, pretend you're a guest, and chat with the concierge—see chapter 5). Follow local newspapers' food columns, skim magazines (at the library), become a devotee of Chowhound. Check blogs like Serious Eats (and the links you find along the way) or your city's local blog establishment

231

(like 600 Block or Localist in Baltimore). Read Epicurious, Saveur, UrbanDaddy. (Skip Citysearch and Yelp—the reviews are often worthless.) Find your own local true foodie network.

Try new places. Mix it up. Cheap eats to white tablecloths. Find your favorites; chat 'em up—it's fun to have a place where "everybody knows your name." Go for just a single appetizer, sometimes two. The different taste explosions are better than a single main course. If you're really, really hungry, control yourself and order just a main course. Try to pass on dessert—if there's a crowd, order one dessert and six spoons. Or grab an ice-cream cone somewhere else. It'll be less pricey than coffee and dessert at the restaurant.

Cruise around town looking for new places. It's free. You're bored. You can just tell where the chef is loving what he or she does by peering at the menu and peeking inside. University neighborhoods are always filled with inexpensive, tasty, and fast options. Or head over to the parts of town still gentrifying, where space is cheap, interiors cool, and food often outstanding. (One of our faves is in a refurbished Burger King now serving the best grilled fresh sardines we've ever had!) Head over to immigrant neighborhoods, walk around, look into storefronts, see which are busy. Be open to new tastes. Ask what they recommend and go for it. Or try going into a nice restaurant, telling them what you can spend, and saying, "Feed me." You'll make new friends and eat better than ever. Chefs love a true foodie.

## WHERE TO GO: The Guides

For years we subscribed to Zagat. Or, more to the point, for years we received gifts of Zagat guides at Christmas from random acquaintances or business contacts. We liked them as handy references for all the restaurants in our area sorted by random things: most romantic, best brunch, best outdoor dining. Being the foodists we are, we didn't always agree with the general reviewing public about best in show, but that didn't stop us from thinking the book a gold mine of lists. When they went online it was even better, because they were outstanding at keeping up with the latest, newest, buzziest places in town.

Then we were no longer gifted with Zagats. We had to spend our own money? Hmm. We just couldn't do it. Yes, we know we're missing out on that single, simple compendium of a dining resource, but we're clever bitches with other tools at our disposal—and we're just not shelling out.

Everyone knows about booking through OpenTable. It's the handiest *free* way to jog your memory about your restaurant options, see who actually has a table for four people at seven p.m. when you decide to go out at six thirty. Or if you're on the run you can just hit the app on your iPhone and—presto—the dining world is at your fingertips. Earn points for booking that translate into gift certificates. They even offer a review/rating service. (Although—you guessed it, we don't rely on these.)

Even if OpenTable denies you (like you need more of that in your life), call to double-check. What you need to remember is that not all restaurants are listed, and often a restaurant that looks booked online actually *does* have open tables. Stay on top of those little cool, out-of-the-way places you want to try (keep a list on your computer or in your drawer), but actually use the telephone.

## BE A FOODIE—SAVE DOUGH, THINK OUTSIDE THE BUN

Don't consider yourself a foodie yet? Not sure what you like, or how to start figuring it out? Need to get out and not spend a lot? Search and lust for a single kind of food. Spend time, not big bucks, in your quest for the best gnocchi, spicy tuna hand rolls, or steak frites near you.

Pizza is still a bargain food. Start a Monday-night pizza hunt. Compare and contrast, travel farther afield, go to the joint by the airport, the old ethnic neighborhoods, hip, small places. Sometimes that funky strip mall in an out-of-the-way suburb has the best kimchi outside of Seoul, or the most delicious veal Florentine this side of Fiesole. Rents are cheap, proprietors present, prices low. Do a hamburger investigation. Are carcinogenic char-grilled burgers tastier than griddled? Swiss better than cheddar? Raw or smothered onions? How about a search for the best pad thai, best tofu, best raw food?

Consider identifying all the restaurants in town where the chef in the kitchen is a woman. Go out of your way to support her. For too long those kitchens have been dominated by macho men—only now are women taking charge in large number.

Break the mold. Must you have omelets just at breakfast, sushi for lunch or dinner, pot roast after dark? Think globally when you're eating locally. Travel around the world and see that other cultures eat their fish or chicken in the morning, or serve their main meals at lunch (followed by a magnificent siesta). Save money by mixing up mealtimes. Have your big meal at lunchtime for half of dinner pricing. Oh, and dessert can be a meal unto itself (talk about bargain dining). Why not a hot-fudge sundae topped with healthy walnuts for lunch?

## PRICE AND TIME ADJUSTMENTS

Expensive restaurants are adapting. These days, the smart guys know that to survive they must cater to you thrifty eaters. Their strategies? Turning out smaller, less expensive plates, hoping to turn the tables more often (just like the retail outfits turning goods to make a profit—see chapter 1), buying less expensive cuts of meat, poultry, and fish and doing really interesting things to spice them up. A good struggle gets the creative juices flowing, often leading to better, tastier results.

Go online to those restaurants that have been out of your budget and see how menus have changed. You'll even find lots of places offering three courses for under twenty bucks! Many are offering a version of early-bird pricing, hoping to drive traffic and turn tables early or late in the evening—book between five and six thirty or after ten and get a deal.

Saturday night is the busiest at most restaurants. You might even go out and wonder, what bad economy? Yes, lots of restaurants are struggling not because weekends suck, but because the rest of the week is bad, or they aren't turning two or three seatings a night but just one or two (hence early and late special pricing!). For the best food, skip Friday and Saturday. Try different nights of the week, when the chef and kitchen aren't overwhelmed—you'll have a better meal. (Stay home; do your own cooking on Saturday—see chapter 9.)

For bargain eating and innovation, check out restaurants that have a Lehman Brothers memorial dining room—you know, those private dining rooms that were once filled with hedge-fund and investment-banker types struggling to outboner one another with $1,000-plus bottles of wine and exotic hand-massaged beef (don't get us started on that one). Those rooms are sadly (for them) now empty, and some chefs have put them to creative use, serving tapas-style or experimental new fare.

Consider eating at the bar or the more casual side of a fancy restaurant. Often a great restaurant will offer a less expensive bar menu, but the same chef and same kitchen are turning out the meals. Our all-time favorite is Nougatine in NYC (walking distance to the Beacon, see page 156). We love this "other"

235

side of the Jean Georges Restaurant. While celebrity chefs are often not our thing, every single time we've been in this place (and we're embarrassed to say how often that has been), Jean Georges is there supervising. He's our hero.

---

O━━ *Thrifty Splurge*

### combine the world's greatest pleasures

LUNCH IS cheaper than dinner. Food is food. If there's a place you have been dying to eat at and it's just too much moola, go for lunch. Pretend you're on vacation. Play hooky. Go with your lover. Drink champagne. Eat too much. Rent a room (okay, that's pushing it). Go home for an afternoon siesta and the world's number one pleasure.

---

O━━ *Splurgeworthy*

### restaurant as mecca

YOU'RE PART of the crowd that lives to eat. Yes, we know who you are, for we're fellow travelers. James Beard Award winners, *Gourmet* feature stories, *NY Times* reviewer Frank Bruni's picks . . . they all beckon you, titillating your taste buds with descriptions of perfection, innovation, service, decadence. We have good and bad news. They're all much nicer now than they ever were before. Prices are moderating—but are still high. You can get a table without getting on speed dial exactly thirty days in advance (except, of course, for Momofuku Ko—where we have yet to snag a table). Save up. This is the kind of indulgence that is a real treat.

## BE BITCHY—GET SERVICE(D)

What is there about being a woman and getting bad service?

We've all been there—whether on the airplane, at the auto dealer, or at the restaurant. Bitch, it's time to stand up. Don't take it anymore. Your money is just as good as the next guy's.

Recently we celebrated the twenty-first birthday of a friend—a young woman, yes, but one with an experienced palate, one who grew up identifying tarragon from chervil, appreciating the subtle flavor difference between roasted and boiled beets, and baking a celeb chef's killer Falling Chocolate Cake recipe. Her birthday request? To go to the eponymous restaurant of the chocolate-cake maven. A gang of women of all ages and sizes converged from all over to toast and dine with her.

The place was pricey. Phone calls were placed to remind the restaurant it was a big occasion . . . we asked them to hold a special table, to make a fuss. The birthday girl arrived first, was ushered to a table in the corner by the kitchen door. The worst table in the whole house. The rest of the party arrived, older and ballsier, and requested a better table. It was "not possible."

The evening was a disaster.

The waiters rushed back and forth, scraping against the birthday girl on their way in and out of the kitchen. Dinner, rushed out of the kitchen, was nothing special. Dessert service, which should have been slow and multicoursed, arrived in a puddle all at once. Candles were lit. Not once did any of the staff smile or even wish the young lady happy birthday. Then they all disappeared . . . no one asked if we needed more tea, coffee, or a nightcap. We had to beg for the check.

We wrote to the owner describing our experience. We imagined that such a distinguished chef would not want anyone to leave his restaurant with such poisonous thoughts, our letter said. We told him we had been seated at the girls' table, the tourists' table, the out-of-towners' table. (You know it, bitch; you've all sat there.) We asked, Did he employ only unhappy waiters? We told him we had seen him emerge to chat up Matt Lauer and Mario Batali, but what of the little girl who had grown up cooking his recipes and idolizing his food?

Then we shared how we had learned to appreciate great food at the same age as the birthday girl . . . on our first trip to France. Unworldly, wide-eyed, naive to good food, we'd stumbled into a restaurant where the owners were so taken by our complete food ignorance and our obvious delight in their delicacies, they brought us taste treat after taste treat. They took *pleasure* in our pleasure. So began our love affair with food. (Ironically, we discovered that this was the very same restaurant where the famous chef had himself apprenticed.)

A testament to the power of the pen, one month later, as a guest of the chef, the birthday girl and her college roommate returned to the scene of the crime to be treated to a seven-course dinner. Each course was paired with the appropriate wine, and this time *the birthday girl* scraped the back of the person in the worst seat in the house on her way to a private tour of the kitchen. The meal ended with so many desserts that their entire college dorm floor satisfied their munchies at two a.m. with gourmet treats.

The point of this story?

Do what you do best.

Bitch, bitch.

238

## DRINKING OUT

Where you go to imbibe is all a matter of intention—are you looking to live on Boardwalk, hustle the crowd, see and be seen? Or are you just looking for a little medication?

Pricey, alcohol-infused Shirley Temples are not part of our drinking lexicon. We pass on the $17 juiced cosmos and gold-infused margaritas—but that's just us. If we're going to consume alcohol, purists that we are, we like to taste what we're drinking. Every bitch needs to find her own moj(it)o. Know what you want to get what you need. Control your bar bills by doing your down-and-dirty drinking in a real down-and-dirty bar. While they won't have lovage-infused designer gin on the menu, they'll have the real stuff straight up, at a fraction of the price you'll find at the sleek places. On those cold and stormy nights, after a bad day at work, at home, at life—take a cab, bring a friend to watch your back, and drink your meds.

Then there are the times we're feeling festive. We want to dress up. We want to be seen. We don't want to be real. We want to feel like we're at the center of the action holding court at the hottest place in town. Then we head out to the kind of places that match who we would like to be. (Never mind that we always leave those bars feeling kind of depressed.) Order your drink carefully and always get a glass of water on the side. Nurse the drink; drink the water. Keep your wits. Try your best to ignore those other bitches, skankier than you, dresses cut straight down to their Brazilians and boobs lifted so high you'll be staring them in the eye. Remember how expensive these bars are, and how you'll hate yourself in the morning if you rack up a big, big bill in pursuit of nothing but a hangover. Indulge your fantasies, but at least be real.

239

## be a budgetbitchsta

*Y*ES, YOU need to get out; yes, you want to see a friend after work. Doesn't mean you have to be such a boozer. How can you really work out your angst if you can't remember the next day what you talked about? Whatever happened to meeting at an old-fashioned coffee shop? Pass on the Antichrist and check out some of the new microroasters. How about a tea shop? Spend less than three bucks. Socialize. Breathe in different air, chat, just hang. (Although you might have to short-circuit the electricity to get those hogs who are roosting on their computers to leave.)

Chapter 8

......................

# Get Comfortable
## THE CHEAP PLEASURES
## OF HOME

*S*O WE TOLD you it was time to separate comfort
from pleasure—now you know how to go out
without blowing your wad. But what about staying in? It's time to find pleasure in the comfort
of home. Look, bitch, you've cleared the clutter; you've painted
the walls white; it's like you're a virgin again. It's time to start all
over, fresh, clean, and cozy.

Return to the things you did at home as a kid that didn't cost
a month's worth of hard labor. Baking cakes and whipping up
homemade ice cream. Painting your friend's nails. Playing pretend. Remember how you organized your own games? Got up
early to watch cartoons and Saturday-morning movies? Stayed
up all night at pajama parties? Spent rainy summer days playing
board games? Spun the bottle on Friday night? Kept your elderly
neighbor company and learned those killer card games in return?

Enjoy all the pleasures of home by organizing your own twisted fun. Hold adult book clubs for you, your friends, and significant others. Learn new card games, or remember the old ones—strip poker, anyone? Play truth or dare. Plan potluck dinners—they've moved beyond tuna-and-mushroom-soup casseroles. Don't just watch—make your own reality shows. Organize a scotch night or an alcohol night (complete with pj party; no liability issues—like you need more bad shit in your life). Keep your sex life under house arrest: Find the fantasy that sparks your engine. Start a community garden with your neighbors, plant your own garden in your window, grow and eat, eat and grow. . . .

## FILL UP AT OTHERS' EXPENSE

### POTLUCKS

Think red; think green. No, it's not Christmas; it's environmentally friendly and communist. Recycling, sharing, and group living are not so bad, and elegant potluck dinners (it's not an oxymoron) are the word of the day. No need to go out on a limb alone and spend time and money searching for and buying all the ingredients. No need to spend the day slaving away. It'll be exhausting enough doing the invitations, getting the house cleaned, and selecting those pretty flowers for the centerpiece.

*At Your Fingertips*

**evites**

FOR THE one bitch who doesn't know what an Evite is, we'll save you the embarrassment of asking. Send electronic invitations for your party. Save on stamps. Go to www.evite.com.

Your cost? A little imagination and a lot of organization. People love direction (not us—we're control freaks), but most people do (trust us on this). Getting an assignment allows them to compartmentalize their responsibility. Telling other people what to prepare kicks ass: You get to slough off the things you hate to do, and they'll feel like they have a stake in the finished product.

A word of warning: Require that all food arrives plated and ready to serve (if you're the invitee, feel free to cheat—see Green Style on page 298). There's nothing worse than the bitch who shows up with her goods and commandeers the kitchen, interrupting your work flow so she can smash her avocados and plate her guacamole, or hijacks the oven to bake her eight mushroom caps while you have the tenderloin ready to roast. Shit, it's your kitchen. Besides, you have more important work—like mixing the cocktails.

Our experience tells us that the most successful potlucks are theme-centered. Themes will aid you in figuring out a menu and will allow everyone an opportunity to costume appropriately—upping the air of festivity.

Have a crustacean night, and get your friends to bring the little Larrys and the Coronas. You organize the enormous boiling pots of water, the corn, the butter, and the bibs. Have a return-to-opulence night. Make a huge, elegant dinner party; put out Grandma's china and the tall candlesticks. Assign others to bring pricey, big, gorgeous flowers for the table. Tell everyone to get their best party clothes out of storage (tuxes if the guys have them). Head to Costco to buy a whole tenderloin (a huge bargain). Do not disappoint us and be a wussy bitch—be prepared to trim it up. Make this your only out-of-pocket expense for the evening—you'll look like a hero and it is *so* easy to make. Assign friends the Caesar salad, baby red potatoes with rosemary, horseradish sauce, dessert, and the

243

vintage Bordeaux and Burgundy wine. Or get worldly—cook Chinese stir-fry. Have some other bitch do the annoying work of chopping up those thousands of veggies. You supply the roasted green tea (see page 281).

How about Sunday brunch? Labor Day? Academy Awards night? The Grammys? Family holidays? No need to slave (and pay) solo ever again.


## SPIRITED POTLUCKS

Dinners and food beyond your organizational skill set? Outside your interest range? You like to drink, you say? You can pour wine and spirits? Well, then, organize wine and spirit tastings. Really lazy? Organize tastings in other people's houses.

Go beyond the usual—Syrahs from Languedoc side by side with Australian Shiraz. Compare Chilean and New Zealand sauvignon blancs, then contrast both styles with French Sancerres. Yes, it could be so lovely with Leon Fleisher at the piano playing Beethoven. Maybe you'll even be inspired to cook up *gougères*.

Aren't a wine drinker? You're a tough bitch; you like it hard. Bring on the scotch, vodka, gin. Try this: Do a blind vodka taste test, just like the *New York Times* did (see page 284); see if Smirnoff is *your* winner. Just make sure you compare apples to apples—grain to grain, potato to potato, grape to grape alcohols. Do a single-malt scotch drink-off; the taste variations are strong and delicious. Crank up Janis Joplin, Alanis Morissette, and start dancing.

Add cheese to the tasting menu. Goat, cow, sheep. Soft-ripening, aged. Spread across regions: French goat cheeses, Spanish sheep. Stay in one place: Italy or Scotland. Buy the cheese to match the wine or spirit locale. Stay local: Find wine, spirit, and cheese artisans in your backyard.

Bitch, a tip: Do the tastings the real way. You won't get too far into this if you actually swallow all the liquor and wine you're testing. Be like a pro and get spitting buckets. Taste, swish, spit. While you might be able to hold your liquor, you can never tell about others. Try to invite friends who'll take it with some seriousness—you don't want people getting sick. No money savings will be worth that—not in your house!

Make assignments, have *everyone else* bring *everything*.

## MAKE YOUR OWN REALITY

**YOU'RE WATCHING TOO** many reality shows. You really believe there is a Chairman and a Kitchen Stadium. You're desperate to audition for *The Real Housewives of Fargo* (if only they would come to your town), *The Millionaire Matchmaker* (if only you lived in L.A. and weren't already married), *American Idol* (if only you could sing). The Kardashians have you mesmerized, and you don't even know about their connection to O.J. and are too young to remember Bruce in the Olympics. Not only are

245

you addicted to *America's Next Top Model*, but you're squeezing Tyra's talk show in between Rachael and Oprah on your DVR list.

For all those free fantasies, you get a gold star. For sitting on your ass watching other people living, you really *are* the biggest loser. Bitch, it's time to apply all that hard-earned knowledge to real life. No, you are not going to *join* the cast of one of these live soap operas. No exchanging lives with people in the Ozarks, or making a trade for a new husband or boyfriend (well, maybe you are; who are we to tell you what to do?). Nor will you be sending your children to live in some ill-conceived futuristic experiment in the desert (on second thought, why did they kill that show?).

Play pretend with your own versions of the reality shows. Act them out at home. Like your own version of *The Rocky Horror Picture Show*—but you don't have to start at midnight or follow the script. You could dress the parts of your favorite characters, even play them . . . set the stage and have a banging good time.

## TOP-IRON-CHOPPED-HELL-CHEF CONTEST

Cook this one up with a group of friends. One night a week—try Saturday (it sucks to eat out on a Saturday—see page 235)—combine the attributes of the top cooking shows into a weekly contest. Use three secret ingredients, set the timer for sixty minutes, break up into teams, and start cooking. Rotate between houses. Each hostess is responsible for setting the table, providing the secret ingredients—guests bring their own implements (how many great chef knives can one gal have?). Find judges—invite boyfriends, spouses, even your kids—all could be wickedly funny.

Losers are responsible for cleaning up!

## EXTREME DO-OVERS

Be brave. Start this activity by signing a pact that no matter what, you won't be pissed. Look, you're sick of your environs, your wardrobe, your hair and makeup, yet you can't seem to get it together to paint the walls, re-cover the furniture, or clean out all the shit. Put together a group of like-minded, lazier-than-thou friends. Think of it as a mutually therapeutic group intervention. Spend a month boning up on the shows, glam mags, makeover sites. Set parameters for the makeover.

## HOME EDITION

How much do you trust them? Do you actually want them to bring the goods that you can't pull the trigger on to Goodwill? Is there a makeover budget for fresh paint or flowers? Do you want to give them a color palette that you find acceptable (see Bitchin' Tip, page 120)? Are there untouchables? You know, your art from Tucson. Create guidelines. Be specific. Be creative. Then visit each friend's house or apartment and do a makeover.

The victim—ahem, recipient—of her friends' beneficence leaves. Spend the day at the museum—you really mean to go there, remember? Those left in charge get to work. The make-over team will have met earlier so they can come equipped with a plan. Editors start boxing tchotchkes and trashy paperbacks. Paint squads don their overalls. Furniture movers start lifting and grunting. That side table in the living room is clumsy and awkward; take it up to the spare bedroom. The black-and-white photos, lost in the hallway, would be perfect over the mantel. C'mon, bitches, you don't live here; there are no sacred cows—give her a clean, fresh start.

## RE-DRESS WITHOUT THE GRIEF

Your wardrobe is spilling out of the two closets in your apartment. Stuffed plastic boxes are shoved under your bed. The coatrack in the corner is precariously balanced; God forbid you actually remove anything from an arm or it'll fall like the massive dressed-up oak tree it is, crushing everything in its path. You can't find anything. You're wearing the same black pants daily, the same pilling sweaters, the same scuffed black heels. You need new stuff but can't buy anything until you clean out the old shit.

Call in your wardrobe advisers. Spend a day. Model. Get the thumbs-up or -down (remember that awful *Sex and the City* movie—the scene when they lounge on the bed giving Carrie direction to keep or toss?). Drink lots of frilly cocktails. Laugh. Go to your friends' houses, drink their liquor—oh, and help them out, too. Then when it's all done, consider letting your friends go off and "find your style"—give them a budget. Have them bring back bags of new duds. (Know the return policies!) Follow the same frilly-cocktail formula. Model. Select the style you like best—wait, that may be pushing it. Clean out the shit, drink too much, then give yourself permission to go to J.Crew or Zara and buy new stuff.

⊶━ *Bitchin' Tip*

**XXX**

CONSIDER AN X-rated makeover. Get your partner(s), closely examine your sex toys, movies, naughty lingerie . . . then go shopping together to fill in the holes.

## SPA-RTAN LIVING

Can't get your right pinkie polished evenly? Your eyebrows to match? Trouble distributing hair color without streaking? What are friends for? In *Extreme Makeover: Spa Edition*, they're your new makeup artists and hairstylists extraordinaire.

Our advice? Pick this group carefully. If you have an aesthetician as an acquaintance, maybe this is the time to deepen your friendship. Black spiked hair, face hardware, maroon nails your look? Then it's okay to include your friend who auditioned for the latest vampire movie—in her day clothes—to help in your personal transformation.

Marilyn Monroe envy? Halle Berry or Angelina Jolie your goal? Be realistic. If you're a skinny, thin-lipped, flat-chested, five-foot-tall-in-your-stocking-feet white chick—well, you're bound to be disappointed. As a group, look through pics of people who share your face shape and coloring. Pick several looks you'd be happy with. Subtly remind everyone before they begin that this is a *mutual*-aid pact: Their turns are coming.

Don't worry too much. Hair will grow, color can be corrected, nail polish can be wiped away, henna tattoos fade . . . as for the eyebrows, go to a professional.


# STUFF YOUR MOTHER TOLD YOU TO DO


## BRAIN FOOD

Ever been part of a book group? Was it fun? Are you part of an unfun book group? Quit. Start your own. Make it fun.

First of all, just because it's a book group doesn't mean you

249

always have to read the book. You are not in school. No one is giving you a grade. Do it on your own terms. If all the bitches are way uptight when you don't finish the book—then quit. If they require you to present a short précis of the book, or insist on having a guest lecturer tell you how to interpret the author's motivation and how it relates to Saint Augustine's philosophy . . . hmm, is this really your style? If so, what the hell are you doing with *our* book? How did you get this far? Go on, close it. Now.

Still with us? What about a dirty book club? (Don't tell Mom.) Pick good or bad erotica. There's a whole world of soft porn waiting to be opened up—try *Nauti Intentions* by Lora Leigh or *Wild, Wicked, & Wanton* by Jaci Burton.

How about a coed book group? (Not that we're recommending a coed porn book club—honey, that's just too weird.) Get different perspectives. Alternate between male and female writers; see if you can pick up differences in voice. Are the authors effective in writing from the voice of the opposite sex? See if the men and women agree. Try Nicole Krauss's *The History of Love*, *The Hours* by Michael Cunningham, or (if you really want to confuse things) Jeffrey Eugenides' *Middlesex*.

## VOLUNTEER

Remember keeping your elderly neighbor company when you were a kid? She was such a lovely woman, so patient, so wise; she taught you all those card games you're so glad you know now. Like gin rummy and poker. You gave something away; you got something in return. Yeah, this isn't quite staying in, but volunteer in your community; it's a homey feeling.

If you're the oldest of thirteen and spent most of your life as mini mom—you're excused. No more responsibilities. Go have fun.

Everyone else—you know who you are—step forward. You may not have loads of cash on hand, but you sure as hell have loads of time. So put on your little thinking caps and consider what you can do for someone else. It'll be a hell of a lot more satisfying than that pair of shoes you were dying for that now dig into your heels and pinch your toes—not to mention the spill you took when you turned your ankle, because even with all those crisscrossing straps the damn things don't stay on well and are so fucking high. Gladiator shoes belong in the Dark Ages. But we digress.

Make it fun. Nothing should feel all serious and penance-like. Do something with a friend or a group of friends. Sit around; talk to people—really talk. If this time has taught you nothing else, it should teach you that life spins and turns on a dime; we are separated by only an accident of time and space, and the person on the receiving end of your help could just as easily be you.

Plan a night out a week when you and your friends or family all go work in a soup kitchen, homeless shelter, or food pantry. Maybe babysit for the moms so they can get a night off. Go to a nursing home and read a book to someone who's bedbound, or offer to record his or her life story. Pitch in at a community garden. Do a Habitat for Humanity project for a week or a weekend. Go to immigrant-aid societies and offer practice conversation to those who are studying English. Be a Big Sister. Mentor in a school. Be a coach. We all have something we love to do; find a way to share it with a younger person or an older person or just another person or a dog at the shelter. Or, if you're a complete misanthrope, pick up trash on the side of the road.

251

**grow your own/pick your own**

- It's super easy and cheap to grow an herb garden on your kitchen sill, terrace, or in the yard. Can't you smell it already? Parsley, tarragon, basil, chervil, sage, lemon verbena, lavender . . . Make your own teas (see page 283), scented oils, sauces, delicious caprese sandwiches.

- Look, too, for pick-your-own opportunities. Autumn apple picking should be an annual family event. Come home red-cheeked and make pies or applesauce, or just bite into fresh, crispy apples. Whether it's strawberries or pole beans, farmers often open their fields, and the pricing is amazing when you supply the labor.

## BORED GAMES

Scrabble, chess, backgammon, Monopoly, Parcheesi, Taboo, charades, Rummy-O, hearts. Have you forgotten how much fun these were? Games are *not* just for vacation or random rainy afternoons. Organize evening events around these classics. Need incentive? Consider a lusty game of strip poker. Get bawdy and bare with truth or dare. Change the rules of Monopoly . . . drink to get out of jail; drink when you pass go; drink when it's your turn. Why is it that guys always gamble and girls take their clothes off? A bitch should make some money too. Bring your spare change.

**pajama party**

$\mathcal{M}$AKE IT festive. Make it fun. Keep it safe. When you're adjusting the rules of Monopoly like this, plan to spend the night. Everyone wear horizontal-striped pajamas like the little bald guy on the yellow Chance cards.

Bridge does sound so midcentury, so Dick Van Dyke–and–Mary Tyler Moore–ish, so twin-beds-for-married-couples. Don't let that put you off. After all, midcentury modern style is so chic right now, and we hear that once you learn this you'll be addicted. Since it's complex, it's best learned with a teacher. This could be a good course at your neighborhood adult ed class. Okay, it still seems geezery—but what are you doing that's so much better?

Mah-jongg. Yes, we want to learn how to play this game . . . the tiles and sets are stunningly beautiful. Still, we're a little nervous. Most of the people we know who play are really nice, but also belong to the Red Hat Society. You've seen them: grown-up women, clad for no good reason in purple clothing, going out together to places like Cheesecake Factory and Applebee's wearing red hats. Something to do with having fun as you approach fifty. We're stumped.

We love pretend, fantasy stuff, so charades is always an oldie but a goodie. Remember? You silently act out titles of books, movies, TV shows, or the names of famous people. The last time we played everyone was on the floor howling, wishing they were wearing Depends. Be a provocateur. Force your competitors to act out titles like *The 400 Blows* or *The Joy of Sex* or *Chitty Chitty Bang Bang*. You get the picture. Dick Butkus, anyone?

We can play Boggle or Scrabble for hours. Boggle's great because

253

no matter how bad the letters, there's a new set every three minutes. Scrabble must hook right into some deep-rooted masochism . . . we get Is, Es, Os, and Us in duplicates, triplicates, and as soon as we put one on the board another sadistically replaces it. We make little grunting and moaning sounds, focus on our letters in the carriage with such intensity we must believe we have Merlin-like powers to transform them. Yet as soon as one game ends, another begins. In fact, we have a running Scrabble game with our neighbor at five p.m., with wine and cheese, every day of the week.

## WOOLGATHERING

Old-fashioned crafts are back with a vengeance. Check out the *Stitch 'n Bitch* books to see what cool hipsters are making. Crochet, knitting, quilting . . . A girl on a budget gets smart about what she whips up with her own two hands. Needlework circles may sound like a nineteenth-century form of entertainment— right up there with "hoop and stick" and marbles—but they're a cheap, easy form of social interaction, a perfect way to be connected, meet social obligations, and end up with a cute new scarf. Besides, these skills come in handy in other ways. During a long afternoon at the in-laws', it's rude to put your nose in a book or open your computer—but it's socially acceptable to click your needles and escape to your own private fantasy.

## STUFF MOM DOESN'T SEE

### MOVIE/TV NIGHT

Forget what Mom said, forget what we said: Don't shut off the TV. For pure escapism, relaxation, and passive entertainment nothing beats a great movie or television series. Have you tried Netflix? Have you gone to the premium channel home pages on cable and found a full series of a show you've never watched? You know us, with our little OCD problem—we're easily obsessed by great TV. Not one of your issues, you smugly say. We say you haven't lived until you've tried it—a movie/television series obsession, that is.

You can certainly do this on your own—and believe us, bitch, sometimes we all need to be left to our own deadbeat devices, in our pj's, unshowered, zoned out in front of the tube. But for fun, low-key socializing with your pals, nothing beats a like-minded group of horny, lonely hearts, munching on popcorn, sharing a Johnny Depp marathon. Soft-core porn can add zip to an old engagement or unzip a new friend. Or get a series season's worth of discs and get so hooked that you'll feel like a kid again, conspiring with your significant other to watch just one more, just one more episode, until two a.m. Priceless will be that feeling of delight when you remember no one can make you go to bed because you have school in the morning.

If you haven't watched *Weeds*, *Big Love*, *Lost*, *The Wire*, *Rome*, or *In Treatment*, you're in for a treat. We watched the entire first season of *Grey's Anatomy* over three evenings. It was riveting. (Although we could never watch the show on a weekly basis—it sucked with commercials.) *House*: No more need be said. Or how about some good Brit oldies but goodies, like Helen Mirren in *Prime Suspect*, Clive Owen in *Second Sight*, or all the seasons of *Upstairs, Downstairs* and *I, Claudius*?

Create your own movie festivals. First stop—your public library. Second stop—Netflix. Since you're more or less under house arrest, the Netflix fee is well worth it. Even the least responsible, laziest of bitches can manage this. Go online to set up your account. Create a list of movies/series/shows you want delivered. They'll send you three movies at a time as they become available. Keep them as long as you want. No late charges, no nasty notes, no little elf reminders either. As soon as you watch one, put it back into the bright red envelope, postage prepaid. They send you the next available movie from your queue. Plus, some Netflix movies are now available online if your browser and equipment support the feed. Yes, that id loves immediate gratification.

The Netflix site offers personalized recs based on what you rent and how you rate them. Our recs for your first foreign-movie festival (foreign because we care about you and we know how house- and country-bound you are): *Amelie*; *Monsoon Wedding*; *Jean de Florette*; *Betty Blue* (with one of the all-time sexiest of sex scenes—a definite zip/unzip companion movie), *The Memory of a Killer* (a small, interesting Dutch film); Ang Lee's *Eat Drink Man Woman*; Kurosawa's *Ran* and *Rashomon*. A good cross-section—something for everyone on this list: old, new, weepy, war-y, creepy, sexy.

*Thrifty Bitch*

**pleasure at home**

*A* BITCH can spend a lot of comfortable time at home indulging in the number one pleasure. All for free. You've mastered your squat thrusts, practiced your Kegels, bought your toys. Now get to work. *Whom* you do is your choice; *how* you do it is between you and your partner; *when* you do it—well, as often as you can!

256

*Chapter 9*

......................

# Eating In
## RETHINKING THE DAILY GRIND

N THE DAYS of yore, when your Louis Vuitton handbag runneth over, you worshiped at the altar of the luxe and opulent: Manolo, Mercedes, and Paris (Hilton, that is). And it was good. But now the tide has turned, your income streams runneth dry, and you find yourself seeking the solace and redemption that can be found only at the altar of the virgin: virgin olive oil, virgin tea leaves, virgin asparagus. In subprime conditions you need sustenance. You need warmth and nourishment. You need to keep your senses in peak condition. And above all, you need pleasure: a reliable, daily fix of deeply satisfying, soul-enhancing pleasure, which—trust us—originates in the kitchen rather than the bedroom. We did say *reliable*, didn't we?

Nothing delivers the self-medicating joy you need like great food and drink, but to truly revel in the pleasures of the table,

257

you must first shake up and sex up the daily grind. Yes, we're talking a major overhaul of every facet of the dining-in experience, from where you go to fill your larder and what you do with your new and delicious finds, to what tasty adult beverages you imbibe and what you pick up on the fly. (If it were as easy as it sounds, bitch, your fridge would be free of the overpriced, unsatisfying shit you've been consuming for years and replaced with cabbage and bluefish.)

So say good-bye to the jugs of California chardonnay and pricey, overdressed salads (those were the rock stars of the *last* recession with Bush number one), and lay a big, juicy, wet one on the yummy foods and savvy strategies hallmarking a modern new era of dining in. Hello, offal! Hello, Asian superstores! Hello, rye! Meet your new best friends.

## FILLING YOUR LARDER

**GET THAT CREAM**-of-mushroom soup out of your shopping cart *stat*; it's a recession, not potluck night at the VFW hall! Times may be tough, but that doesn't mean you need to succumb to a life of tuna noodle casserole. Filling your larder with quality food when cash is tight *is* possible if you stay focused and put your hunting and gathering instinct into overdrive to find the *best* ingredients and products at the best prices available. This means knowing how to work the angles and avoid the pitfalls at the best updated traditional market (Whole Foods), best warehouse purveyor (Costco), and best mass niche grocer (Trader Joe's), as well as fun nontraditional Asian and farmers' markets. With just a little insider's intelligence about how to buy your nuts and berries, your fruits and veggies, and your daily catch, you'll be back waving your food-snob flag with pride. So, c'mon, bitches: Let's get shopping!

258

## WHOLE FOODS MARKET: Be a Two-faced Bitch!

There may be few better canvases for creating an amazing meal than Whole Foods, but navigating through all that gorgeous, unadulterated eye candy to find the gems you can afford takes a two-pronged approach. First, stay loose and open-minded about buying whatever seasonal produce, meat, or seafood is on special. This means throwing that shopping list away, because although you may be fantasizing about pan-seared scallops and braised escarole . . . you just may end up with chicken thighs sautéed with Peppadew peppers.

Then hold firm on buying only a handful of all-star staples from the bulk section, along with a few tested and true, reasonably priced 365 Everyday Value products. We realize this is a bit schizophrenic, but if you've ever had a mood swing (and who hasn't?), then mastering Whole Foods should be a piece of organic, gluten-free cake.

## THE LOOSE AND OPEN-MINDED WHOLE FOODS BITCH

Scoring top-quality fish or seafood on special is always possible if you stay flexible and go with the low-priced catch of the day. But what if the specials leave you wan and uninspired? Then step up and try consistently inexpensive trout, skate wings, and flounder, all of which can be the basis for chic Asian-inspired recipes when steamed in coconut milk and fresh basil. Or what about buying the full monty? C'mon, don't be a pussy! Whole fish with heads and tails intact is at least 50 percent less expensive per pound than fillets, and a showstopper when stuffed with fresh herbs, kosher salt, and olive oil and baked at a high heat (four hundred degrees).

Butcher counter specials are easily competitive with the

259

same cuts you'll find at your traditional grocer, only you'll be able to sleep at night knowing you haven't contracted mad cow disease. (Like you need more to worry about, anyway?) When buying chicken breasts, go with the skin-on, as they're easily less per pound than boneless, skinless breasts and, since your princess days are over, you can do the light lifting yourself.

In produce, look for high-volume seasonal goods like tomatoes and artichokes massed up front and on the end caps for the best deals. Or, since you have more time on your hands, why not get acquainted with interesting or seasonally less expensive produce, like kale, dandelion greens, bok choy, and fresh-from-the-forest fungi? Stir-fry them, steam them, and serve them up with garlic and olive oil or butter, or add them as a tasty twist to vegetable soups.

*At Your Fingertips*

## menu planning in real time

KEEP YOUR cell phone or BlackBerry in close proximity as you shop. When you see a fish or meat special with dinner potential, go to www.foodnetwork.com to match the special with their free online recipes. Talk about saving time, money, *and* gas!

## THE RIGID, ANAL-RETENTIVE WHOLE FOODS BITCH

Think of the bulk section as an organic-style casino: Pull a lever here, pull a lever there, and watch the goods—and your hard-earned cash—come tumbling down. So hold your ground and stock up only on these few great quality basics that Whole

Foods does best: preservative-free peanut and almond butter (grind your own for fabulous freshness), arborio and jasmine rice, panko crumbs, couscous, any variety of granola that sends you.

Some of the 365 Whole Foods house-brand items are studies in perfection. Grab the 365 olive oil, the 365 barrel-aged balsamic vinegar, and the 365 peanut sauce (a rocking base for Szechuan peanut noodles or a chicken peanut marinade).

And, of course, nothing beats a warm loaf of crusty bread. Stop by the Whole Foods bakery, grab whatever's hot (bread, ladies, bread), splash the 365 olive oil into a bowl, add chopped garlic and a little balsamic vinegar, toss an endive-and-radicchio salad, slice into a fresh hunk of cheese, open a crisp Kim Crawford sauvignon blanc. Turn a simple meal into something worthy of a discerning bitch who knows the good stuff when she sees it.

## ⚷—🔨 *Splurgeworthy*

### turn on with truffles

JEAN ANTHELME Brillat-Savarin, the most famous of French epicureans, called the truffle the "diamond of the kitchen," and offered up praise for its aphrodisiacal powers. While science has never proven this claim, a bitch needs all the help she can get. Besides, nothing radiates luxury like truffles. Whole Foods stocks bottles of white truffle–infused oil for $9.99 at the cheese counter. Use a few drops to finish off salad dressing, pasta with fresh mushrooms, or sizzling steak right off the grill for a divine taste treat. Who knows . . . maybe you'll also get lucky!

261

## TRADER JOE'S: A One-night Stand, Over and Over Again!

Imagine Trader Joe's as that unreliable boyfriend who can't always give you what you need, but is truly gifted in giving lots and lots of the feel-good things you want. His produce quality may fluctuate, his fresh meat and fish may make random appearances, but most bitches will agree: Nobody gives low-priced, preservative-free dried goods and frozen foods like Mr. Joe.

## DRIED GOODS THAT WON'T HANG YOU OUT TO DRY

Joe's nuts are the freshest, healthiest, best bargain in the world, and you should buy all of them—almonds, walnuts, hazelnuts, and cashews—since a one-pound bag is at least 30 percent less than what you'll find at a traditional grocer. Then there's his seemingly endless variety of trail mix, dried slab apricots, peaches, and mangos, huge containers of cookies, like chocolate-dipped dunkers for coffee and tea, and lemon snaps for the kids' lunches, all of which will drive you insane wondering how so much pleasure could cost so little.

## FROZEN FOODS: We're Not Talking Birds Eye, Baby!

Do frozen dinners make you think of Salisbury steak and Cronkite on the boob tube? They've come a long way. Delicious and healthy frozen entrees do exist. Venture forth to Trader Joe's for an awe-inspiring and affordable freezer section. Cheese enchiladas in creamy tomato sauce . . . chicken tikka masala . . . pot stickers . . . wholesome veggie pizzas. You can't go wrong. Seeking a side dish in the $2-to-$3 range? Grab a bag of ready-to-go fried rice. (No snobbery, bitch—it's frozen fresh and easy to mistake for the stuff from your local Cantonese joint.) Or try their roasted corn and haricots verts that snap perfectly when cooked.

## COSTCO: Attitude and Homework Required

**COSTCO AIN'T NO** Whole Foods, baby . . . so don't even think about taking a pilgrimage to this airplane hangar of bulk buys without first morphing into an unyielding, tightly wound bitch who has done her homework and knows—down to the most minute detail—exactly what to buy. Costco revs up our little lust engine like no one else we know and it's oh so easy to forget that this is not casual neighborhood shopping—they're selling to restaurants and institutions as well as the little guy. The scale of this warehouse retailer is huge, making it easy to overlook that everything is gigantic. The prices are so low, the carts so large, and the food-sampling stations so tempting (especially

263

at lunchtime), a girl can get in big trouble. Bring a list and stay focused so you don't have unwarranted Costco envy every time you pass a shopping cart filled with multiple packages of Chips Ahoy!

## YOUR COSTCO ATTITUDE

Do *not* come to Costco with an open mind. Do *not* come to Costco feeling all warm and fuzzy and flush with an ecumenical acceptance of all God's creatures large and larger from the fifty-pack of sponges to the summer camp–size tub of Crystal Light. It's easy to suddenly think you need that extra-jumbo jar of peanut butter or eight-pack of graham crackers; they seem so inexpensive and for a delirious minute you forget the kids haven't had those kinds of snacks since preschool. So, come to Costco as a raving bitch. Come to Costco with your dukes up and a "get out of my face" snarl aimed at those bags of frozen pot-stickers they're cooking up that taste delicious but once home languish forgotten in the back of your freezer. A Costco shopping bitch needs to stay in control. Impulse shopping here will only cancel out your savings on the stuff you really use.

## YOUR COSTCO HOMEWORK

Check your cupboard, your fridge, and your freezer, see what's running low, and think about the weeks ahead: Out of food wrap? A family BBQ looming? A stay-at-home pot-luck dinner party planned (see pages 242–245)? Then, make a list based on these and *only* these items that Costco does well for so much less than any other grocer on the planet.

We buy mustard and ketchup, but skip the mayo. Heinz Ketchup and Grey Poupon mustard come in two-packs. One for the fridge, one for the cupboard. But that Hellman's jar is cafeteria sized and will be a science experiment before you get to the bottom. We're serious bakers and stock up on sugar and flour. Pass on the spices unless you're a pro; they'll lose their pungency before you use 'em up. Other nonperishables we fill up on when we find them: Barilla pasta, Near East Rice Pilaf, King Oscar sardines (rich in omega-3—see page 76).

Nobody does cheese like Costco, and there is no better deal around than Costco's Parmigiano Reggiano cheese. This is by far the world's best hard cow's-milk cheese and the only kind of Parmesan permitted to cross our threshold. It keeps forever and is delicious to eat au naturel or grated into your favorite sauces. Costco sells so much of it that it's always very fresh, and always cheaper than anywhere else we've ever been. The same concept applies to their Cabot Farms Private Stock cheddar and Montrachet cheeses: great quality, great value!

Other list-worthy bargain items include blister packs of organic greens—spinach, radicchio, and arugula, all prewashed, ready to go, and half the price of supermarkets. Birthday party or graduation coming up? Order up a yummy (and cheap) sheet cake. Peeled garlic is an adrenaline rush, but like other oversized perishable purchases it's best to buy one container and share with friends and neighbors. Prosciutto and salami are the real thing from Italy and come in handy resealable packages, and whole tenderloins and New Zealand rack of lamb in season are the biggest bargains in the universe. Sides of fresh salmon are perfect poached and served cold for a fancy-looking, dirt-cheap meal, but are colored artificially and farm-raised, so know your occasional poison.

Your Costco mantra? Stick to the list.

265

**psssst . . .**

- We'll let you in on a little secret: Costco has one of the all-time great selections of wines and liquors at low prices. Kirkland Vodka kicks ass. Scope them out, but be a smart bitch and don't get screwed. Make sure the vintage on the Wine Spectator rating card matches the vintage they're actually selling.

- Max out your Costco junket by filling up on those things that are a pain in the ass to run out of (like toilet paper) and give you no thrill to buy (like dog food). Stock up on jumbo-size packages of paper towels, laundry detergent, soaps, Tylenol, toothpaste. . . . Save time and gas.

## GET OUT OF YOUR COMFORT ZONE

**IF YOU'VE NEVER** been to an Asian grocery, then, bitch . . . you've got some explaining to do! Asian supermarkets are free entertainment and a great resource for cheap and exotic fare. But, in order to avoid acute sensory overload and purchase paralysis, you need to know the lay of the land, and exactly what items are allowed to grace your shopping cart.

### KNOW THE LAY OF THE LAND

266

A great Asian market will make you feel desperate for a scotch to steady yourself, because suddenly—and without benefit of a thirteen-hour flight—you've been plopped onto the streets of

Shanghai. The smells are a melding of fish and salt water, linoleum, and the green, earthy scent of exotic Chinese eggplant, bitter melon, and dried lily buds. The sounds are voices shouting Chinese against the backdrop of Asian chanteuse Muzak. Close your eyes and pretend for a moment that you're not a mile from your house. Open them again and start exploring. Ask for help. Take some chances.

◑— ⚷ *Bitchin' Tip*

### buyer beware

WE LOVE shopping at these markets, but "organic" is definitely a foreign concept. Buyer beware, and don't be afraid to ask (if you speak fluent Mandarin, that is) what waters the fish jumped out of, what grass the beef grazed on, and what fertilized the bamboo shoots' soil.

## KNOW THE GOODS WORTH BUYING

Most Asian markets have entire aisles devoted exclusively to authentic, inexpensive rice, so leave Uncle Ben at Kroger and turn on to the delicious taste pleasure of rice in a rainbow of colors and flavors. Try yummy red rice, black sweet rice, forbidden rice, or exotic *aged* basmati.

In seafood, pick your own live sturgeon, largemouth bass, or tilapia from the aquatic tanks. If you have the stomach for it, watch as the workers stun it with a mallet, skin it, and fillet it, all in about five seconds. Writhing mounds of fresh crabs, scooped onto the scale, weigh in at only a few dollars per pound, and bags of frozen mixed seafood—an amazing deal—are perfect for stir-fries or soups.

267

Buying cheap and tasty Asian condiments is one of the all-time great shopping highs, but show restraint or you'll end up overspending and your pantry will look like the kitchen at Mr. Chow. Stick to soy sauce, rice wine vinegar, hoisin sauce, garlic chili paste, and whole fermented black beans. When it comes to sesame oil, you should use only the kind made from hulled sesame seeds that have been toasted prior to pressing (the best quality you can buy), and you should buy it *only* at an Asian market, since it will be half the cost of what you'll find anywhere else.

Huge bags of panko at less than $2 a bag shouldn't be passed up, and waking up to packages of cereal and cartons of juice decorated with Korean anime cartoons can lift you out of your morning misery.

0═══ *Thriftiest Bitch*

## make it your lifeline

*A*SIAN MARKETS can help you save big bucks on many of the staples you *can* find everywhere else. How's this for a little compare-and-contrast reconnaissance: six limes for $1; five huge bulbs of garlic for $.79; a quart of strawberries for $1.99; golden pineapples for $2.99, fresh ginger for $.49/pound, a pound of mussels for $1!

## DIRT-CHEAP FARMERS' MARKETS:
### Oh, Really?

**AH, FARMERS' MARKETS** . . . you feel so chic and green, so *in touch* with nature, so much like that *om*-ing Chill Bitch we told you about in the fitness chapter. Picture it: You're wearing those cute clogs and big sunglasses, canvas tote slung over your bare shoulder, cup of coffee in hand, while under bright blue skies you idly roam through stalls of gorgeous, glistening produce. . . .

Let's cut the shit. These places can be *expensive*. You're paying big bucks for the privilege of eating food that hasn't been transported across the world, traumatized by wild temperature fluctuations, bathed in chemical baths, and wrapped in toxic plastic. This doesn't come cheap.

## IN SEASON ONLY

A girl's gotta be wise. Farmers' markets are great, absolutely, but unless you shop carefully you're just a bitch—*not* a bitch on a budget. Buy fruits and veggies when they're in the peak of the growing season. When farmers need to unload surplus, you'll get way better deals. It's simple supply and demand. Cruise the market. Note that all the tables from all the farms are stacked high with tomatoes or cukes or strawberries. It's their time; these are the real farmers' market bargains—perfectly ripe and deliciously cheap.

So many intelligent bitches throw their economic prowess to the wind at the first sight of a few amber waves of grain and a gingham-clad picnic table. Instead of selecting in-season and well-priced produce, they opt for the extra goodies: pies, cheeses, those jams and jellies with the chintz toppers, zucchini breads festooned with grosgrain ribbons (as if a pretty ribbon could make them taste good). Really now. These items offer you *no* savings, are often disappointing, and should be strictly off-limits. If you want to be Daisy Mae for a day, buy yourself some gingham dish towels at Target!

269

## ASK THE FARMER

Another overlooked way to get the best value at a farmers' market is to play "ask the farmer." Ask the farmer friendly questions, like how the crop was this year or whether the produce is organic (many farms may be making the transition to organic farming). Once you've bonded, ask the farmer for discounts on any misshapen produce; ask the farmer if there are discounts for buying in bulk (particularly if you're planning a party and need a crudité tray or fruit platter); ask the farmer for discounts on produce that hasn't sold by the end of the day. This is especially effective if the farmer is *Mr.* Green Jeans. Bend over, let that tank top slide downward, smile a big country smile, and then ask the farmer.

*Bitchin' Tip*

### touchy-feely

As ALWAYS, use those intrepid fingertips to get the pleasure you want. Touch, squeeze, smell, feel the produce up. No fun buying a bushel of apples, only to get home to find bruises and soft spots. If the farmer discourages touching, be suspicious.

## CHIC FIVE-STAR MEALS ANYONE CAN COOK FOR PENNIES: WE'RE NOT BULLSHITTING!

If one man's ceiling is another man's floor, then when it comes to food . . . one cow's offal is another man's caviar. What we're saying is, the food world is changing and it's time to get with the program and eat beyond white meat. In most countries—no, *not* just the third world—every part of an animal or vegetable is used in their cuisine. In China, pickled chicken feet complete with toenails are a delicacy. In France, fattened castrated ducks produce foie gras with their internal organs. In Peru, *anticucho*, made with grilled beef heart, can be found on every corner.

So, get the uncool, overfarmed salmon off the menu and start taking your lead from the world's top chefs, who use only the simplest, most readily available ingredients, especially the kind most bitches stuck in the 2000s reflexively overlook. To live like a queen in this economy, you need to eat like a peasant—cabbages, tomatoes, dark meat chicken, bluefish, fresh fruit. You'll see that it's the cheapest, hippest, healthiest, and most delicious way to dine.

## SWEET-AND-SOUR CABBAGE SOUP

....................................................

*1 head green cabbage (there is nothing cheaper*
    *on the supermarket shelves)*
*1 can best-quality tomatoes (we stock up on organic*
    *San Marzano Italian whenever they are on sale)*
*1 large beef marrow bone (optional)*
*sour salt or lemon juice—1 tbsp.*
*brown sugar—2 or 3 tbsp.*
*8 cups water*
*1 tbsp. kosher salt*
*salt and pepeper to taste*

**(vegan or meaty, it's *très* delish)**

Okay, bitches, this is as easy, tasty, cheap, and healthy as it gets. Wash and chop up the cabbage into chunks—some bigger, some smaller; we like the asymmetry! The soup cooks long enough that some pieces will get very soft while others will stay firmer.

Fill a large soup pot with cold water and add the cabbage, tomatoes, and soup bone (if you are using it) along with a tablespoon of kosher salt (this is *not* sour salt). Bring the water to a boil, then simmer for at least an hour.

Add two to three chunks of sour salt or lemon juice and two to three tablespoons of brown sugar. Taste to check the mixture for an acid/sweet balance (it's up to you how sweet-and-sour you want your soup). Simmer for another twenty minutes. Adjust the seasonings (if you add more sugar or sour salt, allow it to simmer), and add salt and pepper.

Serve in large, beautiful soup bowls with a crusty whole-grain (*never*, ever white) bread for a tasty meal that's filling enough for a dinner.

## Splurgeworthy

### bite the bullet and buy a great pan

INVEST IN one all-purpose All-Clad twelve-inch sauté pan. It's the world's best conductor of heat, and in the long run it will save you time and peace of mind, since it's incredibly easy to clean up—something we care about, since we're now doing *all* the washing up with our own two little hands.

## QUICK-COOK BEST-EVER TOMATO SAUCE

*3 whole peeled and scored garlic cloves*
*2 cans best-quality whole tomatoes (see above)*
*pasta*
*3 tbsp. olive oil*
*6 tbsp. extra virgin olive oil*
*fresh basil for garnish*

Fill a large pasta pot with heavily salted water and bring to a boil. Warm the olive oil in a twelve-inch fry/sauté pan. Add the garlic, which you have scored by taking a small paring knife and adding three shallow slices to each side of the clove to help release the flavor. Turn the heat to a low simmer and gently cook the garlic until it is lightly brown; then remove.

Open the cans of tomatoes and with a pair of kitchen scissors slice their very whole, very firm flesh to smithereens (think of attacking a very old, very bad boyfriend), and pour the pulpy liquid into the warm, garlic-infused oil. You will want a splatter screen to save your shirt from an unnecessary dry-cleaning charge, and to minimize the cleanup mess. Bring to a boil and then shut off the heat. Your sauce is done; really, it is!

When cooking pasta, it should always be al dente. Drain the pasta and finish it in the sauce so it becomes infused by the tomatoes.

Serve this dish very hot with drizzled best-quality extra virgin olive oil (if you can, find bottles with press dates on them, the fresher the better!), freshly grated Parmigiano Reggiano, and hand-torn pieces of fresh basil. Complement with crusty whole-grain bread and a fresh arugula salad drizzled with a simple mixture of extra virgin olive oil, lemon juice, salt, and ribbons of fresh parmesan shaved with a potato peeler.

 *Bitchin' Tip*

## how hot does he like *it*?

We ARE spicy bitches and like our food hot, hot, hot, hot, so oftentimes we'll add a habanero chili pepper to the garlic as it's browning and remove it when the garlic is done. Or more often, because we don't always have fresh peppers on hand, we'll liberally sprinkle the sauce with red pepper flakes while it's cooking. If we think our guest could be a limp-dicked wimp, we may put the hot red pepper flakes out

*(continued)*

273

on the table for him to spice the sauce as he sees fit. Talk about a good first-date test!

## PAN-CRISPED CHICKEN THIGHS

*2 to 3 lbs. skin-on, bone-in chicken thighs*
*¼ cup safflower oil*
*3 cloves minced garlic*
*½ cup dry white wine or chicken stock to deglaze*
*fresh rosemary*
*kosher salt and pepper to taste*

Dark meat is delicious. It holds up to more rigorous searing and braising than white meat, and always stays tender and moist. It's also the least expensive cut of the chicken you can buy.

○━━ *Bitchin' Tip*

### experience matters

WE LOVE our thirty-year-old cast-iron skillet for making this dish. It's dirty and really well used, like a sensual older man—all seasoned, slick, and tough enough for the high heat on top or inside. You can buy them preseasoned at your local hardware store for as little as 10 bucks, or better yet, scour flea markets for more experienced ones.

274

Wash and thoroughly dry the chicken pieces, then liberally sprinkle with kosher salt and pepper. Heat the oil (we love safflower oil; it stands up to high heat and is flavorless) in the skillet on high heat until it gets hot, but does not burn. Place the thighs in the oil, skin side down (depending on how many you are using and how big the skillet is, you might want to work in two batches). After three to four minutes, the skin should be a crisp brown, and the thighs should easily lift off the skillet without sticking.

Turn the thighs over to crisp the other side, but this time, remove the chicken after only two to three minutes. Drain any excess oil from the pan, turn on the heat, and deglaze the pan with the wine.

Add the chopped garlic, a splash more wine or even some chicken stock for moisture, and the rosemary. Put the chicken back in the pan, and leave on the stove at medium heat for a few minutes, or place in the oven at 300 degrees for five to ten minutes.

 *Green Style*

### the whole damn thing

$\mathcal{B}$UY WHOLE chickens on sale at your local market and cut them up yourself. We prefer organic (not that we're inflexible and the types who listen only to NPR, but we do believe that they're better for us and better for the earth around us, not to mention the poor critters . . . but we won't go there or this will become *that* vegan book!). Remember to put all the parts you may not be using—the backbone, frame, and wingtips—into your freezer to be resurrected for stock after you've assembled a critical mass.

275

# BLUEFISH IN OLIVE OIL AND SAGE

.....................................................................

> *bluefish fillets with skin on (if you can find them this way),*
>    *½ lb. per person*
> *fresh sage leaves*
> *4 cloves chopped garlic*
> *½ cup olive oil*
> *salt and pepper to taste*
> *fresh lemon juice*

Mention bluefish as a dinner option and you might as well have suggested raw tripe; everyone crinkles up their noses and says, "I hate bluefish!" C'mon, bitches, this is the best-tasting fish in the sea, and is perhaps the least expensive fish you can buy! The one rule of blues is that they must be *fresh*. So, when you go into your local fish market, make sure that fish is so wet and glistening you could swear it's still alive.

Wash and dry the fish fillets; put them in a glass pan filled with enough olive oil to liberally coat them, along with generous amounts of chopped fresh garlic and fresh sage leaves, which you can rough up a little before adding. Marinate in the fridge for a few hours.

Place the fillets in a fish grill (all kitchen stores sell them) and throw them on your grill. Turn after five minutes and give the other side another five minutes (more or less, depending on the thickness). If you don't have access to a grill, turn the oven up to 450 degrees, place the fish in an enamel-covered, cast-iron roasting pan, and cook for twelve to fifteen minutes.

Serve with tons of fresh lemon juice. The great thing about bluefish, aside from the price, is that it's almost impossible to overcook!

# ORANGES POACHED IN RED WINE

........................................................

*8 to 10 oranges*

*1 bottle full-bodied red wine*

*1 whole star anise*

*1 whole cinnamon stick*

*3 to 4 green cardamom pods*

*3 to 4 whole cloves*

*4 to 6 whole black peppercorns*

*1 cup sugar*

This recipe is gorgeous, sexy, and delicious. When we can find them, we use blood oranges, because they often have a tart red finish to contrast with the sauce, but any orange—or even grapefruit—will do.

Pour the wine into an eight-quart saucepan. Add the sugar and all the spices (if you're using the real deal rather than powdered spices, try wrapping them together in a little bit of cheesecloth or a tea bag filter or tea ball. It will make it easier to take them out of the wine mixture at the end).

Lower the heat and simmer for at least an hour. Allow the mixture to cool.

Take your oranges, which you have completely peeled, white pith and all, and plunk them down right in the middle of the liquid. Turn them over after a few hours and continue to let them marinate. We use a huge glass bowl for marinating and place this bowl on the table as the centerpiece for dinner. It will whet everyone's appetite for dessert and save you money on flowers.

For serving, make a big production of taking the oranges out of the liquid and slicing them across the grain. Lay the slices on pretty white plates with the wine sauce spooned over them and a dollop of crème fraîche or yogurt. Mint leaf garnishes add a nice color contrast and a flash of fresh flavor.

## all used up

*I*F YOU have half-finished bottles of wine standing at full attention, use them for cooking, as long as they haven't acidified. If you need to buy wine for a recipe, don't waste money on the heavy-hitter bottles. If the recipe calls for a full-bodied red, it need not be Château Lafite; any inexpensive red Burgundy will fill your cooking pot!

## STRAWBERRIES IN VINEGAR

*1 quart strawberries*
*best-quality balsamic vinegar*

This may be the easiest recipe you've ever made.

Buy strawberries on sale in season. Wash, pluck the stems, and dry. Place the berries in the most beautiful bowl you own and lightly sprinkle with great-quality balsamic vinegar. Let the berries rest for a few hours, then serve. This is the perfect ending to a full supper!

## NEVER STOP DRINKING

**NEVER STOP DRINKING:** That's our motto. Whether it's eye-opening joe (daily at eight a.m.), organic green tea with roasted brown rice (daily at three p.m.), a Sazerac cocktail with rye (daily at five p.m.), Argentinean Malbec (daily at eight p.m.), or single-malt scotch (daily at ten p.m.), we like to stay hydrated and . . . we like our oral pleasure. What we *don't* like is getting soaked. We don't like wasting our hard-earned cash on milkshake confections masquerading as coffee. We don't like buying tea that's packaged as an earthy, sensual import if it's only glorified Lipton. We don't like making a minor investment in a bottle of boiled grasses and water (otherwise known as designer vodkas) when there are far more interesting, less expensive spirits to discover. And we don't like buying a wine that's merely drinkable if we're told we're buying *fabulous*. When it comes to the thrift/pleasure drinking equation for coffee, tea, spirits, and wine, we have the G-spot figured out. Here's the skinny on how to rethink these classic beverages so they turn you on without sucking you dry.

## COFFEE: WHAT'S HOT, WHAT'S NOT

Have you ever had a great cup of coffee? Would you know it if you drank one? A great cup should be deep, fragrant, bold, complex, eye-opening. It should evoke a tropical rain forest; a misty, craggy coast; the scent of clean, bracing, mountaintop air. It should get your ass out of bed, lift you up in the middle of a long afternoon, offer fresh hope to get you through another day. It should make you breathe. It should make you hum. Seems over-the-top, right? Then, bitch, you've never had a great cup of coffee.

But hold on. . . . How would you know a great cup of coffee? You've been drinking that overroasted dreck for so long, you probably can't distinguish between a full-flavored, delicious bean and one so charred it calls for massive milk and sugar infusions to make the icky taste disappear.

Wake up to a new era. Toss the overroasted, expensive Starbucks down the drain. Start treating yourself to superior beans so you can truly enjoy and appreciate one of the few delicious luxuries you can still afford.

### Kiss the Antichrist Good-bye

If you're a Starbucks bitch, you'd better get over it. The coffee sucks (the March 2007 *Consumer Reports* stated that Starbucks' drip coffee was "burnt and bitter enough to make your eyes water instead of open") and it's a waste of your precious cash. And if that's not enough to get you running into the arms of Rachael Ray peddling "you know what America runs on": a "venti" white chocolate mocha weighs in at over five hundred calories! So, make your therapist proud and end the dysfunction; spend less and turn on to the best.

### Quality Reigns

Discovering great coffee is itself a journey. Not unlike learning about collectibles or wine . . . the more you know about taste and style, the more interesting the journey becomes. Soon you'll find yourself considering soil composition, light, roasting methods. Ready to become a coffee snob? We're with you. For starters, look in your backyard. Microroasters are springing up everywhere. Can't find one nearby? Check out beans from Blue Bottle Coffee Company (bluebottlecoffee.net). This Oakland-based coffee roaster offers exquisite, organic, interesting coffee. Give their Espresso Temescal a go. The folks at Blue Bottle say it's "complex, poetic, finicky—if you make coffee in your garret, loft studio, pied-à-terre, atelier . . . this is your blend." Drink to your fantasies. Yes, a pound will cost more than what you've been paying. But if you consider cost per pound over the number of fantastic cups you'll actually be *enjoying*, you'll come out as the bitch on top.

Another stellar resource, and our personal fave, is Terroir Coffee (terroircoffee.com), operating under the eponymous George Howell Coffee Company name. Our little secret is that for years, wherever we lived we had him send us a pound of Kenyan coffee every month. With heavenly berry undertones and perfect roasting technique, this is pure coffee perfection.

---

*Thriftiest Bitch*

### french fix

MAKE A small $15 investment in the sexiest accessory of them all: a little French press. It's sleek and sophisticated, and makes the best pure, unadulterated coffee for just pennies. Make the time to treat yourself in the morning, plunge away, sip that java, and when you leave the house, walk right past that caffeine temple and let the healing begin.

---

## TEA: The True Afternoon Delight

Does the mention of tea call to mind a dowdy gal in flannel pajamas curled up on a chintz sofa, G-rated mystery on TV, cat purring nearby? If so, you've been hanging out with clueless spinster bitches, bitch.

These days, tea is hip. Tea is chic. Tea is affordable. Tea is a luxury that can pump you up, wind you down, delight and restore your palate. The Standard Hotel, that beacon of cool on Hollywood's Sunset Boulevard, recently brought "Hip Tea" (as opposed to "High Tea") to their impressive menu. Gentrified

281

neighborhoods from Brooklyn to Berkeley are sprouting tea bars. Let's face it: Tea is hot! But to really soak as much satisfaction as you can out of that cup or two or three or four of exotic brew, you need to know the difference between the schlock and quality blacks, greens, and herbals.

## Blacks

If you go with a black tea, make sure it hails from one of two places where it's indigenous. India and southern China produce the most interesting, nuanced black teas on the market. Black Assam tea from India is complex, malty, dense, full-flavored, and delicious, with a nice little caffeine kick that will get your mojo in gear. Tung Ting oolong tea, grown in the mountains of Taiwan, is faintly floral and light in a lovely, aromatic way. Skip the coffee buzz and try it midday to keep your anxiety level in check. At only three to five dollars for two to three ounces of loose leaves, these teas are the cheapest, chicest luxury you can buy.

⊙╍━🔨 *At Your Fingertips*

### loose leaves are the way to go

*I*F YOU don't have a tea café nearby, go to teavana.com or uptontea.com for your loose tea leaves. You heard us: loose leaves, not tea bags! Remember that in parts of the world there is nothing sexier than a woman in a robe pulling out a beautiful teapot, heating it up, swirling the leaves on the bottom to release the intensity of their aroma, and then pouring perfectly heated water over them. There's also nothing easier, and, in *this* part of the world, nothing more recession-friendly.

### Greens

As you've probably read in every article even whispering the words "health, women, wellness," Green tea is soothing and loaded with antioxidants. Our favorite is Long Jing Shi Feng (Lion Peak Dragon Well) organic, which is grown outside of Hangzhou in China, and is traditionally harvested in April by young girls: *Hmmm . . . Let's not go there.* Green tea with roasted brown rice from Japan may sound odd, but has a nutty, earthy flavor due to the roasted brown rice, and is so hearty and satisfying it can be the perfect substitute for that trans fat–loaded chocolate-chip cookie you've been salivating over since two p.m.

### Herbals

You can actually grow herbal teas and brew them all on your own! One of our favorite nightcaps is to get out our clippers and flashlight and step into the garden to harvest herbs for tea. No, you do not need to wear earth shoes or have underarm hair. Aside from spearmint and lemon balm, try growing lemony and buttery lemon verbena, which makes a sublime bedtime brew.

0━━ *Thriftiest Bitch*

**when any herb will do**

FEEL FREE to get in touch with all that pent-up aggression and go crazy, snip like mad, and harvest every weedy herb at your disposal, from lemon thyme, to fennel, to lavender, to lemon verbena, and pour the boiling water over the whole mess for a soothing herbal concoction.

283

## VODKA, SCOTCH, BOURBON, AND RYE, OH, MY!

Just because our economy is in a major recession, that's no reason to be a masochist and deprive yourself of the right to a nice, long, stiff one (drink, that is). In fact, spirits are just what you need during tough times—*real* spirits, not mediocre cocktails with sexy names (pomegranate coconut orgasm) that leave you overspent and underbuzzed. So leave the overpriced couture vodka cosmos back in the nineties (*Sex and the City* is in reruns, ladies!), learn what whiskey is all about (may you never again think scotch is shrouded in some mystery beyond your intelligence), and start enjoying old-school rye, which is destined to resurface as the affordable, hip new drink of the post-Bush era.

### Vodka Is Vodka

In a blind taste test conducted by the *New York Times*, Smirnoff vodka, once the crème de la crème but demoted to Walmart status with the emergence of the fab four—Belvedere, Grey Goose, Stoli, and Absolut—*actually came in first place.* So, for all of you who can't live without your designer vodka: *Yes, you can!* There is no advantage and no cool factor in buying *très* expensive boiled-down-to-rubbing-alcohol grain (potato, beet, grape…) mash and water in a designer bottle. If you're mixing your drink, use cheaper stuff.

## diy

$\mathcal{O}$NFUSE INEXPENSIVE vodka with your own flavor by stuffing bottles with lemongrass, extremely hot chili peppers, vanilla bean, and tree-bark cinnamon, and learn the joys of DIY cocktails.

### Whiskey Is the New Cosmo

Get ready. You're going to be seeing a lot of whiskey—after all, it's the official drink of any recession or depression. So get used to it, and start lovin' it. Like a bitch herself, whiskey is many things at once: earthy, heavy, spicy, robust, delicate. Like wine, it's subtle, nuanced, complex. Like coffee, it opens your eyes and takes you places. It also steadies your nerves in a few sips (like we said, perfect for recession/depression), is high on the buzz/cost ratio (more bang for your buck), and makes a girl look cool as hell (who dares mess with a bitch ordering single-malt scotch?).

Decoding whiskey is way more complex than vodka, so here's a quick tutorial:

- **Is it whiskey or whisky?** American and Irish whiskey are spelled with an e. Scotch, Canadian and Japanese are spelled without an e.
- **Are scotch, bourbon, and rye all whiskeys?** Yes. Whiskey is defined as a spirit made from a fermented mash of grain that is stored in a cask. Scotch refers to whisky produced in Scotland. Barley, corn and rye are the main grains used for whiskey making.

285

Bourbon's main grain is corn. Rye's, well, uh, is rye. Historically, barley was the key component of Scotch and Irish whiskey, although, outside of single or blended malts, most sold today are a blend of grains (barley, corn, rye).

(Stay with us, we know it's a lot, but just think about that next trip to the bar and all those guys pretending they know whiskey who'll be weeping at your feet.)

- **What is a single-malt scotch?** Refers to a nonblended whisky, made in Scotland, from malted barley and produced at a single distillery. The Glenlivet, Highland Park, and Lagavulin are well-known examples.
- **What is malted barley?** Barley soaked in water to facilitate the conversion of starches to sugar, and then dried over a heat source before grinding. Scotch barley is often dried over a smoky peat fire. Typically Irish whiskey using barley is dried in a kiln without peat (be a show-off and order the famous Irish single-malt whiskey using the peat method: The Connemara Single Malt).
- **What is the difference between bourbon, Tennessee whiskey and rye?** Bourbon, although originally produced in Bourbon County, Kentucky, can be made anywhere in the U.S. To be labeled bourbon it must be made with at least 51% corn and stored in new charred oak barrels. Tennessee whiskey is also corn based. Unlike bourbon, though, these whiskeys can be made only in the state of Tennessee and utilize a sugar maple charcoal filtration system before storage that imparts a warm, sweet flavor.

While some high-end specialty bottles will set you back big-time, you should be able to score your very own whiskey bottle that you'd be proud to show off for under twenty bucks. Besides, every red-blooded American bitch needs a bottle of Jack Daniel's Tennessee whiskey, Jim Beam Black bourbon, and for extra-special occasions, Glenmorangie Sherry Wood Finish single-malt scotch, hiding in the back of some cabinet. On tough nights, it's what she reaches for.

*⚷━━ At Your Fingertips*

### i like to watch

BOUTIQUE DISTILLERIES are springing up all over the country. Check them out online and then go for a tour and tasting of their vodka or other spirits for a fun day that will feel like you're on a mini vacation. Here are just a few sites to peruse, which can link you to other distilleries closer to your hometown: www.ciscobrewers.com; stgeorgespirits.com; mountainmoon-shine.com; starlightdistillery.com.

### Rye Whiskey Is the Up-and-comer

We're guessing that, when ordering cocktails, you're not used to requesting Old Overholt with a water back. This just may change. Poor rye has been shunted to the corner of the contemporary liquor cabinet for decades. Just wait—it's poised for a second coming in the New Dark Ages, and it may well pleasantly surprise you. For starters, it's cheap. Let's say that again: It's cheap. For the price of two lattes, it offers a taste that's distinctive and complex. Start out with a bottle of Old Overholt. The funky, original label will provide a nice aesthetic contrast

287

to your liquor collection, and its whiffs of spice and honey go nicely with tonic and Sazerac cocktails.

Recession or no recession, a bitch should make the most of what she's got, and should learn to appreciate the classics. Wine, once opened, goes bad fast. Spirits, meanwhile, like an amazing lover . . . well, they last a long, long time.

*Thriftiest Bitch*

## perfect new orleans sazerac cocktail for bubkes

½ tsp. Pernod (or other absinthe substitute)

1 sugar cube

1 dash Peychaud's bitters

2 ounces rye whiskey

lemon peel for garnish

CHILL AN old-fashioned glass. Coat with Pernod, then pour it out . . . or if you wish, leave a tiny puddle on the bottom. Muddle bitters and sugar to dissolve. Add rye. Use a twist of lemon peel for garnish.

## WINE: Think Beyond the Usual Suspects

Take all the rules you learned about wine back in the nineties, and throw them out the window. There is a delicious wine for every budget and every mood and *there are no shoulds*! In much the same way that you can wear white after Labor Day or jeans to a chichi restaurant, you can drink whatever you damn well please, despite the menu or the occasion: pinot noir with red snapper, rosé with rack of lamb, and Prosecco while watching the Super Bowl. The only wine rules a bitch needs to follow in the New Dark Ages are thinking beyond France and California, and knowing that quality *can* come cheap.

### Getting Out of the France/California Wine Rut

Great wine is produced all over the world, so drink what you like proudly and get reacquainted with wines you once knew but stopped drinking. (There is *nothing* wrong with merlot!) First order of business: Kiss the chardonnay good-bye; California chards can be too oaky, and French chardonnay . . . well, with the euro to the dollar, they're out of your range, baby. Instead, bring home the modern white—crisp New Zealand sauvignon blancs. Next, try an Argentinean Malbec. In blind taste testings, the same people who thought their $100-plus bottles were spectacular were just as likely to pick a $20 Malbec as the best in show. Skip champagne and drink Italian Prosecco or Spanish cava; they sparkle, they bubble, and they are a fraction of the price of the French stuff. Experiment with rosés; no, don't mix red and white wines—try brisk pinks for hot summer days, like all the Manhattan "it" girls.

289

Rate the bottles that work for you and the ones that don't. Designate a favorite red as your little-black-dress wine—always reliable, stylish, works well with everything—and a favorite white as your jeans-and-T-shirt wine—superinexpensive, crisp and casually chic. Make sure you always have both wines on hand. And, for a fun night, organize your own blind testing, pitting the last vestiges of the wines that you can no longer afford against your cheap, and delicious new wines.

## 0—▬ Green Style

### reuse and recycle

*B*uy a bottle of framboise or St-Germain and turn yesterday's opened white into a festive drink by adding eau-de-vie and floating a raspberry or blueberry at the bottom of the glass.

### *Great Cheap Wines for Tough Times and All Times*

These are a few of our favorite things . . . which, despite their reasonable pricing (under $15 per bottle), can firmly stand their ground, even when you're back eating cake.

**South American Malbecs**—savor the bright fullness of a cab and the deep softness known to merlots.

> Viu Manent, Secreto Malbec, Colchagua, Chile— Aromas reminiscent of chocolate and black cherry.

> Gascon Malbec, Mendoza, Argentina—A little spicy, with subtle vanilla and root beer accents. Oh yes!

**South African Red Blends**

**New Zealand Sauvignon Blancs**—crisp, tantalizingly floral, and more refreshing than the blah nineties-era "art gallery opening" chardonnay you drank from plastic cups. Our new basic white.

> Kim Crawford Sauvignon Blanc, Marlborough—Delicious. Our house summer wine.

> Giesen Sauvignon Blanc, Marlborough—Refreshing. Perfect with raw oysters. Easy to find!

---

⚷— *Thriftiest Bitch*

**best for less**

More than a quarter of the Wine Spectator's 2008 "Top 100" bottles received scores of higher than 90 (on a scale of 100), and retailed under $25, nineteen of which retailed under $20!

---

## MASTERING THE TAKEOUT TEMPTRESS

**TAKEOUT IS THE** crack cocaine of dining in. Right when you're at your bitchiest due to a combination of low blood sugar, lunar regularity, and the prospect of a night filled with laundry, a Vegas-style neon sign starts flashing in your head: "yummy—takeout"; "convenient—takeout"; "kitchen stays clean—takeout." Of course, you're a smart bitch and know the inherent risks—wasted cash, wasted calories, and most important . . . addiction—but the impulse for that quick and dirty fix is far too powerful to resist. Aiding and abetting you toward a new takeout high with every click of the mouse are your friendly neighborhood pushers—diningin.com and "free delivery."

We're not suggesting you purge those grease-stained takeout menus from your kitchen drawer and go cold turkey. There are definitely some times that warrant sitting on the sofa in a near-comatose state, wearing fleecy sweats, devouring greasy pad thai out of the white Styrofoam carton, and washing it down with a cheap bottle of wine. We said *some* times, not every other night; those days of obsessive takeout are behind you.

To get control over your compulsion we'll show you a set of takeout rules for a new era. Use them as your holy grail to master those takeout classics—pizza, Chinese food, sushi, prepared foods—that you've been abusing for years.

## THE RULES OF TAKEOUT IN TOUGH TIMES

Confess that you have a little takeout issue, stay loyal to the rules, and you'll never slide down the slippery slope of spending too much on a good thing again.

### Rule #1: The "Pain in the Ass to Make" Rule

You can buy only takeout that is difficult or nearly impossible to cook at home: Think brick-oven pizza, shawarma, deep-fried calamari, unagi, spanakopita. These are dishes that require restaurant-style ingredients, skill, or equipment and, no matter how hard you try, can't be duplicated on your own.

# Rule #2: The Inverse-Relation Rule

The more expensive the takeout, the harder you need to work for it. You *are* allowed to have the $5 national chain pizza delivered to your doorstep. You are *not* allowed to have the $20 sushi delivered, no matter how hot the delivery guy may be. If you feel the need to splurge, you need to get off your ass and pick it up.

# Rule #3: The Dining-Versus-Fueling Rule

If you're starving and don't have time to linger over a lovely meal, you can buy only a fuel fix. This is the cheapest, most easily available takeout you can find: a simple burrito, steaming bowl of pho, or hot rotisserie chicken. If you *do* have time to dine, you can go to your favorite nearby restaurant and order the meal you love—to go. With no tip, no overpriced glass of wine, and no temptation for coffee and dessert, it will be a reasonably priced, thoroughly satisfying treat.

# Rule #4: The "Takeout Only Once a Week" Rule

You can buy takeout only once a week, Monday through Friday. You have no excuse for playing the convenience card over the weekend. Sorry, bitch, but you're cutting back: No pain, no gain.

# Rule #5: The Control Rule

By the time you're jonesing for those familiar white cartons, you're stark raving starving. Everything looks good and one of anything doesn't seem enough. *Stop!* You are allowed to order only one: one entree from the Chinese restaurant, one topping on your pizza, one supersize sushi roll.

## APPLYING THE RULES TO THE TAKEOUT CLASSICS

The four pillars of takeout are everywhere, quietly seducing you to drop another chunk of change. Sometimes submission is exactly what you need and you bless the day that Kung Pao chicken was born. Other times you feel like a skanky ho for having just given away your most precious asset (hard-earned cash) and getting something so meaningless and unsatisfying in return. It's time to get control. Here's how to apply "the Rules of Takeout in Tough Times" to pizza, Chinese food, sushi, and prepared food, so you can reign victorious in your love/hate takeout relationship.

### PIZZA: Perfect in a Pinch

Pizza gets high marks for being a quick, cheap, and satisfying midweek fuel fix. Even though you think you can make pizza at home using premade dough you've bought at the market, by the time you get the red sauce going, grate the mozzarella, and slice the mushrooms or pepperoni, you'll still be screwed because you can never get your regular oven as hot as a commercial pizza oven. Also, buying all the ingredients can add up to more than the cost of a delivered job. Give this one up and order it in.

294

When choosing your pizza, you might be offered that "fabulous, brand-new roasted tomato, avocado, pesto" concoction that has just been added to the menu. Remember, like everything else, the price of flour has doubled and many pizzerias are avoiding direct price increases on their standard offerings by launching new products at higher price points. Don't bite. Stick to pizza as it was always meant to be and you'll avoid both indigestion and getting burned with an inflated bill.

To minimize the risk of devouring the whole thing in one sitting, try throwing together a salad with whatever lettuce and veggies you have lying around. Freeze the leftover pizza for another full meal.

○━━ *Thriftiest Bitch*

### cheap and yummy

$\mathcal{W}$ITH PRICES as low as $5 to $6 for a one-topping pizza at many national chains, you can afford to sit back, buff your nails, and wait for the doorbell to ring. (See rule #2: Dirt-cheap takeout provides the luxury of delivery.)

### SUSHI: The Raw Rub

The *real* risk in ordering sushi is not the mercury content in the tuna; the real risk is in getting carried away ordering *too many* expensive little pieces of Charlie. Don't panic, ladies! Takeout sushi is within the Rules. Spicy tekka maki is not something you can easily make at home; after all, who has twenty-four/seven access to sushi-grade fish, nori-rolling expertise, and ready-made sushi rice at their fingertips at the end of a long workday? So how does a bitch still eat sushi at home and not break the bank? Control: lots and lots of self-control and clever ordering skills.

Start by going to either your favorite neighborhood joint or the prepared-food section of your local supermarket. Every

295

good grocer worth their stock market symbol has a sushi bar; just be a demanding bitch and make sure the fish is still glistening at seven p.m.

Discipline yourself and order just one roll. Go for one large, gorgeous rainbow roll or a fat, crunchy, spicy spider maki. You should be able to come in under twelve bucks and hit all your food groups. The rice, nori wrapper, and fish will help fill your daily starch, vegetable, and protein needs. And if you can handle the heat, bring on the wasabi! The spicy stuff suppresses that starving sensation. If you need a total fill-up, add a miso soup and seaweed salad. Go home, chill out on the sofa, turn on the tube, pull out the chopsticks, eat slowly, sip green tea (now you know which one to buy!), and savor every morsel.

## Thriftiest Bitch

### palate teaser

IF YOU are near a favorite Japanese restaurant at lunchtime, order a luncheon special box of assorted sushi, loaded with lots of daily offerings, rice, miso soup, salad, and pickled vegetables, usually under $12.95; throw it in the fridge at work, and bring it home. Spend the day aroused and salivating over what is to come.

## CHINESE: Use Sparingly in Place of Prozac or Celexa

Restaurant-style Chinese food is brimming with fresh veggies, tofu, lean meat and fish, and it's relatively inexpensive: An entrée can cost as little as $10 to $12. It seems the perfect takeout/delivery food, except for having to change your name to Puffy Bitch after consuming all that sodium.

But sorry: You *cannot* order veggies and tofu for your Chinese takeout meal; it breaks the rules. You can easily and inexpensively stir-fry healthy veggies at home, but who is going to hang a whole duck—beak, feet, and testes—for a week to dry from the kitchen ceiling, and what bitch is going to get a deep-fat fryer filled with lard and sizzle those wings at home?

If you're going the Chinese takeout route, give up the ghost on healthy, and spend your takeout dollars on those nostalgic comfort foods you can't make at home. Order up a *single* entrée of either deep-fried garlicky chicken wings, Peking duck with hoisin and pancakes, or succulent ribs with duck sauce. Revel in the fat, sodium, and sinful flavors. Lose yourself in the wet, warm, sweet, and salty comfort that waits inside that carton. If it was a shitty day that warrants the full-frontal fix, then go for the goopy, yummy stuff. It's cheaper than the therapist and a shorter-term prescription than Prozac.

## PREPARED FOODS: Dodging Disaster

How's this for a familiar scenario? You missed lunch, and now your stomach is growling, your head is pounding, and all you want is something big, hot, and satisfying to fill you up. You enter your local market and suddenly it's as if you haven't gotten it in months and you're in a room full of Brad Pitt look-alikes. You feel that familiar pulse in your lower body starting to stir; everything looks so good you would hop into bed with any crisp, long cucumber! Wait . . . this is your neighborhood grocery chain, and you need a heavy dose of self-control.

Put on the blinders and beeline over to the prepared whole chickens. Since you do not have a home rotisserie and sixty free minutes to cook the bird (basting every ten minutes), a prepared chicken is the perfect fuel fix for a bitch in dire straits.

It's delicious (slow roasting over a spit or fire makes for moist meat), inexpensive (a store-cooked rotisserie chicken at $6 is cheaper than buying a raw, five-pound whole chicken at $1.30 per pound and cooking it at home), and relatively low in calories. It can easily feed a family of four, or leave you with enough leftover for a yummy chicken Greek or Caesar salad the following day if you're dining solo.

Once you've selected your herb- or teriyaki-roasted bird, you *must* vacate the area immediately: so as not to be tempted by insidiously pricey three-bean salads, candied sweet potatoes, or mac 'n' cheese side dishes. If your cupboard is bare, by all means add a bag of prewashed romaine and some Yukon Golds to your basket. Repeat the mantra, "Get me out of here for fourteen dollars or less," as necessary, all the way to the checkout line.

## Green Style

### how *does* she do it?

BRING YOUR own pretty ceramic bowls and platters into your favorite local dive, and ask your buddies behind the counter to use *them* rather than the Styrofoam containers they usually use for takeout. Aside from avoiding gratuitous paper waste, you'll be able to fool any dinner guests into thinking you just whipped up those Thai noodles in peanut sauce all by yourself.

# Chapter 10

# Pamper the Bitch

*N*OT YOU. YOUR dog. After all, hard as it is to believe, not everything is about you, bitch.

## EVERY BITCH NEEDS AN ALTER EGO
......................

YES, LITTLE MAXIE needs to be pampered.

In these times when you aren't getting all the love and attention that you need, when you can't pamper yourself in the style to which you'd have liked to become accustomed, then think of little Maxie as your alter ego. Lavish little Maxie with all the care and affection you're missing.

Take pleasure in her new haircut and mani-pedi—or is it pedi-pedi? Buy her that slick new raincoat (on sale only!). Bring

299

her to the neighborhood doggy store to test the latest treats. Just think, when you ask for the doggy bag at the restaurant you'll have someone to share it with. Doing things for Maxie is as much fun and as satisfying as doing them for yourself.

Who doesn't want someone eagerly greeting you at the door each and every time you return, as if you've been away for years instead of out dumping the garbage? Who wouldn't thrill to the wagging tail and cold, wet nose of a being fully alert and attentive to your every need? If you wake her from her nap or shut off that annoying golf game, do you think Maxie will snarl? No way. She'll respond with boundless joy, eager for your attention. Faithful? That's putting it mildly. Once Maxie bonds with you and you're her alpha, it'll be till death do you part.

No therapist . . . no life coach . . . no man . . . no bank account . . . no cocktail can do as much as little Maxie to lower your blood pressure, enhance your mood, get you exercising, and offer consistent, fun, warm companionship.

That said, *no* canine arm candy allowed. Pets are not a fashion accessory. No one should have the privilege of pets unless they're prepared to invest the time and money to love and care for them the right way. Really, bitches, would you want to be some sleazy guy's moll? We've all been there, and remember how that felt—you're not allowed to perpetrate that kind of abuse on another adorable little bitch.

## NEW PUPPY, RESCUE, OR SHELTER DOG?

No Maxie at home and you want one?

Before you run out and bring a little cutie home, make sure you're a solid bitch ready to make the time and care commitment that a pet requires.

If you never liked dogs, don't even think about it (in fact, skip this chapter). You aren't going to fall in love with the discerning little pooper and pisser as you clean the mess on the brand-new Peace Industry living room rug, find your Balenciaga handbag shredded, and discover the little dickens has an insatiable appetite for your cherished hardcover books. You aren't going to appreciate his need to go out at two a.m. because he can't hold it anymore. And you certainly won't care for the extra expenses when she needs her shots, or requires teeth cleaning, deworming, or deskunking.

Still reading?

Pets are a grounding experience for mature people. They need wholehearted, mindful attention. They require consistency of care and consistency of scheduling. But, unlike that unreliable boyfriend, they *will* return the favor.

Best of all, they offer endless opportunities for free entertainment.

Think of the all the time you'll spend taking pictures of them in cute poses and dressed in adorable outfits (pics you can then text to your unappreciative friends). Fetch will be your new best sport—afternoons well spent getting your arm in shape for softball season. The endless hours of walking little Maxie will provide good exercise and social opportunities for both of you. Just think, now that you have a little pooch you won't have to just watch—you'll be able to participate in all those dog parades: Halloween, Easter, Mardi Gras. Oh, what fun it'll be!

Anyway, caring for a new pup should be easy now that you're passing on the overpriced martini happy hours and spending more time at home. What better way to embrace your new life?

## my buddy and me

$\mathcal{A}$SSIMILATE THE pooch into your life. Check out www.bring-fido.com or www.dogfriendly.com for lists of dog-friendly attractions, restaurants, hotels in your area or in the city you'll be visiting. Get a sense of how easy it'll be to navigate your community with your new friend.

You have three solid choices for finding your new best friend. First, buy a puppy from a reliable breeder. Second, go to your neighborhood shelter and adopt an orphaned canine. Third, once you decide on a specific breed, contact that national club's site to find their rescue locations. Lots of people have strong opinions about getting only a pound pet or a new puppy. This is a judgment call. Do what works for you; there's no right or wrong answer. If you want a little puppy, go for it. If you're happy to adopt from a shelter or rescue organization, that's great too!

Only one rule: Don't be impulsive. (Remember—search and lust.)

## THE NEW PUPPY

How cute is a new puppy?

It should be the acid test for every date—or friendship. If the guy can't gush over pictures of an adorable little Lab, poodle, or mutt, how much heart can he have? What kind of dad will he make? (If you're the kind of bitch who can't gush over a new puppy, why are you still reading? We told you to skip this chapter! Now you feel bad.)

302

We all want a brand-new little puppy at least once in our lives.

But brand-new puppies are like babies—they require continuous care. You'll need to house-train them, survive their teething (put away those Manolos, Louboutins, and Choos—you can't afford to replace them!), and be willing to do midnight walks.

Book still open?

To hone in on the breeds that might work for you, your first stop should be the American Kennel Club site at www.akc.org. Not only do they have an excellent guide to different breeds and their character traits, but they can provide a list of breeders in your area.

Start calling and asking about their dogs to see if they're the right match for you. How active are these particular pups? How much do they really shed? Do they like kids? Are they silent or barkers? What medical or behavioral issues might they be prone to?

Ask if they have litters ready or if they plan on getting the bitch in the family way soon. Chat up the people you talk with to get referrals to other breeders in the area. This is a critical part of your intel. You'll need to make *lots* of calls, double-check, do your homework to find a great breeder. You'll probably find that certain names keep coming up.

Likewise, when you do find a breeder you're interested in, they should turn the third degree back onto you. They should want to know all the details about you and your lifestyle—well, maybe not the last time you had sex or your bank account balance, but close. A reputable breeder wants to ensure that the match is a good one for you and the puppy. If they aren't interested in you, fail to ask lots of questions, it means they're just pumping out the pups for sale and you shouldn't be interested.

Next, as part of this due diligence, visit local groomers, vets, and dog trainers. Groomers, better than just about anyone else, know how a dog behaves in stressful situations. (Think of yourself in the salon chair, how your blood pressure and anxiety level rise. . . .) So ask groomers the same questions about breed and breeders. Keep notes. Triangulate. You may have begun believing that a giant schnauzer was your Justin Timberlake and end up knowing that a Portuguese water dog is your Hugh Jackman.

You'll be surprised at how certain names, dog lines, and breeders keep appearing. Yep, this is a crazy world where Sir Martango of Angora the Fifth's third bitch is related to King Rolie Napoleon of the Buttrick's second cousin. Be careful: Hillbilly inbreeding is not a good thing. But you *will* find that one or two breeders in your area keep getting mentioned as breeding the best dogs for disposition and health.

Finished chasing after info on different breeds and breeders? Sit, stay, and be downright honest about yourself! While any dog will get you out of the house for walks, different breeds require different owners. Don't get the dog that matches the person you *want* to be! If you're not the Peppy Bitch (see chapter 3)—if you hate to walk a block to the drugstore, don't own a pair of sneakers, and find insects of all kinds heinous (ants and black widow spiders are equally horrifying)—well, that gorgeous golden with the long legs and auburn hair, the one who loves to run and run on bucolic country paths, is definitely not the dog for you. If you're the perfect fashionista bitch, always wearing black, obsessively neat, a shedding white pup is *not* the way to go. Know the bitch you're getting, yes. Just as important? Know thyself, bitch.

Once you find a potential litter, make a visit. An outstanding
breeder will help make a match for you among the available puppies. Our favorite way to pick is to sit on the floor and see which
little guys come bounding into our laps. We've passed on little Miss
Perfect Ready-for-the-Show-Ring in favor of the fat little guy who
kept crawling into our lap for a snuggle. (Maybe we were just desperate.) Don't be shallow. Don't be vain. Go for disposition over
looks (yes, your mother told you that, too—why didn't you listen?).

While a new puppy is a delight, a new puppy is also *really
pricey*. Not only will you be paying for the privilege of all the
work ahead, but you'll also be paying vet expenses and shelling
out for training classes. After all, the best dog is a well-trained
dog (somewhere in this there's a life lesson here about mates).

305

breeders that don't discern breed, regulate traits, or necessarily provide humane care and conditions for their animals. They'll breed genetically compromised dogs, meaning bad traits get passed down. Lots of puppy mills are shut down by the ASPCA . . . all too often, females are bred over and over with no concern for their health, deceased dogs are kept in cages with living animals, and other nasty violations occur.

◆ A good breeder will certify that your dog is healthy—or will disclose any potential health problems in advance. But when you buy a puppy at the pet store, you're blind to the health issues you're inheriting. Vets see lots of problems (deformities, pneumonia, hip and elbow dysplasia) in pups bred this way.

◆ The selling price at the pet store may be comparable to the breeder's price, but you'll end up shelling out *a lot* more in the long run—and you'll be an unwitting participant in a gross practice. Steer clear. A pet store promises instant gratification, but resist the temptation. Remember the golden rule: Search and lust, baby, search and lust.

## SHELTER AND RESCUE DOGS

For any number of reasons you may pass on that little bundle of pissing puppy joy, opting instead for a dog from a shelter or rescue organization. While you can sometimes find puppies for adoption, it's more likely that you'll be taking home a grown-up. There's a lot to recommend this course of action.

Shelters and rescue organizations are packed with more dogs than ever before, these canines the victims of their owners' hard times. How many heartbreaking stories have you seen on the evening news? Owners forced from their home by the mortgage crisis can't bring Fifi with them to their friend's place or the homeless shelter.

Or people who've lost their jobs can no longer afford to care for their dogs. Cute dogs, well trained, well cared for, but homeless now too. You can find expensive purebred dogs you might have not been able to afford before. Or you can find a sweet mutt. This is a *much* cheaper route than going to the breeder.

Plus, the benefits are that an adult dog will most likely be housebroken and trained. Your leather goods, books, and carpet should be safe. Shots will already have been administered, a tracking microchip implanted, and you can feel great by doing your part to help out the little pooch.

*Thrifty Bitch*

### help!

*You've hit* upon hard times and are having trouble meeting Maxie's basic needs. Talk to the Humane Society in your area—they've got associated clinics that provide discounted medical services (though you may have to wait awhile for an appointment). PETCO also offers low-cost pet vaccinations—contact your local store for clinic dates and times.

If you choose to adopt, follow the same protocol to identify the right kind of dog for you. Do your homework *before* you go to see who's living at the shelter. It's so easy to be seduced by the watery big brown eyes, waggy tail, and nuzzliness of an orphaned Fido. Just don't. If you're impulsive and it turns out to be a bad match, you'll end up doing more harm to the pup (and yourself) in the long term. This is not like all those fashion faux pas that, while costly, can be hidden in the back of your closet.

If you go the rescue-dog route, you'll already have identified the breed you want. The purebred kennel clubs have rescue organizations for their specific breed, and this may be another good route in your adoption search.

Petfinder.com is *fantastic*. Nearly every shelter dog in the country is listed on this site. Its excellent search engine can help you locate the right dog for you. This is an ethical, affordable route . . . just prepare to be patient. Shelters are swamped with applications—underpaid, overworked employees and volunteers can hardly keep up. It may take a while to connect with your dog, but the wait's worth it.

## *Thrifty Bitch*

### hello, kitty

WHAT SUITS a bitch better than a sleek, sultry, independent-minded feline? Less labor-intensive than Maxie, less expensive to maintain, less needy of constant care and affection. Cats can be amusing bundles of manic energy or warm, sleepy placeholders. Unlike your eager-to-please puppy, cats have such subtly interesting personalities; their behaviors will provide you with endless hours of admiring analysis. They could do the trick if you're lusting for a little playmate but can't make the doggy commitment. How to find your own little kitty? Follow the same route outlined in your quest for Maxie. The only thing you may *not* do is get a collar and leash and walk your little feline friend. While Maxie may be a man magnet, Felix on a leash? Uh, we don't think so.

## SORRY, MAXIE NEEDS TO CUT BACK (JUST A LITTLE) TOO!

Yes, you love her—but times are tough!

Maxie grooms like you do and will have to make some sacrifices too:

- Stretch her grooming time from five to eight or nine weeks.
- Give her a bath yourself—what better way to spend quality time together? (No over-the-top-pricey doggy shampoo and conditioner. Just the basics.)
- If little Maxie is big Maxie, find a local do-it-yourself doggy Laundromat.
- Blow-dry and style her hair yourself.
- Trim around her eyes so you can see their warm adorableness.

- Clip her toenails.
- Brush her hair or fur daily.

Yes, Maxie wears clothes and needs accessories just like you do. And, yes, she needs a little pick-me-up now and then, but:

- No full-priced new clothes.
- No new pop-up doggy mansion.
- No doggy strollers (unless Maxie is three-legged or arthritic).
- No new lavish, logo'd doggy carriers.

As for new accessories: a little leather and diamond-studded collar for $5.99 could be just the pick-me-up she needs now that she isn't moving into a big new house. Head over to your local pet store, and bring Maxie—she should have a voice. *Do not* go online to buy doggy gear. The shipping will cost you more than the item! (By the way, have you seen those fantastic fake dog nails you can get, in righteous shades, to help protect your wooden floors? Oops. We digress.) Okay. Just control yourself. Don't go overboard acting out your own shopping-deprivation frustrations.

## EXERCISE AND HEALTH

Just like humans, exercise and preventive care cut down on medical costs by keeping a body in tip-top health. Maxie needs to run. Take her with you on your daily walks or runs. Get a ball and play catch over and over again. (You have nothing better to do anyway.) Stay on top of vaccinations. Skip the doggy health care insurance—in general it doesn't pay.

Brush Maxie's teeth daily. You need to *do* this, not *mean* to do it. Yes, it does feel silly struggling to get the toothbrush into her back canines as she squirms and chews, but it's good for her. And forget the pricey doggy toothpaste that she sucks down like candy. Forget even the doggy toothbrush. Why do all those manufacturers need to sell pet products like animals have the same needs as humans . . . toothbrushes, peanut-butter doggy treats, over-the-top doghouses . . . ? We aren't dumb bitches. Yes, we love our babies, but we also know they're just animals one generation removed from working in the fields, helping us hunt, guarding the castle, and sleeping in the barn. Really!

Instead of the toothbrush, use a piece of gauze and gently, in a circular motion, go around and around her teeth up into the gum line. Be careful; we don't want to hurt out little princess, do we? Or if it's easier, use a regular old human toothbrush. Besides reducing her hellish doggy breath, you might save big bucks by not having to get her teeth professionally cleaned. There are no doggy dentures, after all, and do you really want a toothless hound? Avoid paying anesthetist and vet dental bills.

## MAXIE-MIZE HER DIET

Baby's gotta eat. But what exactly to put in your precious pumpkin's belly? You've got hundreds upon hundreds of choices. Basically, pup food is as complex and controversial as people food. Raw? Organic? Natural? Wet? Dry?

Every dog is different—and every dog's nutritional needs change over the course of his or her life. Puppy food will probably make a grown dog overweight; grown-up food won't meet a puppy's extensive needs. Evaluate your dog's needs periodically (with the help of your vet), so she doesn't get caught in a nutritional rut.

Generally, dry food is preferred, since it's better for doggy teeth. Organic food is, of course, pricier, but some people claim dogs eat less of it (and find it more satisfying)—as it's more nutritious, purer, free of fillers—so that in the end the cost is the same. Plus, those who argue for high-quality organic food say you'll spend way less on medical care if your puppy eats a premium diet, since organic food may mean fewer allergies, skin problems, and cancers, and less digestive trouble.

Word of warning: "natural" is not the same as organic, in dog *or* people food. Only the USDA can certify something as organic, while "natural" can mean different things. Still, natural is generally better than most, since it usually means fewer synthetic preservatives. If your budget's tight but you want to go the healthiest route, this may be a smart compromise.

Our advice? Same as always. Do a little research. Don't obsess. Get a recommendation from your vet. Then offer Maxie the best food you can afford.

○━━ *Bitchin' Tip*

## essential ingredients

- Avoid buying food that lists "by-product meal" or "meat and bone meal" on the label. These are cheaper sources of animal protein, and can vary from batch to batch, so they don't offer reliable or consistent nutrition.

- Select food with *named* meat or meal as the first ingredient. Meaning you should go for a bag that says "lamb" or "chicken meal" rather than merely "meat." Really, what does "meat" mean? Would you order simply "meat" off a menu?

(continued)

312

We all need a treat now and then. Occasional trips to the doggy bakery are fun, but just mooching free treats is shameful, and buying healthy goodies gets pricey fast. Since you're doing more cooking for yourself these days, you should have no problem whipping Maxie up a little home-cooked indulgence. She'll feel oh-so-adored! Wrap some treats up individually, tie cute ribbons around them, and offer them as gifts to the dog owners in your neighborhood. Cheap, social, and in no time you'll be the leader of the pack.

## MINI-MAXIE TREATS

1½ cups liquid (water, chicken, or beef stock)

½ cup lukewarm water

6 cups whole-wheat flour

1 egg

3 tbsp. honey

½ cup peanut butter (optional)

Preheat oven to 350.

Proof yeast in ½ cup lukewarm water.

Mix together 1½ cup liquid, 1 egg, honey, peanut butter if using, and yeast mixture. Stir in the dry ingredients. If you have an electric mixer with a dough hook, stir until mixture is smooth and elastic. If not, flour a big board and turn the mixture onto it and knead by hand for five to eight minutes—again, until it is smooth and elastic.

Split dough in half and shape into balls. Roll them out to about ¼-inch thickness. This is where it gets fun. Buy outrageous cookie cutters in tiny sizes and fun shapes—cats, rats, people, and, if you must, bones (how boring). Place on ungreased cookie sheets and bake approximately fifteen to twenty minutes on each side (depending on their size). They should be golden brown but, trust us, perfection is not prized. Unlike your mother-in-law, Maxie and her friends will not be critical.

For maximum crispness, leave them in the oven (shut off, of course) overnight.

## MAXIE-WARE

Yes, Maxie needs clothes too. Although we advise that if Maxie is really a big Max of a dog, keep her wardrobe to a minimum. Raingear can be a plus to keep the poor beast dry—and your house from smelling rank. Also, on a sub-sub-frigid winter day, consider a snuggly coat. Not all Fidos are bred for the arctic.

But for the most part, it's the little ones that really look cute in doggy duds. After all, those little guys are close to the ground, so when it's cold and wet their duds are just the ticket to keep them from freezing to death or drowning in a puddle.

We would *never* buy full-price, brand-new, brand-name doggy duds. Just like we wouldn't be caught dead pimping a designer logo, why should little Maxie—unless they want to *pay* her. Plus, lest we remind you, you just can't afford the overpriced stuff. Unless you are gifted (not smart, just given something by a friend) or find it at Doggy Consignment, take a pass on Juicy Couture. Instead, swing by PetSmart, PETCO, Target . . . and browse the clearance racks. Remember what we've taught you? Wait for the season to change. Keep an eye on sales. New merch comes in; old must go. Doggy clothes work just like people clothes, so keep on searchin' and lustin'.

## TURN MAXIE INTO A MAN MAGNET

Remember, Maxie is just your dog. Let us repeat it: D-O-G. Yes, you love her like a child, and would never use a child to pimp a date for you. It's anathema just to think about it. But she's *not* your child, so you can use her without guilt.

Max out your assets. You'll both have so much fun.

First, you need to strategize. Select the right outfit for the walk down the busiest, chicest street in town. While her pink puffy with the white faux fur collar is one of *your* all-time favorites, unless your future husband is totally comfortable with his manhood, he's not likely to stop and bend over and gush over prissy Maxie as she charmingly jumps up on his leg and smiles. Careful of the camo jacket and studded collar as a tool for attraction—you may make some of your new best gay friends (this may be a better deal in the end, but it's not your goal for this exercise). Instead, consider a tasteful blue or red jacket with a black felt lining, a simple black harness, and a black lead. Keep it neutral. (Haven't you learned anything?) It'll contrast well with the color of her hair or fur—we've yet to see a bright blue- or flaming red-haired little one. She'll look cute because she's attired, but you won't look like a nut.

Try it and let Maxie do her magic!

## MAXIE FUN

Learn from Maxie.

Have fun like a dog. (Can you keep your mind clean for just one minute?) In these tight times dogs are the perfect companions. They remind us what's important. They teach us to appreciate *free* things: friendship, play, the natural world. They require absolutely nothing but company, good nutrition, and exercise.

So enjoy having Maxie. Get humble. Let her teach *you* a new way of being—this is a valuable lesson anytime at all, but particularly in a rough economy. Find pleasures in the little things—you know, snuggling, stroking, black leather collars.

An adorable pet should be a shared experience. Find your local doggy park and head on over. Maxie will benefit from being social, learning to share, and not always being the alpha in the pack—she's in charge at home, isn't she?

*You* will benefit because you'll be able to show off how adorable Maxie is and how beautifully you dress her. Doggy parks are amazing places to meet people. No entry fees. Easy social interactions, since you've always got something to talk about and something to look at.

So let Maxie off the leash and direct her to the cutest guy in the park. We're certain he'll have a Lab. Go racing over, blush, and apologize as you tell him how Maxie never does that, but his dog is just *so* cute (hopefully she's not a bitch). Since you've carefully selected and trained Maxie, she'll be just so adorable and charming—your new friend(s) will be all over her.

## PLAY THE MATCH GAME

Few places rival a doggy park for free entertainment.

Play the match game. Notice how alike dogs and their owners

are. See the guy in the far corner with the bulldog? Both outfitted in their leather jackets, each has a chain around his neck, and both share a remarkably wide, frowny face. While the dog has an obvious underbite, it's hard to see whether the owner shares this attribute. . . . Maneuver a little closer—yes, those bottom teeth are sticking out.

Or how about that chick with the Chihuahua? So skinny—wonder what she's been reading? Dressed in her brown suede leggings, with the red vest and that funny, skinny leather thong thingy wrapped around and around her scrawny little neck. All those jangly little X and O bangles announce her every move. Ignore the ferocious little pooch by her side, slide in a little more, and focus—notice how her face is a little pointy and her head nearly shaved under the cap? So nervous in her movements.

Check out the way people infantilize their dogs or need to be the big boss. The woman with the toy poodle wrapped around her neck so that the dog has his head hanging back over her shoulder. My God, is she burping him? Of course, she's got really wiry, gray curly hair, and that poodle is silver, so it's hard to see where his head ends and hers begins. The guy with the boxer, so proud of himself because the poor schnook dog is obeying each command. Notice how tightly the owner holds his body, how he moves each muscle with precision and keeps his head up high, but you can see him glancing from side to side to make sure everyone is watching.

Check out that insecure couple with the yapping, out-of-control little shih tzu. It's barking up a high-pitched storm and they're so tense and embarrassed. Do they think they share DNA with the animal?

Nothing like a dog park to get in touch with the weirdness of (other) people . . .

317

Be happy with little Maxie: She's perfect. And if this is the first time you've really looked closely at owners and their pets, be thankful that while *she* is wearing her Burberry raincoat, you decided to leave yours at home.

⚷⚟ *Bitchin' Tip*

### a bitchin' good time

WE'VE ALL seen the Westminster dog show on TV—and the hilarious mockumentary film *Best in Show*. (If you're unfamiliar with this, rent it immediately . . . and just try not to see yourself.) Now join the fun. Find local dog shows where your own glorious pup can strut her stuff. A recent show at a campground in our area featured barbecue and educational booths for the grown-ups, while the dogs got to sniff one another, socialize, and roam in the sunshine. A positive, lighthearted competition lets *all dogs* (not just the pricey purebreds!) impress a riveted crowd. Once-orphaned shelter dogs picked up high honors: our friend Judah, a white German shepherd, won "best coat"; sweet mutt Cujo's vivid peepers earned the title "wildest eyes." We went home wickedly proud. Which raises the question: Are we like those freaky *Best in Show* characters if we admit to believing our pooch got a self-esteem boost?

## PARADE AROUND

Mardi Gras, Easter, Halloween, Valentine's Day, the Fourth of July . . . any holiday is a perfect occasion for a dog parade. Wouldn't gentle, sweet-faced Tulip look adorable in a devil costume? Wouldn't pudgy Jasper just exude patriotism in a sparkling red-white-and-blue leotard? At a Mardi Gras parade we once attended, a naughty chow named Mimi, strings of beads around her neck, cheekily showed off her doggy bustier. Just something about human nature . . . no one can resist a sheepdog in a beret, a poodle in a fire hat, a trudging dachshund dressed like a cowboy, holster and all. Get creative. Our favorite was when little Lizzie (unresolved Oedipal issues) donned a Freud beard and chewed a rubber cigar. Or when stolidly masculine Preston the bulldog went as Ernest Hemingway—turtleneck sweater, shaggy beard, dragging a line with a massive rubber fish behind him. See the potential? Time you'd spend shopping, watching bad TV, or worrying about your budget can be spent sorting through junk in the attic for homemade doggy costumes. What fun! This is the height of budget bitchdom.

No dog parade in your town? Organize one! Throw up some flyers; send a flurry of e-mails. (Check in with city hall to get a permit.) Be the weird dog lady. Add this tradition to an annual block party or fireworks demonstration. Trust us: The crowds will come. The cost to you? Very little. Amp up your civic pride, meet dog lovers, take pictures, *ooh* and *ahh* at your extraordinary pups.

No dog? Go and laugh your ass off.

○—━ *Thrifty Bitch*

## use the neighborhood

CONSIDER HAVING a doggy clothing swap with all the new friends you made at the park. It'll freshen up her wardrobe and give you a chance to get to know your neighbors better.

Keep track of Maxie's littermates. Make new friends with similar sized/aged/temperamented dogs and trade care

*(continued)*

## LET MAXIE GUIDE YOUR ADVENTURES

You've already heard us wax poetic about the joys of the American road trip (see chapter 5). Next time you get the urge to hit the road, consider making your destination the annual Incredible Dog Challenge. For over ten years, in various U.S. cities, this Purina-sponsored event brings us amazing dogs doing utterly amazing things. Enjoy dog diving, freestyle flying disk, various agility competitions. If Westminster is a beauty pageant, this is the Olympics. A perfect destination for you and your furry friend. Find a dog-friendly hotel and you're in business.

Or do some research and locate a dog show in a city you've been dying to visit. Friends of ours, hard-core dog lovers, were itching to see the Windy City. They arranged their trip for February: Hotels and airfare were cheaper in the postholiday, cold-weather lull. They got a good deal, traveled with their spaniel, Mister Bister, and scored tickets to the International Kennel Club of Chicago show. They came home and told all their high-brow friends it was the Art Institute that *truly moved* them, but we know better.

Let your love of pooches give shape to your thrifty vacations. Why not? Follow your passion, bitches.

## pussylicious

*Y*ES, CAT people can join the fun, too. Visit the Web site of the Cat Fanciers' Association (www.cfa.org) for a schedule of their cat shows. The CFA visits a wide array of cities, so you're likely to find yours—or one nearby—on the list. We took a couple of feline-obsessed kids to the show when it came to our civic center . . . a perfect and inexpensive way to spend a drizzly afternoon. The kids were delighted, and we were too, until they decided to meow instead of talking for a solid week. ("Would you like some milk?" "Meow." "I'm serious, honey, milk or juice?" "Meow." "I mean it, now." "Meow, meow.") But we digress. Cat shows are fun, cheap, and endearingly weird, whether you're a participant or an observer. Think you've got a prizewinning kitty? You'll find rules, regulations, registration guidelines, and lots of info about breeds on this site.

## BUDDHA DOGGIE: Train Maxie, Train Yourself

Remember, Maxie is your alter ego. You've got a lot to learn from her.

Dogs live in the moment . . . they're not fretting about the future, not mourning the losses of the past. The simplest things give them pleasure.

Fortunes change; traumas happen. Even little Maxie can have bad things happen to her, things outside her control. Like the time that rottweiler approached her as though she had a "late-afternoon snack" sign stuck on her back. It could have left her terrified of going out, forever fearful of big dogs. Yes, she became

321

rightfully wary of big dogs that could gobble her in one bite, but you kept a steady, calming hand and didn't let this get in the way of her becoming best friends with that goofy Newfie.

Let go of the past; let go of the mistakes and disappointments that are part of everyday life. Work on staying relaxed and finding pleasure in everyday living. Don't give up on hanging with the big dogs—just pick the right ones.

After all, shit happens. Life's a bitch. The economy's down, up, down again (good thing you're a born-again search-and-luster). Your friends move away (good thing you know how to get cheap airfare). Your car breaks down once and for all (good thing you know about Zipcar). You can't stop worrying about what tomorrow will bring (good thing you've got Maxie to keep you centered).

Maxie reminds you to move on. She isn't dogged by the past, obsessed by inane, everyday minutiae. She doesn't live with house or clothing envy (we hate to break it to you, but she would rather be a nudist). With some sunshine, exercise, good food, an occasional treat, and calm and consistent love, your canine companion is Buddha incarnate, master of the present moment.

You want some sage advice? You want the secret? Live in the moment. Keep it simple. Use only what you need. Have fun!

Open your eyes. Look at that wagging tail. Maxie's got it covered.

Bitch.

## About the Author

......................

**ROSALYN HOFFMAN** is a former buyer for Bonwit Teller, Filene's, and Lord & Taylor in New York City. She was also a marketing executive for Avon and Lillian Vernon. She speaks Chinese and has traveled extensively in China. In addition to being a serious cook and wine collector, she has lived and studied cooking in France and has traveled the world cataloging changing markets. Aside from food and cooking, her other passion is design and architecture. She has worked with award-winning architects in the building and design of several modern homes that have garnered awards and international recognition.